Schriften zur Kriminologie

Edited by

Prof. Dr. Katrin Höffler, Georg-August-Universität Göttingen
Prof. Dr. Johannes Kaspar, Universität Augsburg
Prof. Dr. Jörg Kinzig, Eberhard Karls Universität Tübingen
Prof. Dr. Ralf Kölbel, Ludwig-Maximilians-Universität München

Volume 23

Lucia M. Sommerer

Self-imposed Algorithmic Thoughtlessness and the Automation of Crime Control

A study of person-based predictive policing and the algorithmic turn

Nomos

The Deutsche Nationalbibliothek lists this publication in the Deutsche Nationalbibliografie; detailed bibliographic data are available on the Internet at http://dnb.d-nb.de

ISBN 978-3-8487-8900-9 (Print)
978-3-7489-2955-0 (ePDF)

British Library Cataloguing-in-Publication Data
A catalogue record for this book is available from the British Library.

ISBN 978-3-8487-8900-9 (Print)
978-3-7489-2955-0 (ePDF)

Library of Congress Cataloging-in-Publication Data
Sommerer, Lucia
Self-imposed Algorithmic Thoughtlessness and the Automation of Crime Control
A study of person-based predictive policing and the algorithmic turn
Lucia Sommerer
260 pp.
Includes bibliographic references.

ISBN 978-3-8487-8900-9 (Print)
978-3-7489-2955-0 (ePDF)

Onlineversion
Nomos eLibrary

1st Edition 2022

Source: Petrarch, Remède de l'un et l'autre fortune prospère et negative (Paris, 1524); Courtesy Bibliotheque Nationale, Paris.

Fortuna, the Roman goddess of destiny (left), and the goddess of science Sapientia (right) are depicted in the above image in their traditional opposition. Fortuna's wheel lets human fate rise and fall seemingly by chance, while science promises certainty. The investigation of the 'taming of chance' and thus the specifically modern unification of the arch-rivals Fortuna and Scientia through algorithmic predictions forms the core of this book.[1]

1 Illustration from *Gigerenzer* 1997, xiii, xviii, Gigerenzer 2015, 44 et seq. ('By 'taming chance in Ian Hacking's evocative phrase, probability and statistics had reconciled Scientia to her arch-rival Fortuna.')

Acknowledgements

'A scholar is just a library's way of making another library.'
– Daniel Dennett

Scholarly work is never the feat of just a single person. My thanks therefore go to all those who have personally supported me in the past years and enabled me to write this book, but also to those authors whose library of works formed the basis and source of inspiration for this book – in particular, Mireille Hildebrandt, Bernard Harcourt, Tobias Singelnstein, Lucia Zedner and Dan McQuillan, who coined the term 'algorithmic thoughtlessness'.

Special thanks go to my thesis supervisor, Professor Katrin Höffler, for the outstanding support and freedom I was given during my doctoral studies. Always encouraging, she accompanied me along my path, placed a great deal of trust in me and taught me the art of science. She is the best mentor I could have imagined. Her love and passion for criminal law, criminology and sociology of law is truly contagious. I would also like to thank Professor Johannes Kaspar and Professor Jörg-Martin Jehle for their support.

I am further deeply indebted to Eva Marguerite Herzog, Maximiliane Berger, Elena Rittinghausen, Felix Butz and Henrike Kruse, without whose contribution this work would not have been possible.

I am also grateful to Yale Law School, particularly the Information Society Project, which during my LL.M.-studies gave me the opportunity to deepen the international perspective on this topic. I would like to thank Professor Jack Balkin and Professor Tom Tyler for their helpful feedback.

I also want to thank the staff of the Yale Law School Graduate Program, in particular Maria Dino, Allegra Di Buenaventura and Gordon Silverstein, as well as the extraordinary librarians of the Law School, in particular Lucie Olejnikova.

Finally, my thanks go to the Studienstiftung des deutschen Volkes for financing my research, especially to Professor Florian Jacoby and Professor Henning Ernst Müller, who placed their trust in me at the very early stages of my research.

The initial ideas for this book became crystallized – far removed from the constraints of everyday life – in the summer of 2017 on the Maltese island of Gozo. I would like to thank the owner of the lonely beach house in the bay of Ghajn Barrani for their hospitality.

This book constitutes an abridged translation of the author's German doctoral thesis. The thesis was awarded 1st place in the Körber Prize and the young scholars' award of the German Foundation for Law and Informatics. The book includes literature and case law up to January 2021.

Table of Contents Overview

Table of Contents

List of Figures

List of Tables

Chapter I. Foundations of person-based predictive policing

A. Introduction

'Had Pyrrhus not fallen by a beldam's hand in Argos or Julius Caesar not been knifed to death. They are not to be thought away. Time has branded them and fettered they are lodged in the room of the infinite possibilities they have ousted. But can those have been possible seeing that they never were? Or was that only possible which came to pass?'

– James Joyce, Ulysses[2]

To what extent is our future predestined? What will happen next? These questions have always vexed humanity. From consultations of the Delphic Oracle of Antiquity to the modern data-driven state – we have always wanted to know what the future holds. For some years now, predictive algorithms[3] have been employed to help answer these questions, including in crime control.[4]

Predictive algorithms, (computer systems with the goal of predicting human behaviour) are in fact omnipresent in our daily life. Have you ever used a search engine, applied for a loan or indulged in online shopping? If so, you have been exposed to predictive algorithms. They predict which search results we are most interested in (personalized browsing), whether we will be able to repay our credit (credit scoring), and what we want to buy next (personalized advertising).

Forecasting criminal behaviour seems to many the logical next step in this evolution. Worldwide, more and more police departments are using 'predictive policing' and courts are increasingly relying on predictive algorithms for decisions on pre-trial detention, probation[5] and sen-

2 *Joyce* 2000, 30.

3 For the term see fn. 20 and accompanying text.

4 On the long-standing fascination of the science fiction genre with crime prediction, see *Dick* 2013 [1956], 223.

5 See overview at *Mayson* Yale L.J. 2018, 490, 512.

tencing.[6] Computer-aided predictions have penetrated all levels of crime control.

At first glance, making decisions based on mathematical-statistical calculations is nothing new in crime control. Statistical methods of crime forecasting have been used in courts for decades to support, for example, probation decisions.[7] However, the acceleration and simplification of previously lengthy procedures with the help of algorithms is now not only opening up new avenues of application in policing with its notorious needs for rapid response; rather, it is fundamentally changing crime control as a whole. This 'algorithmic turn' of crime control is more than a simple continuation of the 'actuarial turn', which Feeley and Simon attested to the criminal justice system at the end of the twentieth century.[8] The actuarial turn was characterized by the emergence of a new discourse on probability and risk. Instead of focusing on the individual perpetrator, statistical models were used to focus on aggregated information on large groups of perpetrators. The algorithmic turn, however, poses further challenges for the system of crime control with the advent of artificial intelligence and the predictive focus on behaviour ever more removed from the actual perpetration of a crime.[9] In particular, the new technologies threaten to diminish the role of traditional criminological research and may lead crime control into 'self-imposed thoughtlessness' (a term inspired by Hannah Arendt; see Chapter III).[10]

These challenges, which originated in the US, reached Europe in 2014.[11] Since then, predictive policing has been used in Germany to predict locations of future crimes (location-based predictive policing). It was first used in Bavaria, but this was followed by numerous other federal states.[12] Further, the German Air Passenger Data Act (Fluggastdatengesetz – FlugDaG), which took force in 2017,[13] provides the first legal framework for personal-based predictive policing in Germany. Finally, German policing

---

6 Cf. international overview in de Keijser et al. 2019; *Eaglin* Emory L.J. 2017, 59, 61; *Slobogin*, in: Petersilia/Reitz 2012, 196, 203-05; see on 'sentencing databases' *Kaspar* 2018, 114 et seq.

7 For Germany see below p. 38 et seq.; see detailed overview in *Boetticher et al.* NStZ 2006, 537, 538; *Tondorf/Tondorf* 2011, 4 et seq.

8 *Feeley/Simon* Criminology 1992, 449.

9 Cf. *Wischmeyer* 2020, mn. 5.

10 See below p. 198 et seq.

11 See *Sommerer* NK 2017, 147, 152 et seq.

12 See below p. 30 et seq.

13 See below p. 80 et seq.

programmes such as Palantir Gotham[14] and RADAR-iTE[15] act as clear precursors to person-based predictive policing, paving the way for fully automated crime prediction in the near future. However, algorithms are not just used to prevent future crime; they are also used to help solve past crimes. The German Federal Criminal Police Office (Bundeskriminalamt), for example, reports that it already uses artificial intelligence and automated pattern recognition for the evaluation of mass data in certain investigations.[16] The German capital of Berlin announced that it would use artificial intelligence to uncover corruption.[17] There are also indications that artificial intelligence in the form of neural networks is already being used today to search for certain forms of tax evasion in Germany.[18] The premise that all of these algorithmic applications follow is one of increased precision, efficiency and objectivity in policing.[19]

The following critically examines this premise, and evaluates the changes associated with the algorithmic turn. Although this book focuses primarily on the use of person-based predictive policing in Germany, many of its conclusions may be generalized beyond national borders and its findings transferred to other areas of the governmental use of algorithms. Since the new algorithmic tools are still in their infancy in Germany, this book is necessarily of a partly prospective nature. However, the conclusions presented here should not be confused with mere speculation about future developments. The book is grounded in evidence in the form of legislative activities and statements by decision-makers in the police and politics. It thus limits itself to realistic and plausible future developments.

Pyrrhus of Epirus and Julius Caesar were regarded as nascent tyrants by their murderers. In accordance with prevailing narratives, their opponents believed that the killings were in the interest of future freedom and security. In the introductory quotation, James Joyce asked about the significance of such tyrannicide as well as the predicted tyrannies that were prevented by the murderers. Were the 'ousted possibilities' of a Pyrrhus in power in Argos or of a Caesar as Roman autocrat ever possible in the first place,

---

14 See below p. 75 et seq.
15 See below p. 71 et seq.
16 BT-Drs. 19/3714, 10.
17 See *Krempel* Heise Online of 20.8.2018, accessible at https://perma.cc/CRK2-4KUL, last accessed 1.1.2022.
18 *Wischmeyer* 2020, mn. 27.
19 *Creemers/Guagnin* KrimJ 2014, 134, 141; *Garzcarek/Steuer* arXiv 2019, 6; cf. on the hopes for the administration in general also beyond the police *Wischmeyer* 2020, mn. 3 et seq.

or, he asks, 'was that only possible which came to pass'. These questions about the determination and predictability of human behaviour must also be addressed by modern police officers in Germany and around the world.

B. Chapter structure

This book is divided into four main chapters: I. Foundations of person-based predictive policing, II. Legal limits of person-based predictive policing, III. The algorithmic turn in crime control, and IV. Minimum requirements for algorithmic crime predictions. These chapters are supplemented by concluding remarks in Chapter V and a summary of the theses in Chapter VI.

Chapter I explains the terminologies used in this book and distinguishes person-based predictive policing from other forms of predictive algorithms used in the field of crime control. Then the research design is laid out. Subsequently, the technological background of predictive policing is explained and differences between traditional statistical methods and algorithmic methods are described. Finally, seven example projects from predictive policing from the US, UK and Germany are presented. The chapter concludes with a reference to the factual limits of the new technology: a lack of overall assessment, causality and neutrality.

Chapter II analyses person-based predictive policing for its compatibility with constitutional values regarding privacy, non-discrimination, transparency, and the presumption of innocence.

Chapter III explains how person-based predictive policing not only fits into existing trends towards risk orientation in crime control, but also leads to fundamentally new challenges, which are critically examined under the headline of the 'algorithmic turn'. The following elements are examined as part of an algorithmic turn: the loss of legitimacy of the police due to a lack of procedural justice, the loss of relevance of criminology vis-à-vis computer science, the lapse of crime control into 'self-imposed thoughtlessness' and the subjugation of law to machine logic.

Finally, Chapter IV proposes 'minimum requirements' on which algorithmic crime predictions should be based in the future. In particular, the minimum requirements emphasize a duty of transparency and impartiality of the procedures used and stress the importance of establishing a central, interdisciplinary government body to set standards and control person-based predictive policing.

C. Terminology

Predictive policing is a dazzling term. It is often used in the media as a catch-all phrase for all algorithm-based procedures in crime control. A clear conceptual distinction between the different types of predictive policing and differentiating the algorithms associated with predictive policing from other types of algorithms, however, remains important. Only after this has been done can the respective necessary legal requirements be assessed.

In this book, predictive policing is understood as algorithmic crime predictions in preventive police work (Fig. 1). Predictive policing is used to avert crimes that have not yet occurred. The fact that it is algorithmic means that it is the result of an algorithm-based decision-making process. An algorithm-based decision-making process is a set of rules that is executable by computers. The rules are written into computer code by programmers or 'learned' by the system itself during machine learning processes. Ultimately, the set of rules assigns a certain value to objects or people (e.g. a high or low probability of committing future violent crimes).[20]

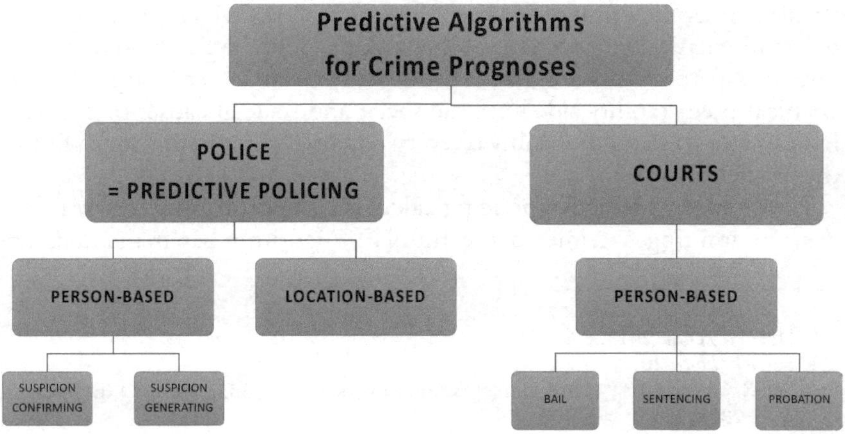

Fig. 1. Overview of predictive algorithms in crime control

20 Cf. *Krafft/Zweig* 2018, 471, 471 et seq.; see also *Pomberger/Dobler* 2008, 29 (An algorithm is essentially a 'guide to solving a problem', which is 'formulated so precisely that it leaves no room for interpretation' and its 'mechanical' execution leads to the desired solution').

I. Types of predictive policing

1. Person-based and location-based

There are two types of predictive policing: location-based and person-based (Fig. 1). Location-based predictive policing has been used in the US since 2005[21] and in Germany since 2014 (currently in six federal states).[22] It identifies *places* with a high probability of becoming the scene of a crime. Identification takes place, among other things, through an analysis of past crime statistics and the use of criminological theories such as the Near Repeat Theory[23] or, in the US, using methods originally developed for earthquake prediction.[24] Police resources, such as patrols, can then be concentrated on these locations to deter offenders.[25] The aim is to use existing police resources as efficiently as possible. At present, location-based predictive policing, internationally as well as in Germany, still concentrates predominantly on predicting burglaries.[26]

A problematic objectification and mechanical image of people even emerges from location-based predictive policing. This is the case for example, when a founder of the American predictive policing company PredPol describes crime as a mere 'physical process', which can be calculated mathematically,[27] or when high-ranking police officials in Germany state that perpetrators are 'like a bad weather front'.[28] This jargon of mechanical predictability side-lines the social and societal causes of crime. It ignores free will and the ability of every potential perpetrator not to follow the prediction.

Person-based predictive policing calculates the probability of an *individual* committing a crime in the future.[29] Algorithm-based methods are

---

21 See *Perry et al.* 2013, 69.
22 See *Knobloch* 2018, 13.
23 See *Knobloch* 2018, 11, 16; *Balogh* Kriminalistik 2016/5, 335; *Johnson* J. Exp. Criminol. 2008, 215.
24 See *Mohler et al.* J. Am. Stat. Assoc. 2011, 100.
25 *Knobloch* 2018, 17.
26 Cf. *Sommerer* NK 2017, 147, 151.
27 *Rubin* LA Times of 21.8.2010, accessible at https://perma.cc/SXX7-9VYF, last accessed 1.1.2022.
28 *Borchers* Heise Online of 2.2.2016, accessible at https://perma.cc/PB9J-T7VG, last accessed 1.1.2022.
29 See also *Rademacher* AöR 2017, 366, 368: 'With the aid of big data technologies, statistical methods are applied to the most comprehensive possible databases of past human behaviour in order to filter out as many variables as possible and

used to analyse volumes of data on past offenders to identify characteristics and behavioural patterns shared by many known offenders prior to their crime. These characteristics and behavioural patterns then form the rules by which the algorithm judges new individuals. Individuals who display characteristics and behavioural patterns that are like those that were identified by the algorithm are classed as more likely to commit a crime.

The likelihood of committing a crime is expressed as a probability score (also known as a risk score). This score can take the form of a percentage, e.g. a 20 per cent probability of committing a violent crime within the next two years. Or it can take the form a risk category, e.g. a person is said to have a low, medium, or high probability of committing a crime. Finally, it is also possible to express a probability score by the measure of deviation from an average population norm, e.g. a score of 500 means that a person has 500 times the probability of committing a crime compared to the average in the population.[30] In contrast to classical statistical methods of crime prediction, algorithm-based crime prediction calculates the probability score automatically, not manually.[31]

Person-based predictive policing, just like location-based predictive policing, is used to allocate resources efficiently. It is aimed at identifying the people who pose the greatest criminal threat, while using as few resources as possible to do so. Follow-up measures (such as observation[32] or telecommunications surveillance)[33] can then be put in place to investigate the threat and ultimately avert it. Person-based predictive policing systems, therefore, do not make decisions about *how* to avert risks; they merely support police decision-making by identifying where risks are assumed to exist.

combine them into patterns that preceded this behaviour'; see also *Wischmeyer* 2020, mn. 19: 'Police analysis systems that evaluate databases using more or less adaptive systems in order to identify impending deviations from standards'.

30 See below p. 66 et seq.

31 For details of the differences, see p. 52 et seq. below.

32 § 16a PolG NRW.

33 § 20c PolG NRW.

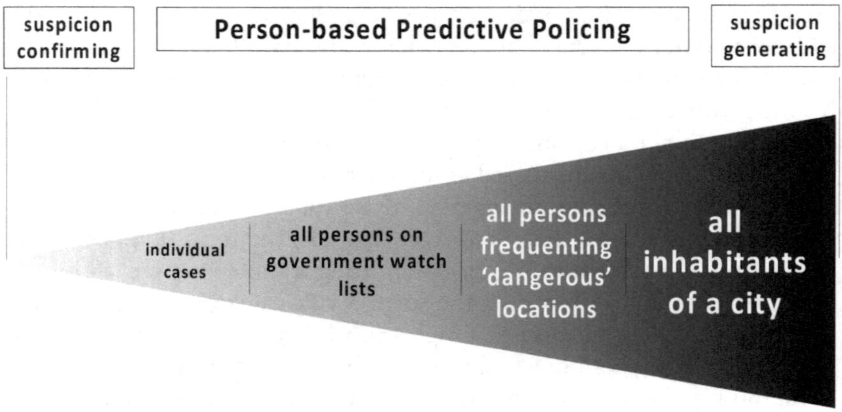

Fig. 2. Impact breadth of different predictive policing approaches from 'suspicion confirming' to 'suspicion generating'

2. Suspicion confirming and suspicion generating approaches

Within person-based predictive policing, a further distinction can be made between applications that merely confirm a suspicion of a crime risk and those that generate suspicions about previously unidentified individuals (Fig. 1, Fig. 2). The approaches differ in terms of impact breadth, i.e. the number of people affected.[34] Suspicion-confirming predictive policing involves the use of algorithm-based crime prediction on data from people that the police assume pose a potential crime risk. Suspicion-confirming predictive policing may be conducted using data from individuals or a small group of people suspected of committing crimes in the future. For example, predictive policing may be conducted using data from the individuals on a government watch list of potential terrorists. In these cases, individualized suspicion existed prior to the application of predictive policing and one can speak of the predictive policing system being used like a magnifying glass to take a closer look at people already known to the police. This category of predictive policing includes, for example, the DyRiAS program used in Switzerland[35] and – as a precursor of predictive

34 Cf. BVerfGE 115, 320 (536).
35 See below p. 76 et seq.

policing – the RADAR-iTE program used by the Federal Criminal Police in Germany.[36]

In contrast, suspicion-generating predictive policing involves the examination of data on large groups of people with the aim of determining whether a person who is not yet known to the police poses a crime risk (Fig. 1, Fig. 2). In the US, for example, predictive policing was used in the Beware programme to create risk scores for all residents of a city.[37] In the Strategic Subject List programme, risk scores were compiled for all Chicago residents who had been arrested by the police in the previous five years.[38] Finally, flight passenger data pattern analysis allows the automated comparison of the data of all air passengers in Germany with patterns that are assumed to indicate future crimes.[39] In these cases, the authorities have no suspicions about specific individuals prior to the application of predictive policing. Rather, the predictive policing system is used to identify people who the system classes as suspicious. In this case, predictive policing 'filters out' dangerous people from the crowd. This is a form of preventive dragnet investigation.[40]

It can be hard, however, to draw a clear line between suspicion-generating and suspicion-confirming predictive policing in practice. The two categories should not be understood as clearly distinguishable, but rather as forming two endpoints on a continuous spectrum. The demarcation between the two categories is fluid, for example, regarding the question of when one may speak of the application of a system to a 'large number' of individuals, or of the application to individual cases. Thus, a system initially used for suspicion-confirming purposes may be transformed into a suspicion-generating system merely by extending the pool of people that it assesses, without the need for significant technical modifications.

36 See below p. 71 et seq.
37 See below p. 64 et seq.
38 See below p. 66 et seq.
39 See below p. 80 et seq.
40 Cf. *Arzt* DÖV 2017, 1023, 1023 et seq.

II. Crime algorithms beyond preventive policing: court proceedings, the penitentiary system and *ex post* police investigations

Algorithms are used in countries like the US[41] for predicting recidivism in pre-trial detention, sentencing and probation decisions. While these algorithms rely on similar algorithmic methods, they do not constitute predictive *policing* due to their *judicial* context (Fig. 1). In addition, *predictive* policing does not involve the use of algorithms designed for *ex post* police work to identify the perpetrator of a crime that has already been committed.[42]

D. Research design

Automation in crime control is an extensive topic that raises many fundamental questions. The breadth of the topic requires a clear analytical framework. This book focuses on the use of person-based predictive algorithms by the police for crime prevention. The use of predictive algorithms in court proceedings and *ex post* police investigations, as described above, do not fall under the concept of predictive policing and lie beyond the scope of this book. The same applies to location-based predictive policing. The research design is based on considerations (1) of topicality, (2) of the transformative potential of person-based predictive policing for crime control as a whole, and (3) of the current research gap on person-based predictive policing.

1. Topicality

Since 2017, the German Air Passenger Data Act (Fluggastdatengesetz – FlugDaG)[43] has permitted person-based predictive policing in Germany

---

41 See above fn. 5, 6.

42 See on tax evasion *Wischmeyer* 2020, mn. 27; on corruption *Krempel* Heise Online of 20.8.2018, accessible at https://perma.cc/CRK2-4KUL, last accessed 1.1.2022; see internationally *McCrank* Reuters of 25.10.2016, accessible at https://perma.cc/VA8R-XL7N, last accessed 1.1.2022, *Hastie/Group* Legaltech News of 19.4.2017, accessible at https://perma.cc/2NEG-S98Z, last accessed 1.1.2022.

43 Act on the Processing of Passenger Data to Implement Directive (EU) 2016/681 of 6 June 2017 (BGBl. I, 1484).

in the form of the automated pattern analysis of passenger data.[44] Data processing commenced in 2018.[45] Further, in 2017, the Federal Criminal Police Office introduced the RADAR-iTE system, a precursor of person-based predictive policing,[46] and in 2018 the German federal state of Hesse amended its police law[47] to permit the use of the Palantir Gotham software, which had already been used for person-based predictive policing in the US.[48]

When location-based predictive policing was abruptly introduced in Germany in 2014, it could not rely on any legal or criminological analyses by the German scientific community.[49] Thus, the first location-based predictive policing system in use in Germany, Precobs, was developed and implemented entirely without the involvement of legal scholars.[50] The implementation of a new technology – even if only in a temporary trial phase – without preceding and accompanying[51] scientific discourse (not to mention democratic discourse) can anchor problematic modalities and key assumptions into the technology and its use. Many of these modalities will be difficult to overcome once they have been established.[52] This is not only a question of ensuring the legality of the technology, but also of which value judgements should be embodied in the technology in the first place. Once a technology has been introduced, *ex post* discussions can no longer have the same impact on the technology's design. Key decisions will have been made without taken legal and criminal considerations into account. This book is intended to help prevent a repeat 'ambush' of society and the scientific community when it comes to person-based predictive policing.

---

44 See § 4 FlugDaG.

45 See *Bundesministerium des Innern* 2018; see in detail p. 80 et seq.

46 See *Bundeskriminalamt* Presseinformation of 2.2.2017, accessible at https://perma.cc/Z89V-CF75, last accessed 1.1.2022; legal basis for the deployment is § 18 (1) no. 4 BKAG; see in detail p. 71 et seq.

47 New introduction of § 25a (1) HSOG.

48 See below p. 75 et seq.

49 See on hot spot policing, fn. 64.

50 The inclusion of data protection officers only once after completion of the system cannot be equated with the involvement of lawyers as early as the development phase.

51 The project has been academically accompanied in Baden-Württemberg since 2015, but only with regard to the efficiency of the system, see *Gerstner* 2017.

52 *Wischmeyer* 2020, mn. 6 generally warns with regard to the use of algorithms by the executive that technological development will have an unreflected effect on the administration, and he calls for 'responsive regulation' of the development process.

More than merely offering a definitive analysis of person-based predictive policing, this book is aimed at encouraging further scientific analyses and discursive processes.

This is even more urgent in view of the problems reported from countries like the US in connection with person-based predictive policing, such as regarding the discriminatory effect of algorithms.[53] These problems are inscribed into algorithmic systems during the early stages of development and can subsequently only be eliminated with great effort. Raising awareness about these challenges among decision-makers in police and politics as well as the scientific community is thus of particular importance and should be done as early as possible.

2. Transformative potential

The impact of person-based predictive policing on citizens' constitutional rights is more far-reaching than that of location-based predictive policing. At the same time, person-based predictive policing deviates significantly further from existing police practices and laws than location-based predictive policing does.[54] Whereas location-based predictive policing can be conducted without the processing of personal data and thus without interfering with constitutionally guaranteed rights to privacy and informational self-determination, person-based predictive policing necessarily intervenes deeply in the right to privacy.[55] By reducing individuals to risk percentages and by using algorithms that are too complex for people to understand, person-based predictive policing even threatens to infringe upon the non-alienable fundamental right of human dignity.[56]

Person-based predictive policing threatens to limit police officers' decision-making corridors to such a degree that it encourages a displacement of responsibility (see 'Self-imposed algorithmic thoughtlessness' in Chapter III).[57]

Further, once introduced, person-based predictive policing technology has the potential to migrate to other areas of crime control. A system

53 See e.g. *Angwin et al.* ProPublica of 23.05.2016, accessible at https://perma.cc/LA-E9-A656, last accessed 1.1.2022.

54 See also *Singelnstein* NStZ 2018, 1.

55 For details see p. 103 et seq.

56 For details see p. 153 et seq.

57 See below p. 198 et seq.

implemented by the police for preventive purposes could, for example, be transferred without major technical changes to *ex post* police work to investigate past crimes[58] or to recidivism prognoses in courts.[59] A detailed examination of the legal and factual limits of predictive algorithms in preventive policing, and answers, for example, to the question of which control infrastructures should be set up around person-based predictive policing promises insights useful beyond a policing context.

Finally, an extrapolation of person-based predictive policing that attaches numerical risk scores to individuals may also be imagined outside of crime control. As Franz von Liszt warned, escalating prevention may lead to 'social hygiene'.[60] Initial examples of this can be seen in China's plan for a 'Social Credit Score' (社会信用体系 – shèhuì xìnyòng tǐxì). This Chinese 'super-score' is intended to merge data from various online and offline sources in order to comprehensively evaluate the social behaviour of the population[61] and to support government decisions on university admission and promotions. There is currently no danger of *total* state surveillance in either Europe or the US. However, it is impossible to rule out the fact that private companies could offer similar super scores for commercial reasons.[62]

3. Research gap

Person-based predictive policing is of greater novelty for police work from the viewpoint of the historical development of police practices. This is the case, because there is no body of 'historical' scholarly research into person-based predictive policing. Location-based predictive policing,[63] on the other hand, can look back on predecessors known as hot-spot policing

58 See *Saunders et al.* J. Exp. Criminol. 2016, 347, 365.

59 Cf. very similar systems in the US, e.g. COMPAS *Angwin et al.* ProPublica of 23.05.2016, accessible at https://perma.cc/LAE9-A656, last accessed 1.1.2022; cf. also the concern of the German Data Protection Commissioner *Datenschutzbeauftragte des Bundes und der Länder* 2015, 1.

60 *von Liszt*, 25, 62.

61 *Kostka* New Media & Society 2019, 1; further evidence from *Zalnieriute et al.* Mod. L. Rev. 2019, 425, 439 et seq.

62 *Gigerenzer et al.* Wirtschaftsdienst 2018, 860, 867.

63 See *Gluba* Kriminalistik 2014, 347; *Kriminologische Forschungsstelle Landeskriminalamt Hamburg*, Projektbeschreibung Prädiktionspotenzial Schwere Einbruchskriminalität, accessible at https://perma.cc/AW7Y-5H6R, last accessed 1.1.2022; *Gerstner* 2017; *Knobloch* 2018; *Hauber et al.* 2020; publications that address person-

and crime mapping. Both have already received detailed treatment in the scholarly literature.[64] Therefore, some areas of location-based predictive policing have at least been subjected to critical analysis by the scientific community. In contrast, person-based predictive policing has yet to be properly examined in scientific and social discourse. Moreover, the current efforts to introduce person-based predictive policing in Germany and around the world seem to have gone largely unnoticed. It is this research gap that this book aims to address.

E. *Technological background*

The following section presents the traditional statistical methods of crime forecasting before providing an overview of the new methods of algorithmic predictions and their core differences.

I. Traditional statistical methods

As mentioned in the introductory chapter, statistical methods for predicting crime are nothing new in crime control. For decades, statistical approaches have been used in sentencing and probation contexts along with intuitive prognoses by judges[65] and clinical-psychiatric prognoses[66] by doctors.[67]

These tools for statistical prognostics are based on empirically proven predictors of recidivism, which have been obtained from scientific studies, for example, through court file analyses using data from offenders. Whether certain predictors are present in an individual case is determined by

---

based and location-based predictive policing together often focus on the latter, see *Singelnstein* NStZ 2018, 1; *Rademacher* AöR 2017, 366; *Egbert/Krasmann* 2019.

64 See *Bowers et al.* Brit. J. Crim. 2004, 641; *Johnson et al.* 2007; *Groff/LaVigne* Crime Prevention Studies 2002, 29;*Farrell/Sousa* 2001, 221.

65 See *Kaiser* 1996, 960; *Eisenberg/Kölbel* 2017, 223.

66 See *Nedopil* Forensia 1986, 167; *Nedopil/Gross* 2005.

67 For an overview of the various forecasting methods see *Rettenberger/von Franqué* 2013, 20 et seq.; in detail *Pollähne* 2011; on the classification of forecasting instruments into 'generations' *Andrews/Bonta* 2017, 192 et seq., see also the 'Method of ideal-typical comparative individual case analysis' (MIVEA) *Bock* 1995 founded by *Göppinger* and further developed by *Bock*; on the superiority of statistical methods at any rate over clinically intuitive ones: *Andrews/Bonta* 2017, 193 m. w. N.

specially trained prognosis experts (psychiatrists, psychologists or criminologists) who study individual case histories and interview the individual involved (anamnesis). Statistical approaches can look back on a long tradition in the penal and probation system and their preventive paradigm. Tools for statistical prognostics have been used in probation decisions in the US since the 1920s.[68] In Germany, the use of statistical forecasting tools has been increasing since the 1980s, especially in the case of violent,[69] sexual[70] and extremist crimes.[71] At present, at least 150 statistical forecasting tools are available.[72] Numerous instruments have been developed by commercial providers and one may even speak of a forecasting industry.[73] These tools serve the sole purpose of predicting recidivism in judicial sentencing and probation contexts. They are not used to identify future criminals outside of court settings.

In essence, the tools used for statistical crime prognosis compare individuals to groups of people who are known to have committed a heightened percentage of crimes in the past. A 20 per cent risk of recidivism means that an individual shares characteristics and behaviours with 20 individuals out a group of 100 people who recidivated. This method cannot specify whether the person under assessment will go on to commit a further offence.

In the following, the development and application of statistical forecasting tools is explained in six steps using the example of the forecasting tool Violence Risk Appraisal Guide-Revised (VRAG-R),[74] which is frequently used in many countries including Germany to predict violent behaviour:[75]

1. compiling database
2. defining target variable

---

68 See *Burgess* 1928, *Hart* J. Am. Inst. Crim. L. & Criminology 1923, 405.

69 See e.g. VRAG – Violence Risk Appraisal Guide: *Quinsey et al.* 2006; HCR-20 – Historical-Clinical-Risk Management-20 Violence Risk Assessment Scheme: *Douglas et al.* Int. J. Forensic Ment Health 2014, 93 et seq.

70 See e.g. RRS – Risk of relapse in sex offenders: *Rehder/Suhling* 2006; SVR-20 – Sexual Violence Risk-20: *Boer* 1997.

71 See e.g. VERA – Violent Extremism Risk Assessment: *Pressman et al.* 2016; *Sadowski et al.* Kriminalistik 2017, 335; TRAP-18 – Terrorist Radicalization Assessment Protocol: *Meloy et al.* Journal of Threat Assessment and Management 2015, 140, 140 et seq.

72 *Fazel et al.* BMJ 2012, e4692, 2; see also *Rettenberger/von Franqué* 2013, 21.

73 *Pollähne* 2011, 2 fn. 15.

74 *Rettenberger et al.* 2017; *Rice et al.* Psychological Assessment 2013, 951; *Quinsey et al.* 2006.

75 Cf. *Eaglin* Emory L.J. 2017, 59, 76 et seq.

3. defining predictive input variables
4. deducing a predictive model
5. risk translation and risk communication
6. application to the individual case

1. Compiling database

First, a database of past cases is collected. It contains all the information from which rules for predictions are to be derived by statistical analyses. In the case of VRAG-R, this was data on 1,261 male offenders in Canada.[76] All of the individuals included in this database had a mental illness. The data set includes people who are considered fit as well as unfit for trial due to their mental illness and people in prison who require psychotherapeutic treatment.[77]

2. Defining target variable

The next step is to determine what the data is to be used to predict, i.e. the target variable. If the aim is to predict criminal behaviour, three points must be defined: the type of offence (e.g. theft, robbery, rape), what is meant by perpetration (arrest, indictment or conviction), and the period under consideration for recidivism (e.g. 6 months, 2 years, 10 years). VRAG-R defines the target variable as follows:[78] type of offence: (attempted) murder, kidnapping, deprivation of liberty, assault, any kind of offence that led to injury on the victim's part, robbery, rape and any other sexual assault that involved physical contact between offender and victim. Indicator of the commission of a crime: being formally charged with one of the offences. Measured time period: recidivism during a period of 5 and 12 years.

The choice of target variables is also guided by practical considerations, such as how easily the manufacturers of a prognosis tool can obtain data. For VRAG, for example, the manufacturers deliberately defined perpetrati-

---

76 *Rettenberger et al.* 2017, 7.

77 VRAG-R also postulates a transferability of the instrument generally to perpetrators of violence despite the special design of the case basis to people with a mental illness, *Rettenberger et al.* 2017, 7.

78 *Rettenberger et al.* 2017, 8.

on of a crime as a formal charge instead of a conviction. They considered it too time-consuming to wait for final conviction judgments for the individuals in the case database.[79]

3. Defining predictive input variables

The next step is to determine which of the offender's characteristics (predictive input variables) are associated with future criminal behaviour.

The predictors are regularly based on empirical and theoretical criminological knowledge of general recidivism factors[80] and usually fall into one of four areas: (1) history of antisocial or delinquent behaviour, (2) an antisocial personality, (3) antisocial attitudes and (4) antisocial environment.[81]

First, many variables are selected, which are then reduced to the most predictive variables during model construction. In VRAG-R, around 50 initial variables[82] were reduced to the 12 most significant (e.g. growing up with one parent, behavioural problems in school, drug use, marital status).[83] Both risk-increasing and risk-reducing (protective) variables can be considered as input variables. At this stage, a decision needs to be taken on whether only static, i.e. unchangeable variables should be included in a prediction (e.g. age, parental divorce), or if dynamically changeable variables (e.g. attitudes, social environment, impulsivity) should also be included. It is much more time-consuming to objectively determine the status of dynamic variables. However, if dynamic variables are included, a tool can be used to identify possibilities for active risk-reducing therapeutic interventions, instead of merely statistically calculating individual risk. Although VRAG-R also uses dynamically changeable variables (e.g. marital status), it focuses heavily on static variables. Some other instruments take more dynamic factors into account including the Juvenile Sex Offender Assessment Protocol-II (J-SOAP-II),[84] Static-99, Stable-2000 and Stable-2007[85] in the context of sexual offences.

79 *Rettenberger et al.* 2017, 8.
80 *Kröber et al.* 2006, 83.
81 *Kröber et al.* 2006, 83.
82 *Kröner* 2005, 16.
83 *Rettenberger et al.* 2017, 45 et seq.
84 *Prentky/Righthand* 2003, 21 et seq.
85 *Rettenberger et al.* Forensische Psychiatrie, Psychologie, Kriminologie 2011, 45, 45 et seq.

4. Deducing a predictive model

In the case of VRAG-R regression analysis,[86] statistical analysis is used to determine correlations between an input variable and the 'recidivism' target variable. The statistical model is unable to determine causal relationships between the variables and instead determines correlations and extrapolates them for the future. Statistical analyses are used to derive 'if-this-then-that' relationships between input variables and target variables from the data, e.g. *if* a person has drug problems, *then* they are 2x more likely to recidivize; *if* a person grew up with only one parent, *then* they are 3x more likely to recidivize. The different probabilities can be reflected in the model by weighting individual input variables.

Finally, more complex models can consider the way in which the variables influence each other. The probability of recidivism in people with drug problems *and* growing up with one parent, for example, does not simply add up, but forms a new probability factor, e.g. of 3.5x. When greater numbers of variables that influence each other are considered, more if-this-then-that rules need to be developed and this increases the complexity of the model.

Finally, at this stage it is also possible to influence the errors that a model produces. Every statistical forecast contains a certain error rate; it is impossible to provide forecasts with absolute certainty. Absolute certainty in a prognosis would presuppose behavioural determinism that cannot be justified epistemologically.[87] There are two kinds of error that a model can produce: false-positives and false-negatives. False-positives occur when people who do not actually go on to commit a crime are identified as high risk – these are, so to speak, 'harmless' individuals who are falsely marked as high risk. False-negatives occur when people who do go on to commit a crime have been marked as low risk. False-positives are particularly problematic from the view of the constitutional right to freedom; false-negatives are problematic with regard to societal security considerations. Statistically, both errors are interwoven in such a way that they cannot both be minimized at the same time. Attempts to reduce the number of false-negatives ('dangerous individuals at large') automatically increase the number of false-positives ('harmless people locked up').[88]

---

86 *Rettenberger et al.* 2017, 8 et seq.

87 *Hoffmann et al.* 2017, 35.

88 *Hoffmann et al.* 2017, 36; for an interactive simulation of this see *Grossenbacher* SRF of 5.4.2018, accessible at https://perma.cc/7ZY8-6HCS, last accessed 1.1.2022.

5. Risk translation and risk communication

Once a model with all input variables, their weighting and the calibration of the error rate has been deduced, the model must be converted into a form that is easy for users to understand and handle.

a) Percentages

With VRAG-R, this is done by converting the twelve input variables into twelve questions that can be answered by an operator in writing. The questions regard the existence or absence of specific input variables. Each answer is assigned a point value that reflects the weighting of the characteristic (e.g. growing up with both parents: -2 points, never married +1 point). At the end, the operators manually add up all points to gain a total score (e.g. 10). The total score corresponds to one of 9 defined risk categories[89] (10 points correspond to risk category of 6). The operators can then use a table to determine the person's predicted rate of recidivism for the next 5 and 12 years (a person with a risk score of 6 is said to have a 34 per cent and 60 per cent risk respectively).[90] This means that 34 per cent and 60 per cent of the people who in the past fulfilled the characteristics of risk category 6 recidivized. However, it also means that 66 per cent and 40 per cent respectively did *not* recidivize. As mentioned above, it is impossible to statistically determine which subgroup a person is closer to.

The paper-based checklists, in which operators manually add up points, have also been adapted for completion on computers and web browsers.[91] In these cases, the scores for each answer are clearly visible to the operator but everything is added up by the computer at the end. This method is not a complex system of algorithmic decision-making.[92]

b) Probability of crime in comparison to the average population

A display of risk percentages is not the only way of communicating risk. It is also possible to use the factor by which a person's risk of crime

89 *Rettenberger et al.* 2017, 11.
90 *Rettenberger et al.* 2017, 11.
91 See for example https://perma.cc/5YA3-95QE (last accessed 1.1.2022).
92 See below p. 49 et seq.

deviates from the norm (the average population). In this way, people can be assigned a 2x, 10x, or 500x higher risk than the average population.[93] However, such risk display is not used for VRAG-R.

c) Base rate

Finally, the base rate can also be used as a reference value. The base rate refers to the occurrence of certain offences in the general population or in certain narrower population groups (e.g. among men, convicts, people with a mental illness, people on a 'watch list'). The base rate is an important aspect of overall risk assessments.[94] Without awareness of the base rate, misjudgements of risk may occur.[95]

It is generally accepted that very low base rates, such as for terrorist offences,[96] automatically lead to more false-positives in any statistical system, and operators should be aware of this. However, it is difficult to determine reliable base rates for many offences.[97] It is particularly difficult to determine recidivism base rates for people in prison, as no data are available on whether prisoners would actually commit an offence if they were not being held in custody.[98]

VRAG-R reports a recidivism base rate for the 1,261 people with mentally illness in its case database as 47 per cent over ten years (592 individuals).[99] However, it does not state the recidivism base rate for people without mental illness. Despite this, the designers of VRAG-R also recommend that their tool be used for people without mental illness.

Although the base-rate information is contained in documents accompanying VRAG-R, it is not made available to operators when calculating a risk.

---

93 See below for the Strategic Subject List p. 66 et seq.

94 *Kröber et al.* 2006, 84.

95 *Gigerenzer* 2000, 251 et seq.; *Ginosar/Trope* J. Exp. Soc. Psychol. 1980, 228, 228 et seq.; see also *Kahneman/Tversky* Psychol. Rev. 1973, 237, 237.

96 Cf. *Albrecht* Journal für Konflikt-und Gewaltforschung 2003, 97, 104; *Polläbne* 2011, 242.

97 See *Kröber et al.* 2006, 84 et seq.

98 See *Volckart* Recht und Psychiatrie 2002, 107.

99 See *Rettenberger et al.* 2017, 14.

d) Error rate

Finally, it is possible to indicate the error rate for false-positives and false-negatives to help operators properly judge the meaning of a risk score. However, virtually no prognosis tool currently provides error rates. Despite this, the Supreme Court of the State of Wisconsin in the US ruled that risk scores developed with the COMPAS prognosis tool must be accompanied by general information about a prognosis system's susceptibility to errors.[100]

e) Cut-off

It is also possible to define the 'cut-off' between 'dangerous' and 'harmless' individuals, i.e. the threshold above which a person should be classified as dangerous or even 'highly dangerous'.[101] VRAG-R does not do so and instead leaves the decision to the operators. In contrast, other prognosis tools make these assessments to ensure that the tool is applied consistently. For example, they always classify people with an X-percent risk as 'highly dangerous' irrespective of their individual circumstances.[102]

6. Application to individual cases

Statistical prognosis tools such as VRAG-R have been used solely in the context of prognosis decisions in court. They are not used in policing. However, attempts to produce statistical crime prognoses have not always been limited to sentencing and probation: in the 1960s, US criminologists Sheldon and Eleanor Glueck attempted to identify potential offenders among toddlers using statistical characteristics.[103] Elmerings attempted to transfer this approach to Germany and posited that every child should

---

100 The results of the instrument should be accompanied by warnings concerning, inter alia, susceptibility to errors particularly for African Americans: State v. Loomis, 881 N.W.2d 749 (WI 2016) (mn. 66).

101 See *Pollähne* 2011, 237 et seq.; see also *Mayson* Yale L.J. 2018, 490, 497; *Eaglin* Emory L.J. 2017, 59, 87.

102 For example, RADAR-iTE (see below. p. 72 et seq.

103 See *Glueck/Glueck* Brit. J. Criminol. 1963, 215; *Glueck/Glueck* Int. J. Soc. Psychiatr. 1966, 5.

be assessed for their future risk of committing a crime.[104] Nevertheless, statistical predictions of crime beyond the court setting have yet to become widely established. Preventive policing cannot look back on any tradition of statistical forecasting. Instead, the area is dominated by the subjective-intuitive risk prognoses developed by police officers in the field. The need for rapid responses in traditional policing is hard to reconcile with the time-consuming development of statistical prognoses. The police do not usually have the time to examine statistical crime predictors, either through detailed individual interviews or through court file analyses. Even if there were time for such lengthy procedures, a conversation with the person concerned would draw attention to their status as a person suspected of committing future crimes. Moreover, files for analysis on the general public are not kept to the same extent as court files on criminals are. All this contributes to the fact that the compilation of standardized crime prognoses in preventive policing has so far been considered impractical. To make standardized crime prognoses attractive for preventive policing, automation and acceleration through algorithm-based decision-making is needed.

a) People affected by crime prognoses

Despite the special nature of the case database used by VRAG-R, which only contains data on people with a mental illness, follow-up studies have confirmed the transferability of the tool to the general prison population without mental illness.[105] However, VRAG-R only applies to people who have already been charged or convicted once. According to the developers, the prior offence must not have been a violent offence.[106] Independent studies have shown, however, that the predictive power of the tool decreases significantly when applied to people convicted of non-violent offences.[107]

In German judicial practice, statistical forecasting tools are not applied to everyone in the criminal justice system. There is no generalized application of statistical crime prognoses in Germany, unlike in some US states,

---

104 *Elmering* 1969.
105 *Rettenberger et al.* 2017, 7 et seq. with further references.
106 *Rettenberger et al.* 2017, 9 et seq.
107 *Kröber et al.* 2006, 40 with further references.

for example.[108] There is also no 'general screening' of all defendants or prisoners, aimed at using statistical means to identify the most dangerous prisoners.

Although the option for judges to obtain an expert crime prognosis report is laid down in various paragraphs of German law,[109] judges rarely do so and usually make their decisions without seeking expert opinions and thus make no use of statistical procedures. For reasons of procedural economy, experts are only commissioned for particularly grave cases where[110] prognosis reports are expressly required by law: such as when dealing with offenders with a mental illness who may be unfit to stand trial,[111] or if an offender has committed a particularly serious offence that could lead to life imprisonment or preventive detention.[112] Even in these legally prescribed cases, the type of prognosis is not specified by law, which means that it is up to an expert to include or leave out statistical prognoses in their assessments. It is therefore impossible to speak of statistical crime forecasting as a 'standard measure' in criminal proceedings in Germany.

b) Prognosis tool operators

The manual accompanying the German version of VRAG-R clearly states that the tool should only be used by people who have received appropriate training in statistical prognosis. Operators are expected to have precise knowledge about the evaluation rules used in VRAG-R as well as general knowledge about statistical relationships in forecasting tools.[113] In the context of a risk prognosis in court it is not judges themselves who use tool but expert psychiatrists, psychologists or criminologists. It is important that the risk assessment should not be based *solely* on the results of a statistical prognosis tool. The list of minimum standards for forensic progno-

---

108 See *Mayson* Yale L.J. 2018, 490, 497; *Pretrial Justice Institute* 2017, 4; use of the Public Safety Assessment Tool (PSA) in New Jersey, Kentucky and Arizona.

109 See overview in fn. 7.

110 *Schneider et al.* 2015, 264

111 §§ 63, 64 German Criminal Code in conjunction with § 246a German Criminal Procedure Code; § 67 d II German Criminal Code in conjunction with § 463 German Criminal Procedure Code.

112 § 57a German Criminal Code in conjunction with § 454 German Criminal Procedure Code; § 57 German Criminal Code in conjunction with § 454 German Criminal Procedure Code; §§ 80a, 246a German Criminal Procedure Code.

113 *Rettenberger et al.* 2017, 5.

sis reports in Germany published in 2007[114] considers prognoses developed *solely* with statistical methods as inadequate.[115] The German Constitutional Court (Bundesverfassungsgericht – BVerfG) and the Federal Court of Justice (Bundesgerichtshof – BGH) have also stated that recidivism prognoses may not be based exclusively on statistical findings.[116] For example, the BGH declared as insufficient expert opinions developed *solely* with SVR-20[117] and HCR-20.[118] These focus the clinical recidivism assessment process strongly on statistical predictors.[119] In addition to a forecasting tool, experts must carry out overall assessments of the circumstances surrounding an individual case.[120] At the international level, however, we find opposing approaches to prognoses, some of which promote the exclusive use of statistical tools in crime forecasting.[121] Since 2017, judges in the US have been permitted to make decisions about pre-trial detention solely on the basis of statistical prognoses.[122] Moreover, prognosis instruments have been deliberately developed that completely dispense of the use of interviews between experts and the people being assessed.[123] In Germany, however, statistical forecasting tools are only *one* component in a holistic recidivism prognosis.

---

114 *Boetticher et al.* NStZ 2006, 537.

115 *Boetticher et al.* NStZ 2006, 537, 542 ('Prognostic instruments do not replace hermeneutic or hypothesis-driven individual prognosis' and '[it] is intended to generate an individual theory against the background of empirical knowledge').

116 See BVerfGE 109, 190 (759) ('A mere abstract forecast decision based on statistical probabilities is not sufficient'); BGH NStZ 2007, 464 (465); NStZ-RR 2009, 323; 2009, 499; 2010, 203 (204); NStZ 2010, 504 (506); see also *Dessecker*, in: NK-StGB, § 66 mn. 89; *Heger*, in: Lackner/Kühl, § 66 mn. 17.

117 See BGH StV 2008, 301 et seq.

118 BGH Resolution of 16.12.2015 -2 StR 469/15.

119 SVR-20 and HCR-20 do not belong to the class of 'pure' statistical forecasting instruments in the narrow sense, but to the 'Structured Professional Judgement' class. However, they still have a focus on statistically proven risk factors. *Kröber et al.* 2006, 44 et seq. also state that SVR-20 and HCR-20 also 'largely meet the requirements of statistical methods'.

120 BVerfGE 109, 133; see the landmark decision of the BGH on standards of credibility assessment BGHSt 45, 164 et seq.; see also BGH NStZ-RR 2005, 39; BGH NStZ-RR 2005, 232; on statistical forecasting instruments in particular BGH StV 2008, 301 et seq.

121 *Wiseman* Geo. Wash. L. Rev. 2016, 417, 458 ('Fixing bail requires [...] to craft and impose guidelines based on validated risk assessment tools'); see also *Andrews/Bonta* 2017, 193 et seq.

122 In the state of New Jersey, *Mayson* Yale L.J. 2018, 490, 497 fn. 25, 26.

123 *Mayson* Yale L.J. 2018, 490, 512.

II. Algorithmic predictions

The following demonstrates how the use of algorithmic predictions can change the processes described above (Tbl. 1). An algorithmic predictive system is, as described in the chapter on terminology, a computer program that assigns values to objects or people based on properties of that object or person.[124] Values can either be assigned according to rules written into the computer code by humans (rule-based) or according to rules learned by the system itself (machine learning).

Traditional statistical approach	Algorithmic predictions	
	Rule-based	Machine learning
1. Compiling database	similar to traditional	larger database; greater diversity of data sources; possibly big data
2. Defining target variable	similar to traditional	Similar to traditional
3. Defining predictive input variables	similar to traditional; greater number of variables possible	greater number of variables possible; more dynamic variables
4. Deducing a predictive model If-this-then-that relationships deduced by humans	similar to traditional; more complex correlations possible	automatic deduction of if-this-then-that relationships from case database by AI; more complex, correlations; self-learning; greater lack of transparency
5. Risk translation & risk communication - Risk translation: Paper questionnaires & points system	risk translation: translation of if-this-then-that relationships into computer code	risk translation: not necessary; if-this-then-that relationships already in computer code
- Risk communication: Probability, base rate, error rate, etc.	risk communication: similar to traditional	risk communication: similar to traditional
6. Application to individual case Filling out paper questionnaires & manual point addition	data entry into software, automatic score generation greater lack of transparency, e.g. due to trade secret protections acceleration; automation of data input possible	data entry in software, automated score generation greater lack of transparency, e.g. due to trade secret protections acceleration; automation of data input possible

Tbl. 1. Comparison of traditional statistical and algorithmic crime predictions (differences in thicker frames)

124 See above fn. 20.

1. Rule-based algorithmic predictions

The 'simplest' forms of algorithmic predictions are rule-based, also known as theory-based or knowledge-based. The term 'Good Old-Fashioned Artificial Intelligence' is also commonly used.[125] Rule-based algorithms are now so widespread in our everyday lives in computers, mobile phones, cars, etc., that they are often no longer perceived as artificial intelligence at all. They are often not even called AI by laypeople. However, computer scientists would certainly describe certain rule-based systems as artificially intelligent.

Rule-based prediction systems are systems in which people develop a criminological theory and prove it with traditional statistical calculations. The algorithm does not come into play here until the developers have derived a complete statistical model from the database. The resulting statistical model contains all the if-this-then-that relationships between different input variables and the target variable. Steps 1–4 in the development of a traditional statistical prediction tool (see above)[126] must be completed by humans before, in step 5, risk translation, the (weighted) if-this-then-that relationships of the statistical model are translated into computer code (instead of paper-based questionnaires in the case of traditional statistical models). The algorithmic prediction system comprises the totality of all humanly derived if-this-then-that relationships (rules) and the formation of these rules into a software application. The software will then automatically output a risk score using the input variables entered for each individual case.

If the algorithm-based prediction system is applied to individual cases, the software prompts operators to answer the same questions about certain input variables (e.g. age, drug abuse) that would have been asked in the case of a paper-based questionnaire. The operator must enter or click on the answers manually. The algorithm then assigns point values to the answers independently in the background and uses them to calculate an overall risk score, which is then presented to the operator.

Theoretically, the software could even do without the manual entry of input variables by humans. The status of each variable could instead be read automatically from a database. In Chicago, for example, the Strategic Subject List produced criminal forecasts for almost 400,000 people.[127] In

125 *Haugeland* 1989, 112.
126 See above p. 40 et seq.
127 See above fn. 100.

this case, the data were collected automatically from the police database without the need for police officers to fill out 400,000 computer questionnaires manually.

The core differences between the rule-based algorithmic approach and traditional statistical models are particularly clear, however, from step 6: Application in individual cases (Tbl. 1).

First of all, the prediction procedure greatly lacks transparency for operators, as they no longer assign point values to variables themselves as was the case with manual addition. Moreover, software manufacturers may now invoke trade secrets[128] to deliberately conceal the way in which the results are calculated. This is the case with numerous prediction tools used by courts in the US to make decisions about probation.[129] Another difference is the processing speed of the software compared to manual calculations and the inherent potential of further automation not only for the data output, but also for the data input stage.

However, step 3, Defining predictive input variables, and step 4, Deducing a statistical model, also provide for new opportunities. In a traditional statistical paper-based questionnaire, the number of input variables and the complexity of their weighting are limited by researchers' abilities to add up point values. If a computer carries out the weighting and adds up the point values, a larger number of variables can be used[130] and more complex relationships between variables can be studied.

Finally, it should be mentioned that while the calculations in rule-based algorichtmic predictions may appear intransparent to the operator in individual cases, they are easily comprehensible in themselves for experts who are granted access to the data base and the underlying statistical model. Comprehensible in this context means that experts can gain an understanding of the input variables used and their correlation with the target variable, but not of causality. Comprehensibility decreases with a rising number of interlocking if-this-then-that relationships, i.e., more complex computer code. For example, the rule that determines a decision in an individual case may be 'hidden' in hundreds of lines of code, or the code may be written in a confusing way by using superfluous elements

128 See critical analysis at p. 149 et seq.

129 *Eaglin* Emory L.J. 2017, 59, 112.

130 However, the number of possible variables is further limited by the fact that the more variables one queries in a model, the larger the case base must be in order to achieve valid results; the 'curse of dimensionality' see *Lehr/Ohm* UCDL Rev. 2017, 653, 700.

or numerous patches. Computer scientists describe rule-based code that is hard to understand as 'spaghetti code'.[131]

The Deep Blue algorithm, which defeated the chess world champion Kasparov in 1989, is a rule-based algorithmic system.[132] Another example of this type of system is the computer-based questionnaire used for the DyRiAS system, which was developed in Germany and deployed in Switzerland.[133]

In summary: knowledge contained in a rule-based algorithm is limited to the if-this-then-that relationships that people have inscribed into it. Rule-based algorithmic predictions are associated with innovation at the application stage of a predictive tool, but not when deducing a statistical model. This changes, however, when we turn to machine learning predictions.

2. Machine learning algorithmic predictions

Machine learning, which is also called pattern recognition or correlation-based artificial intelligence,[134] is a more complex form of algorithmic prediction. In this case, if-this-then-that relationships are not inscribed into the system by people, but automatically by the system which analyses information in the database (also called the training dataset). The degree to which these if-this-then-that relationships are comprehensible to humans depends on the exact method of machine learning used. Some are more comprehensible than others. The independent derivation of rules from a training dataset is referred to as 'learning' of the algorithm. The algorithm identifies patterns in the training dataset and compares new cases with these patterns.

---

131 Cf. the fatal accident of a Toyota driver in 2007. The error in the rule-based 'spaghetti code' of the on-board system was only discovered after almost two years of investigation by a multi-member team of experts. This code is to be considered difficult to understand even for experts; Trial Transcript of Expert Testimony, Bookout v. Toyota, Case No. CJ-2008-7969, Oct. 14, 2013, accessible at https://perma.cc/3M9S-L4R6, last accessed 1.1.2022; *Barr* Embedded Gurus 2013; see also Wischmeyer, who states that even rule-based systems can have a large internal complexity, see *Wischmeyer* 2020, mn. 4.

132 See for details *Pandolfini* 1997.

133 See below p. 76.

134 For a generally understandable introduction to the technology see *Alpaydin* 2016; cf. also *Gesellschaft für Informatik* 2018b, 45 et seq.; *Lehr/Ohm* UCDL Rev. 2017, 653; *Berk* 2019.

Although the algorithm 'learns' the patterns independently, people still have the important task of selecting the training dataset, defining the target variable, specifying the input variables and calibrating and monitoring the learning process. These are central steps that have a decisive influence on the quality of the if-this-then-that relationships derived by the algorithm.[135]

An example of a machine learning prediction system in crime control is the HART program in the UK, which supports police custody decisions.[136]

a) Differences: Compiling training dataset (step 1)

Differences from traditional statistical methods first arise regarding the database, i.e. the training dataset. Traditional statistical prognosis tools are usually developed using a case database of several hundred to one thousand people. The scope of a database in machine learning, however, is theoretically unlimited (and could include data, for example, from the last 5 years on all offenders in a city, in a certain province or a whole country). The scope is only limited by the (constantly increasing) computing power of a particular system.

In addition, a greater diversity of data sources can be considered. For example, commercially available data from private data brokers[137] or publicly accessible data from social media can be included. The information obtained via data brokers can be extremely detailed. In 2016, for example, Norddeutscher Rundfunk, a German public radio and television broadcaster, succeeded in obtaining data records on the detailed Internet browsing

135 See also p. 87 et seq. and *Lehr/Ohm* UCDL Rev. 2017, 653, 655.
136 See below p. 65 et seq.
137 Data brokers are companies such as Deutsche Post, Acxiom, Experian, Oracle or Equifax that collect as much offline and online data as possible about individuals (e.g. through cashback cards, e-commerce platforms, website trackers, social networks) and process them into personal profiles. These profiles are then sold on in bulk to trading companies for advertising purposes or to the banking and insurance industries for 'risk assessments'. Detailed information on data brokers in Germany at *Goldhammer/Wiegand* 2017, 50 ff; *Palmetshofer et al.* 2016; short overview at *Sachverständigenrat für Verbraucherfragen* 2018, 65 et seq.; see also concern about the integration of data from the private sector at *Eisenberg/Kölbel* 2017, 455 et seq., mn. 62.

behaviour of three million Germans from a data broker, the majority of whom could easily be identified.[138]

Because of its ability to process such large amounts of diverse data, machine learning is often discussed in the same breath as big data, which is characterized by volume (a large amount of data), velocity (the speed at which data is added and processed), and variety (the fact that data can come from different sources that have different formats and structures).[139] Mayer-Schönberger and Cukier describe big data as forming the core of the 'informational revolution' of the twenty-first century.[140] However, big data is not required for machine learning. Machine learning can also work with smaller, less diverse databases. Nevertheless, the possibility of being able to process large amounts of data is likely to fuel governments' 'hunger'[141] for more and more data and may lead to the spread of the view that 'more data is better data', which conflicts with the data protection principle of data minimization.[142]

b) Differences: Defining target variables (step 2)

There are no differences from the traditional statistical approach when it comes to defining the target variables.

c) Differences: Defining predictive input variables (step 3)

As with traditional statistical approaches, in machine learning people select a large number of potential input variables, which are then reduced to the most meaningful during model formation.

However, the number of variables ultimately used in the model may be greater than in traditional statistical methods, as there is no need to consider the human capacity to process variables. The forecasting algorithm COMPAS, which is used in the US to support judges' sentencing decisions,

138 See *NDR*, Nackt im Netz: Millionen Nutzer ausgespäht, accessible at https://perma.cc/G8D2-ZKH9, last accessed 1.1.2022.

139 See *Laney* META Group Research Note 2001, *Gandomi/Haider* IJIM 2015, 137, 138 m. w. N.

140 See *Mayer-Schönberger/Cukier* 2013, 13.

141 See also concern about 'insatiable thirst for knowledge' at *Singelnstein/Stolle* 2012, 69; *Pütter* Bürgerrechte & Polizei / Cilip 2007, 3 10.

142 *Martini* DVBL 2014, 1481, 1483 et seq.

uses about 137 variables.[143] Single assessments in the private sector process even more information. According to the now insolvent online credit company Kreditech, the company used an algorithm to calculate credit scores that processed up to 20,000 individual pieces of information about a person, including location-based data, social graphs (likes, friends, posts on social networks, etc.), online shopping behaviour and electronic device data.[144]

Finally, big data makes it possible to infer the presence of certain input variables automatically (especially dynamically changeable input variables such as attitudes or impulsivity) by analysing online behaviour (such as publicly accessible social media data). Without big data, such variables would have to be gathered through time-consuming personal interviews.

Various studies have postulated that Facebook 'likes' are enough to predict characteristics such as drug use and relationship status, and that they can also be used to deduce whether a person's parents separated before the individual's twenty-first birthday.[145] All of these characteristics are also important for crime prognoses, as shown by the use of these factors in statistical prognosis tools such as VRAG.[146] Similarly, the Big Five Model of Personality Psychology stresses that certain personality traits can be deduced using data on social media behaviour. An algorithmic analysis of more than 150 Facebook 'likes', it is argued, are enough to make a more precise judgement about a person's personality than could be provided by close friends and family members.[147] Such online data could soon arouse the interest of police decision-makers when it comes to predicting terrorist acts, since a large proportion of radicalization takes place online.[148]

143 See *Dressel/Farid* Science Advances 2018, 1, 1; *Northpointe*, COMPAS Risk-Assessment Sheet, accessible at https://perma.cc/VAS7-UPX5, last accessed 1.1.2022.

144 *Sachverständigenrat für Verbraucherfragen* 2018, 62.

145 See *Kosinski et al.* PNAS 2013, 5802, 5803; see also *Kosinski et al.* PNAS 2013, 5802; *Youyou et al.* PNAS 2015, 1036; *Nave et al.* Psychological Science 2018, 1145; *Ortigosa et al.* J. Comput. Syst. Sci. 2014, 57; *Quercia et al.* PASSAT and SocialCom 2011, 180; *Williams et al.* Brit. J. Criminol 2017, 320; *Aghababaei/Makrehchi* IEEE/WIC/ACM International Conference on Web Intelligence 2016, 526; *Balasuriya et al.* IEEE/ACM International Conference on Advances in Social Networks Analysis and Mining 2016, 685; *Wang et al.* ACM SIGKDD 2016, 635.

146 See e.g. VRAG-R Item No. 3 and No. 4, *Rettenberger et al.* 2017, 45.

147 *Youyou et al.* PNAS 2015, 1036, 1037.

148 See *Höffler et al.* NK 2017, 424, 425 et seq.

Another important difference is that the selection of predictors in a machine learning system no longer necessarily has to rely on existing empirical and theory-based criminological knowledge.[149] This diminishes the relevancy of the disciplines of criminology and psychiatry for the construction of prognosis tools.[150]

d) Differences: Deducing a predictive model (step 4)

The largest difference from traditional statistical methods regarding deducting a predictive model from the data is that machine learning independently derives if-this-then-that relationships from the training dataset. The machine learning system can 'discover' new complex correlations between the input and target variables, which were previously invisible to humans (e.g., purely fictitious: such as identifying a relationship between a past conviction for shoplifting and the separation of parents before the age of 18 as multiplying the risk of committing violent crimes).

Correlations with high predictive power may result from a combination of the most innocuous personal characteristics. For example, a machine learning algorithm at the Target supermarket chain in the US made it possible to detect whether a woman is pregnant from mere changes in her purchasing behaviour.[151] Kreditech claimed to be able to infer the creditworthiness of a person by analysing, among other things, the apps and fonts that a person had installed on their mobile phone.[152] This ability to uncover new, unexpected connections in large amounts of data has the potential to further trigger the 'hunger' for more data mentioned above,[153] as more and more input variables supposedly lead to ever greater predictive accuracy. The culmination of this development may well be an 'all data is crime data' mind-set.[154] In this view, every piece of data, however

---

149 *Kröber et al.* 2006, 83.

150 On the challenge of big data for criminology as a discipline see *Chan/Bennett Moses* Theoretical Criminology 2016, 21.

151 See *Duhigg* The New York Times of 19.2.2012, accessible at https://perma.cc/UU4W-YVPH, last accessed 1.1.2022.

152 See *Seibel* Die Welt of 17.4.2015, accessible at https://perma.cc/N9XU-98DC, last accessed 1.1.2022.

153 See also concern about 'insatiable thirst for knowledge' at *Singelnstein/Stolle* 2012, 69; *Pütter* Bürgerrechte & Polizei / Cilip 2007, 3 10.

154 Cf. also *Singelnstein/Stolle* 2012, 35, 69 ('The quest for the most accurate forecast possible inherent in this approach leads to the permanent "discovery" of

trivial, has the potential to – in combination with other characteristics – form unexpected correlations with criminal behaviour.

A further difference from traditional statistical systems is that machine learning may adapt to changes in the database almost in real time (self-adaptation of the system). The system 'learns' continuously with each case added to its database over time.

Finally, a core difference from traditional statistical methods is that machine learning systems tend to be particularly non-transparency due to their complexity. The rules by which an algorithm reaches a prediction may not always be comprehensible, not just for outsiders but even for experts.[155] Different machine learning algorithms show different degrees of transparency. While decision trees, one of the numerous subgroups of machine learning, are relatively comprehensible for experts,[156] neural networks are viewed as barely transparent.[157] However, even decision tree algorithms become more incomprehensible the greater the numbers of variables considered by a model, i.e. the more decision trees that are used in a system ('random forest').[158]

---

new risk factors and thus generates new risks' and 'The techniques used in this process constantly produce new forms of threats, risks and deviations by discovering new risk-creating factors'); cf. also the related expression in the banking sector 'All Data is Credit Data', *Aitken* Competition & Change 2017, 274; cf. in contrast, however, the prohibition of 'Totalerfassung' in German law in BVerfGE 125, 260 (839, mn. 218) ('Conversely, the storage of telecommunications traffic data must not be understood as a step towards legislation aimed at the most comprehensive, precautionary storage possible of all data useful for criminal prosecution or averting danger.[...] It must also not lead to the reconstructibility of practically all citizen activities in interaction with other existing data.'); on 'Totalerfassung' see also p. 102.

155 On system inherent non-transparency p. 127 et seq.; see also *Matthias* Ethics and Information Technology 2004, 175, 179, *Kroll et al.* U. Pa. L. Rev. 2017, 633, 638 ('even experts often struggle to understand what software code will do, as inspecting source code is a very limited way of predicting how a computer program will behave.').

156 *Pedreschi et al.* arXiv 2018, 1 et seq.; *Berk* 2019, 75 et seq.

157 *Pedreschi et al.* arXiv 2018, 1 ff; *Guidotti et al.* ACM Computing Surveys (CSUR) 2018, 93 93 et seq.; *Berk* 2019, 101 et seq.

158 For details on the legal aspects of a lack of transparency, see below p. 120 et seq.

e) Differences: Risk translation and risk communication (Step 5)

Machine learning no longer requires humans to undertake the step of risk translation. As the rules are already contained in the system in the form of computer code, the statistical model does not need to be translated into a paper-based questionnaire or written up as computer software by humans in a separate step.

For the step of risk communication, however, no differences to the traditional statistical methods arise.

f) Differences: Application to the individual case (step 6)

Differences arise when applying machine learning algorithms to individual cases. As with rule-based predictions, input variables are queried via software input masks, which results in the automatic output of a risk score. It is also possible to dispense with the manual input of individual case data and, instead, to automatically read in data from a database. Although this accelerates the development of crime prognoses, it also increases the lack of transparency of the correlations and input variables for the operators.

aa) People affected by crime prognoses

The new possibilities offered by machine learning can also lead to changes in the group of people to whom crime predictions are applied. In the past, the data used to develop and apply prognosis tools were usually only available for people who had already committed crimes. Today, the police in many countries keep lists of people considered to pose violent threats to society (e.g. in Germany the police maintain the following lists 'Gewalttäter-Sport', and 'Politisch motivierte Kriminalität links'; in the US, the police have a list of 'Black Lives Matter activists'). These lists may also contain persons who have not yet committed any crime, but whose crime risk the police want to assess in a standardised manner.[159] Further, as soon as trivial personal characteristics, such as shopping behaviour or Facebook likes, are associated with crime, it becomes possible to expand crime prognoses to the entire population. It should therefore not be surprising that the police have begun purchasing commercial data from private 'data

159 See below fn. 233.

brokers' for prognoses such as for the HART project in the UK and the Beware project in the US. If the law were to subordinate itself at this point to mere 'machine logic',[160] this could possibly result in calls to extend the reach of criminal prognoses beyond former offenders. The speed and processing capacity of new technology means that mass crime prognoses are certainly feasible. Algorithmic prognoses are already being applied to anyone taken into police custody (as in the HART project in the UK)[161], to anyone in custody (as in New Jersey in the US),[162] to anyone living in a city (as in the Beware project in California),[163] and to anyone engaged in high-risk activities such as flying (passenger name record analysis).[164] It is to be feared that the inhibition threshold to create risk scores for a large number of random persons could decrease the faster and easier automated prognoses can be carried out by police officers.

bb) Prognosis tool operators

(1) From prognosis experts to prognosis laypeople

Finally, the new technology may also change the circle of people who undertake crime prognoses. The simplified handling of prognoses by computer software may give the impression that no specialist background knowledge is necessary to achieve reliable results. This impression may be particularly arise with prognosis tools for which data input is fully automated and individual risk scores calculated without the need for operators to enter data themselves.

The use of algorithms could thus move crime prognoses away from experts and towards laypeople. These may be judges, police officers or prison officials. This places specially trained experts at risk of being pushed out of the prognosis process. If, however, crime prognoses are no longer supervised by experts the prognosis process lacks people with sufficient knowledge to be able to spot and, where necessary, correct a questionable algorithmic result.

---

160 See on 'machine logic' p. 207 et seq.
161 See p. 65 et seq.
162 See above fn. 108.
163 See p. 64 et seq.
164 § 4 FlugDaG; see detailed below p. 80 et seq.

(2) Automation bias

This is all the more ture, as studies of algorithmic decision-support systems in medicine and aviation have already shown that people find it very difficult to make decisions that contradict the results of algorithmic calculations.[165] This phenomenon, known as 'automation bias' leads people to refrain from obtaining and evaluating information themselves, and even to deliberately ignore evidence that clearly conflicts with the result produced by an algorithm. This phenomenon is located, in the broadest sense, in the trust people place in automated systems.[166] This can be defined as 'the tendency to use automated cues as a heuristic replacement for vigilant information seeking and processing'.[167] This can result in two types of error: either a user of an algorithmic system fails to recognize a critical situation that has been overlooked by the algorithm (*omission errors*) or they follow faulty instructions provided by the algorithmic system (*commission errors*).[168] Examples of the occurrence of 'automation bias' in algorithmic decision-support systems have been identified in highly sensitive areas such as intensive care units, nuclear power plants and aircraft cockpits.[169] The studies worth mentioning in this area, such as by Skitka, Mosier and Burdick, mainly come from the Anglo-American region.[170] In Germany,

165 See *Manzey* 2012, 333, 333; *Skitka et al.* Int. J. Hum. Comput. Stud. 1999, 991; *Mosier et al.* Int. J. Aviat. Psychol. 1998, 47, 63; *Cummings* Journal of Technology Studies 2006, 23, 25 ('humans have a tendency to disregard or not search for contradictory information in light of a computer-generated solution that is accepted as correct'); fundamentally *Mosier et al.* Int. J. Aviat. Psychol. 1998, 47; *Skitka et al.* Int. J. Hum. Comput. Stud. 1999, 991; *Skitka et al.* Int. J. Hum. Comput. Stud. 2000, 701, see also *Parasuraman/Riley* Human Factors 1997, 230; on approaches to counter automation bias through targeted user sensitization: *Ahlstrom/Longo* 2003, Kap. 3, 20; see, however, critical of long-term successes of these approaches *Skitka et al.* Int. J. Hum. Comput. Stud. 1999, 991, 1004.

166 *Bahner* 2008, 40.

167 *Mosier et al.* Proceedings of the Human Factors and Ergonomics Society Annual Meeting 1996, 204, 205.

168 *Bahner* 2008, 40; *Skitka et al.* Int. J. Aviat. Psychol. 2000, 85.

169 *Skitka et al.* Int. J. Hum. Comput. Stud. 1999, 991, 991; *Mosier et al.* Int. J. Aviat. Psychol. 1998, 47, 47; *Alberdi et al.* Academic Radiology 2004, 909; Gigerenzer/Engel 2006, 14.

170 *Skitka et al.* Int. J. Hum. Comput. Stud. 1999, 991, 991; *Mosier et al.* Proceedings of the Human Factors and Ergonomics Society Annual Meeting 1996, 204, 205; *Skitka et al.* Int. J. Aviat. Psychol. 2000, 85, 85.

Bahner's dissertation is particularly noteworthy.[171] These studies show that machine results are often regarded as 'error-resistant' and that recommendations provided by computer systems are often followed even if operators have doubts about their correctness.[172]

Similar patterns of behaviour can be expected when dealing with algorithmic crime predictions: precisely because the complex process behind the algorithmic 'black box' is not fully understood and its assumptions cannot be verified, people attach particular importance to algorithmic results and find it difficult to use their own observations to question algorithmic indications of high risk. Time pressure and the need for justifications probably also play a role here: making decisions *against* 'the machine' involves a greater expenditure of time and explanatory effort than making decisions *in line with* 'the machine'.[173]

3. Conclusion: technological background

In summary, rule-based algorithmic prediction entails a number of innovations in crime control (particularly in the application stage of prognosis tools). Only machine learning, however, has the potential to fundamentally change the process of crime prognosis. Algorithmic prognoses not only promise to contribute to a society's safety and security; they also entail risks and challenges for the rule of law. This emphasizes the 'dangerousness of the prediction of dangerousness', so to speak.[174]

This chapter has further demonstrated that the most important decisions impacting a person's risk score are not taken during the application of a predictive policing system, but long before, during the algorithm design stage.

---

171 *Bahner* 2008, 40; despite these studies, there is still need for further research cf. *Goddard et al.* J. Am. Med. Inform. Assn. 2011, 125 , who say that the effect of the 'automation bias' lacks clear empirical evidence.

172 *Citron* Wash. L. Rev. 2007, 1249, 1254); *Parasuraman* Ergonomics 2000, 931, 936; see also *Sheridan* 1996, 449, 458 ('It is so tempting to trust to the magic of computers and automation. ... [I]f a computer program compiles, we often believe, the software is valid and the intention will be achieved.').

173 Cf. 'The computer then cranks and heaves and gives an answer, and there is some temptation to obey the computer. After all, if you follow the computer you are a little less responsible than if you made up your own mind.', *Bateson* 1972, 481 et seq.

174 *Pollähne* 2011, 4.

Chapters II and III explore the legal and criminological challenges posed by the use of algorithmic crime prognoses in policing. First, however, examples of predictive policing from Germany, the US and the UK are provided for further illustration.

F. Examples of predictive policing

The following section contains examples of person-based algorithms in police work. Before discussing four examples from Germany, this section provides an overview of the situation in the US and UK.

It will become clear that the legal foundation for the use of predictive algorithms by the police in Germany has been laid out by the Passenger Name Record Act (Fluggastdatengesetz – FlugDaG). Further, this section demonstrates that several other German police projects constitute at least preliminary stages of person-based predictive policing. Although the use of algorithms in Germany currently lags behind the technical possibilities seen at the international level and in the private sector, efforts are clearly being made to expand person-based predictive policing in the future.

I. US and UK

The technological developments in Germany should not be viewed in isolation. They are embedded in an international trend towards automated predictive policing. In particular, Germany is following the examples of the US and UK. This applies to police technology in general,[175] but especially regarding prognosis tools.[176] The German police keep a very close eye on international developments[177] and often seek to exchange experiences with their counterparts in other countries.[178] An analysis of

175 See e.g. use of body cameras in the US since before 2014, *Joh* Surveillance & Society 2016, 1 and in Germany since 2016, *Martini et al.* NVwZ - Extra 12/2016, 1, 2 et seq.

176 Cf. introduction of location-based predictive policy in the USA almost 10 years before deployment in Germany, see above p. 30.

177 As early as 2014, the BKA was informed about numerous data-mining applications belonging to companies such as IBM, NetApp, Fun Communications, CED Consulting, IABG and others.

178 See *Ministerium für Inneres und Kommunales des Landes Nordrhein-Westfalen* 2014, 2 ('The State Criminal Police Office has been commissioned to collect informa-

developments in the US and UK can thus contribute to an understanding of the German predictive policing market.

Three predictive policing approaches from the US and UK, Beware, HART and the Strategic Subject List, are selected from the large number of applications globally[179] to illustrate international trends.

	Data Input	Data Processing	Data Output
Beware	*inter alia* convictions, arrests, land register entries, private data broker, social media data, health data	machine learning	suspicion-generating risk assessment of whole city population; retrieval of risk score on an as-needed basis in the event of an emergency call
HART	34 points, including age, gender, postal code; also initially included data from private data brokers	machine learning	risk assessment of everyone taken into police custody; decision on whether they should remain in custody
Strategic Subject List	age at last arrest, arrests for violent crimes and weapon possession; victim status in firearms crimes and grievous bodily harm, 'trends' in other criminal behaviour	co-arrest, theory-based & machine learning	suspicion-generating risk assessment (factor 0–500) of anyone who has been in police custody; identification of the 'most dangerous' individuals

Tbl. 2. Overview of selected algorithmic crime prognosis projects in the US and UK

tion on the methods of "predictive policing" [...] used by police authorities in Australia, Great Britain, the Netherlands and the USA').

179 See overview of other different systems at *Rich* U. Pa. L. Rev. 2016, 871, 872 et seq., 878 fn. 40; see also examples of criminal intent recognition at *Kölbel/Selter* Eur. J. Crime Crim. L. & Crim. Just. 2010, 237.

1. Beware

The Beware system[180] was developed by a private company[181] and has been used since 2012 in various US cities[182] to assign a 'threat score' (provided in red, yellow or green) for people to whose addresses the police are called out to. The threat score is assumed to indicate a resident's propensity for violence. To be able to immediately retrieve a threat score in the event of an emergency call, data on all[183] residents of a city are collected, including data on previous arrests, land register entries, data acquired from private data brokers,[184] publicly available social media data, and health-related data, particularly on mental illness.[185] High threat scores do not authorize the police to arrest or observe a subject. Rather, the scores have an informational character, and are used to prepare police officers in the field for particular situations. However, high scores do have a negative impact on people in so far as the police may act more aggressively towards people considered violent and the police may be more willing to use violence themselves.

The precise risk assessment processes within Beware are a trade secret and are not provided to people outside of the company, even to the police. Subsequently, it is unclear which probabilities are associated with a red risk, and the mathematical approach on which the algorithm is based is unknown. There is no publicly accessible definition of the target variables, i.e. which offences are covered by the term '[has a] propensity for violence'

---

180 See *Intrado*, BEWARE Werbebroschüre, accessible at https://perma.cc/8JQL-WU7D, last accessed 1.1.2022.

181 See https://perma.cc/2JYA-26X5 (last accessed 1.1.2022).

182 For example, 2015–2016 in the Californian town of Fresno, public criticism of the system was voiced, and city council members unexpectedly received an increased risk assessment from the system during a demonstration of Beware, which led the system to be no longer used. In other cities, the system is still in use, *Jouvenal* The Washington Post of 10.1.2016, accessible at https://perma.cc/P4FG-6WH8, last accessed 1.1.2022; *Sheehan* Fresno Bee of 31.3.2016, accessible at https://perma.cc/KP2P-YZBM, last accessed 1.1.2022.

183 In the town of Fresno, Beware provided information on practically every adult resident of the town, *Sheehan* Fresno Bee of 31.3.2016, accessible at https://perma.cc/KP2P-YZBM, last accessed 1.1.2022.

184 See fn. 137.

185 *Jouvenal* The Washington Post of 10.1.2016, accessible at https://perma.cc/P4FG-6WH8, last accessed 1.1.2022; for attempts in Germany to use data of people with a mental illness, see Gesetzentwurfs der Staatsregierung für ein Bayerisches Psychisch-Kranken-Hilfe-Gesetz, Bay-LT-Drs. 17/21573 v. 10.4.2018.

or information about the time period that the threat score refers to. It is also unclear how data on an individual is weighted and how data from social media are processed. Local media reports suggest that a woman's threat score increased after she had repeatedly tweeted about a card game called 'Rage'. The algorithm interpreted these tweets as expressions of rage and therefore classified the woman as having a heightened propensity for violence.[186] No scientific studies on the Beware system are currently available.

Even if individual threat scores are only retrieved if an emergency call is made, the system still creates comprehensive threat scores for the entire population of a city and keeps them in stock. The scope, i.e. the number of people affected by this predictive policing system, therefore, is rather large.

2. HART (Harm Assessment Risk Tool)

In the UK, the forecasting tool HART, which was co-developed by statisticians from Cambridge University,[187] is used to decide whether people should be detained until they can be brought to trial.[188] Each person is assigned one of three risk categories: high risk (highly likely to commit serious crimes such as murder, violent crimes, sexual crimes or robbery over the next two years), a moderate risk (likely to commit minor crimes), or a low risk (unlikely to commit crimes). The prediction is based on machine learning in the form of a random forest approach.[189] Thirty-four behavioural predictors are used as input variables, most of which were derived from criminological theories. In addition to previous convictions, age, gender and postal code are used.[190]

The training dataset, on the basis of which the algorithm learned crime relationships, contains data on the subsequent behaviour of 104,000 people arrested in the last five years.[191] Data from the data broker Experian was also purchased for part of the project.[192]

---

186 *Jouvenal* The Washington Post of 10.1.2016, accessible at https://perma.cc/P4FG-6WH8, last accessed 1.1.2022.
187 *Oswald et al.* Information & Communications Technology Law 2018, 223, 225.
188 *Oswald et al.* Information & Communications Technology Law 2018, 223, 225.
189 *Oswald et al.* Information & Communications Technology Law 2018, 223, 227.
190 *Oswald et al.* Information & Communications Technology Law 2018, 223, 228.
191 *Oswald et al.* Information & Communications Technology Law 2018, 223, 228.
192 *Big Brother Watch* 2018.

The model has an accuracy level of 62.8 per cent. However, the algorithm is devised in a manner that ensure that errors are not evenly distributed. The algorithm is deliberately calibrated to commit false-positive errors ('harmless people classified as risky') twice as often as a false-negative error ('dangerous people classified as harmless').[193]

The project describes itself as 'risk-need-based': it does not solely focus on the security interests of society, but rather in keeping people with a low risk out of custody and transferring people with a moderate risk into extrajudicial intervention.[194] As such, the system is said to be beneficial to people with a low risk score. However, the flip side of a police project that favours low-risk individuals is that it discriminates against people who have not been categorized as low-risk. This is true even though the manufacturers stress that the system is for guidance only and that final decisions on detention should be taken by police officers.[195] A first accompanying study has shown that the algorithm is more likely to classify people as high-risk than police officers do.[196] Moreover, it is important to remember that it can be difficult for people to go against recommendations provided by algorithms.[197]

HART falls into the middle of the spectrum between suspicion-generating and suspicion-confirming predictive policing. The instrument is applied to a large number of individuals (anyone who the police arrest). Moreover, the two-year period to which the prediction of crime refers is very long, since the system is initially only concerned with the issue of the likelihood of a person attending their next court hearing if they are released. Although this system is limited to people placed under arrest, it still has a relatively wide scope.

3. Strategic Subject List[198]

Since 2013, the police in Chicago have been using the Strategic Subject List, also known as the Heat List, as a tool against gang crime. It was

193 *Oswald et al.* Information & Communications Technology Law 2018, 223, 228.

194 The so-called Checkpoint Program *Oswald et al.* Information & Communications Technology Law 2018, 223, 225

195 *University of Cambridge* 2018.

196 *Oswald et al.* Information & Communications Technology Law 2018, 223, 233.

197 See above for 'Automation Bias' p. 60 et seq.

198 Anonymized data from the Strategic Subject List from 2012–2016 can be viewed online: Strategic Subject List, Chicago Data Portal, https://data.cityofchicago.or

developed by the Institute of Technology at the University of Illinois. The list is based on data from all individuals who have been arrested in Chicago over the past five years.[199] A machine learning[200] algorithm uses this training dataset to calculate the probability that a person will become a perpetrator or victim of firearm violence. A person is assigned a risk score between 0 and 500. The number indicates the factor at which a person's risk is higher than that of the average population. A risk of 500 therefore means a 500 times higher risk of gun violence than the average population. It is not clear what base rate the system works with and what percentile probability a risk score of 500 corresponds to.

By 2016, the system had produced risk scores for almost 400,000 people.[201]Although risk assessments are principally intended for people who have been arrested, the system also assesses people who have had no contact with the police.[202] The approximately 1,500 individuals with the highest risk scores are listed at the top of the Strategic Subject List and are considered 'persons of interest'. The police visit these individuals at their home addresses[203] to let them know that they are 'on the police's radar'.[204] Further, social workers accompany the police to offer help.[205]

Input variables used by the system include age at the last arrest, arrests for violent crimes and illicit firearm possession, victim status in firearms confrontations, grievous bodily harm and an increase in other forms of criminal behaviour. An earlier version of the system further used the cri-

---

g/Public-Safety/Strategic-Subject-List/4aki-r3np (last accessed 1.1.2022); see also *Richardson et al.* N.Y.U. L. Rev. 2019, 192

199 See *Dumke/Main* 2017.

200 Cf. Website of a developer of the Strategic Subject List: Miles Wernick, Ph.D. https://engineering.iit.edu/faculty/miles-wernick ('In this program, machine learning, social network analysis, and methods drawn from image processing are being applied to produce forward-looking analysis of crime data to promote data-driven policing').

201 See *Posadas* Medium of 22.6.2017, accessible at https://perma.cc/2A9A-8LMG, last accessed 1.1.2022.

202 See *Posadas* Medium of 22.6.2017, accessible at https://perma.cc/2A9A-8LMG, last accessed 1.1.2022.

203 Sog. 'Custom Notification Letters' *Saunders et al.* J. Exp. Criminol. 2016, 347, 356, 360; *Chicago Police Department* of 17.8.2016, accessible at https://perma.cc/7A9H-97U8, last accessed 1.1.2022.

204 See *Davey* The New York Times of 23.5.2016, accessible at https://perma.cc/MCL2-EZXN, last accessed 1.1.2022.

205 The theoretical basis for interventions with high-risk offenders has existed since the 1980s, See *Sherman* Crime and Justice 1986, 343; *Saunders et al.* J. Exp. Criminol. 2016, 347, 349 m. w. N.

terion of 'co-arrest' (the people who were arrested at the same time) an important role.[206]

As the project is focused on 'risk-need', it is not only aimed at potential criminals, but also in offering help to potential victims. The idea may be well-intentioned, but in practice this aspect becomes lost: no distinction is made between potential perpetrators and potential victims, instead, they are pooled and provided with one risk score. It is therefore impossible for the police to use the score to understand whether they are dealing with a high-risk perpetrator or victim. As such, in case of doubt police officers will likely assume they are dealing with perpetrators to err on the side of caution.[207]

The effectiveness of the list has yet to be clearly demonstrated. An independent evaluation of the initial project phase (2013–2014) showed no clear success in predicting victims or perpetrators of armed violence.[208] In 2015, however, project participants reported a success rate of 29 per cent for correctly predicting whether someone would be involved in armed violence (for the 400 most dangerous individuals on the Strategic Subject List).[209] It is unclear whether the use of the list has had a general impact on the rate of armed violence in Chicago. According to the police, 70 per cent of the people shot in Chicago in 2016 were on the Strategic Subject List.[210] However, no details were provided about how high up on the list these individuals were ranked.[211]

---

206 This criterion based on the work of the sociologist Papachristos has been dropped, since its predictive power has proven to be low, *Chicago Police Department* of 17.8.2016, accessible at https://perma.cc/7A9H-97U8, last accessed 1.1.2022; see on the theoretical background *Papachristos* Am. J. Sociol. 2009, 74; *Papachristos et al.* Researchgate 2011; *Papachristos et al.* J. Urban Health 2012, 992.

207 This would not be possible in Germany, since § 72 No. 2, 4 German Federal Aata Protection Act stipulates that data on perpetrators and victims must be stored separately.

208 *Saunders et al.* J. Exp. Criminol. 2016, 347, 363 et seq.; although the study found that people on the list were arrested twice as often as people who did not appear on the list, given the total average of nine shootings for people on the list and five shootings for people not on the list, the predictive power of the list is still low.

209 *Lewin/Wernick* IACP Conference 2015; *Saunders et al.* J. Exp. Criminol. 2016, 347, 366.

210 *Davey* The New York Times of 23.5.2016, accessible at https://perma.cc/MCL2-EZXN, last accessed 1.1.2022.

211 Since a score is created for such a large number of people (400,000), the police's statement could theoretically also refer to people with only a small score.

This system displays a particularly wide scope of application, since predictive policing is carried out without individual suspicion. In contrast to Beware, the score is not only retrieved on a case-by-case basis, but the system *actively* brings a person with a high score to the attention of the police. Unlike HART, it is not only people held in police custody who are assessed, but anyone who has been arrested in the last five years.

The fact that, in contrast to Beware, the system in Chicago only assesses people who have been arrested before only marginally limits its scope; further, it was shown that persons without prior police contact are also occasionally included in the Strategic Subject List.

Finally, the fact that a prognosis system once established only for preventive purposes has the potential to have an effect on *ex-post* policing, too, can be seen with the Strategic Subject List: Police officers in Chicago have also used it as a tool in order to find suspects for crimes already committed.[212]

4. Summary US and UK

These examples show person-based predictive policing at an advanced stage. In each case, data is automatically read from a database into the predictive system and it automatically produces a risk score. All the systems lack transparency with regard to the development of the model and the exact weightings and correlations used. Moreover, the effectiveness of the systems is by no means clear.

II. Germany

The following sets out four examples of person-based predictive policing in Germany: RADAR-iTE and hessenDATA are precursors of fully automated predictive policing, while DyRiAS and Flight Data Pattern Recognition constitute full-blown predictive policing.

212 *Saunders et al.* J. Exp. Criminol. 2016, 347, 365.

	Data Input	Data Processing	Data Output
RADAR-iTE	73 questions, including attitude to violence, family ties, employment	checklist, manual addition of points	suspicion-confirming risk assessment (high, increased, moderate) of people known to the police for Islamic violence
Palantir Gotham - hessenDATA	police databases, telecommunications data, data from seized mobile phones, social media data	keyword search; link analysis; (additional Ava module for machine learning)	factual basis for follow-up measures regarding known and newly identified perpetrators; (in the US also: suspicion-generating identification of unknown perpetrators and victims of future crimes)
DyRiAS	30–40 questions, e.g. housing situation, consumption of media that glorifies violence, interest in military and weapons	rule-based system (50 individual rules)	suspicion-confirming risk assessment (levels 0–5) concerning people already known to the police for acts of violence
Flight Data Pattern Recognition	20 points, including contact details, email address, date of birth, payment information, travel companions, date of booking and ticket issue, hotel reservation	automated pattern matching	suspicion-generating risk assessment, identification of people unknown to the police but with a high risk of committing terrorist offences

Tbl. 3. Overview of algorithmic crime prediction systems and their precursors in Germany

1. RADAR-iTE (Rule-based analysis of potentially destructive perpetrators to assess acute risk – Islamist terrorism)

The RADAR-iTE system has been developed by the German Federal Criminal Police Office (Bundeskriminalamt – BKA) and the Forensic Psychology Working Group at the University of Konstanz since 2015.[213] It has been in use throughout Germany since 2017 to assess the risk (that individuals who are known to the police pose) of committing Islamist-motivated terrorist offences.[214] The aim is to provide a nationwide uniform evaluation of Islamist threats and to apply the results to prioritize the use of police resources (such as telecommunications surveillance).[215]

The use of the system is based on §§ 16, 18 Bundeskriminalamtgesetz (BKAG), which deals with data processing.[216]

a) Prognosis tool development

This is the first time that a prognosis tool for Islamist terrorism has been developed in Germany,[217] and the first time that a prognosis tool has been developed specifically for the police.

While the ERG-22+ (Extremism Risk Guidance)[218] and VERA (Violent Extremism Risk Assessment)[219] tools have been used internationally for some time to predict extremism,[220] these tools require operators to have a

213 Among others, Professor Jerome Endrass, who is developing a similar instrument with the Swiss police called Octagon, *Endrass/Rossegger* format magazine - Zeitschrift für Polizeiausbildung und Polizeiforschung 2017, 36.

214 *Bundeskriminalamt* Presseinformation of 2.2.2017, accessible at https://perma.cc/Z89V-CF75, last accessed 1.1.2022.

215 § 51 German Federal Data Protection Act.

216 BT-Drs. 19/1558, 11.

217 Cf. however shortly thereafter the development of DyRiAS-Screener Islam from 2017, *Böckler et al.* Kriminalistik 2017, 491; see below p. 76 et seq.

218 *Lloyd/Dean* Journal of Threat Assessment and Management 2015, 40.

219 *Pressman* 2009; *Pressman et al.* 2016.

220 Both instruments are of the 'Structured Professional Judgement' class, in which clinical assessment by an expert (psychologist, psychiatrist, criminologist) is based on certain scientifically founded predictors; on the problem of empirical foundation of terrorism predictions in general, *Hoffmann et al.* 2017, 36

high level of psychological and criminological expertise;[221] they are therefore unsuitable for mass deployment in police stations.

It has not yet been possible to develop a purely statistical prognosis tool, as too little data are available on terrorist offences as these occur rarely. RADAR-iTE does not rely solely on statistical factors but derives its risk predictors from criminological-theoretical considerations of radicalization.[222] However, no information has been made public on the exact criminological considerations that RADAR-iTE takes into account.

b) Prognosis tool application

The tool consists of 73 questions that operators need to answer in order to gain an individual risk assessment. The questions are only partially publicly known and include risk-increasing and risk-reducing[223] features derived from criminological studies.[224] The focus is on objectively observable behaviour, not on attitudes or religiosity.[225] Unlike traditional prognosis tools, where operators answer the questions after interviewing the person concerned, in this case, they rely on analyses of police files.

---

221 Another instrument that requires high user skills is TRAP-18 (Terrorist Radicalization Assessment Protocol), which is not a forecasting instrument in the narrower sense, but rather a looser evaluation structure, *Meloy et al.* Journal of Threat Assessment and Management 2015, 140, 140 et seq.; also *Vollbach's* proposed application of the MIVEA method (see fn. 67 above) to terrorists would require a great deal of time and expertise, *Vollbach* NK 2017, 62 62 et seq.; overview of other methods not suitable for mass use by untrained persons at *King et al.* Kriminologische Welt in Bewegung 2018, 191, 193 et seq.

222 *Endrass* Frankfurter Allgemeine Zeitung of 19.7.2017, accessible at https://perma.cc/6XY2-H6H8, last accessed 1.1.2022.

223 *Flade* Die Welt of 12.6.2017, accessible at https://perma.cc/2MLX-A6ST, last accessed 1.1.2022.

224 For example, questions are asked about family, friends, education and prison sentences, possible access to weapons, military service, and psychological problems such as attempted suicides. It is also asked whether the person has already participated in jihadist activities in a war zone, whether there are indications of violent and aggressive behaviour or whether the person cooperates with the prosecution and maintains relationships with people outside the Salafist community, see *Endrass* Frankfurter Allgemeine Zeitung of 19.7.2017, accessible at https://perma.cc/6XY2-H6H8, last accessed 1.1.2022.

225 *Bundeskriminalamt* Presseinformation of 2.2.2017, accessible at https://perma.cc/Z89V-CF75, last accessed 1.1.2022.

The risk assessment leads the individual to be classified as a red (high), orange (increased) or yellow (moderate) risk of committing Islamist-motivated offences. The operator is not told how likely it is that a person classified as red will commit a terrorist offence; and the Federal Criminal Police Office maintains no data on this.[226] Since terrorist offences are very rare events, it can be assumed that even a low single-digit probability of a future offence could be enough to categorise someone as high risk.[227] No information is available about the base rate used or on false-positives in addition to the risk categories.

Although the tool is described as computer-based, this only means – at least for now – that the questionnaire is answered on a computer instead of on paper. The only software systems that were still in use for RADAR-iTE in March 2017 were Word and Excel.[228] And even in April 2018, the system was described as having 'no automated decision-making'.[229] This means that the results are not provided automatically,[230] and that the necessary data are not read in automatically from databases. Instead, questionnaires are completed manually on a computer before each answer is assigned a score. Operators then add up all the points and assign risk categories in accordance with the total score. However, the system is constantly being developed, so a greater level of automation is expected in the coming years.

aa) Prognosis tool operators

The instrument is used by police officers after a short training.

---

226 BKA in *Rath* Vorwärts of 17.8.2018, accessible at https://perma.cc/AT2B-TEQE, last accessed 1.1.2022; see also *Endrass* Frankfurter Allgemeine Zeitung of 19.7.2017, accessible at https://perma.cc/6XY2-H6H8, last accessed 1.1.2022.

227 Cf. *Saunders et al.* J. Exp. Criminol. 2016, 347, 351 ('Indeed, a "very high risk" person for homicide might have a risk rate of 1 per cent per year'); cf. also studies in the US which have shown that the category 'high risk' in algorithms for determining recidivism is already applied to people with merely an 8 per cent probability of an act of violence *Mayson* Yale L.J. 2018, 490, 514.

228 BT-Drs. 18/11578, 7.

229 BT-Drs. 19/1558, 11.

230 BT-Drs. 19/1558, 11.

bb) People affected by crime prognoses

The instrument is applied to people who are already suspected of posing a threat, including everyone listed on the Federal Police's watchlist for dangerous Islamists. This list includes people who have not committed a crime. By 2018, 466 individuals had been assessed.[231] Of these, less than half (40 per cent) were classified as high risk.[232]

Although the system is only applied to people on police watchlists, the system could – from a technological point of view – easily be extended to other people. For example, it could be used to help decide who should be placed on a watchlist in the first place. This technologically easy possible expansion should be kept in mind when considering future developments of the system.

Importantly, police watchlists regularly include people who have ended up on them by mistake.[233] Ruch and Feltes speak of a worrisome expansion of those affected by police watchlists.[234] Against this background, the application only to people on a watchlist must be considered an unsatisfactory criterion for restricting the use of predictive policing.

cc) Lack of transparency

Despite the relatively simple technical means used by the prognosis tool, it completely lacks transparency: hardly any details about the tool have been provided since its widespread use in 2017.[235] The developers call the instrument 'the only tool available in the German-speaking world that meets strict scientific criteria'.[236] However, the composition of the case database and the theoretical basis are unknown, and although the input variables are partially known, nothing is known about their weighting, exact definition or about the base and error rates. No evaluation studies of

231 BT-Drs. 19/1558, 8

232 *Jansen/Fiedler* Bundeskriminalamt of 19.12.2018, accessible at https://perma.cc/6HPV-4HYU, last accessed 1.1.2022.

233 See Zeit Online of 30.8.2017, accessible at https://perma.cc/6Z45-CSRZ, last accessed 1.1.2022; *Ferguson* U. Pa. L. Rev. 2015, 327, 398; in detail on databases, *Ruch/Feltes* NK 2016, 62.

234 *Ruch/Feltes* NK 2016, 62, 62 et seq.

235 *King et al.* Kriminologische Welt in Bewegung 2018, 191, 194.

236 See *Knight* Deutsche Welle of 19.12.2017, accessible at https://perma.cc/3QQC-7MDC, last accessed 1.1.2022.

the instrument have been published. This lack of transparency is already present in the non-automated preliminary stage of predictive policing and it threatens to set the tone for the future of more complex technical developments. These problems will multiply when the evaluation and data entry processes become automated.

2. Palantir Gotham – hessenDATA

The hessenDATA project, which uses the Gotham software from the US company Palantir,[237] has been running in the German federal state of Hesse since 2017.[238] The project was introduced as a tool in the fight against Islamist terrorism. The software is already said to have prevented a planned attack by a 17-year-old in the German town of Eschwege.[239] The use of the software is based on § 25a HSOG on 'automated data analysis', which was inserted into Hessian police law.[240] The new paragraph permits automated data processing for preventive purposes in 'justified individual cases'.[241]

The software, known in the media as 'Robocop-Google',[242] can be used in different ways. It is primarily designed to automatically link information from different data sources in the shortest possible time using 'link analysis'. This enables keyword searches of all data sources to be conducted simultaneously, and the visualization of data connections and patterns. In this way, complex networks can be mapped and relevant individuals can be highlighted from the data. The resulting information can be used to anticipate threats and to take action against individuals who have been identified as such. However, the results of automated data analysis, as is the

---

237 Nota bene: see on the connection of Palantir to the Cambridge Analytica Scandal s. *Confessore/Rosenberg* The New York Times of 27.2.2018, accessible at https://perma.cc/4E2X-2CKD, last accessed 1.1.2022.

238 *Hessischer Landtag* 2019, 17 et seq.

239 *Hessischer Landtag* 2019, 17.

240 The amendment was only introduced in June 2018. Previously, the system operated without a sufficient legal basis.

241 § 25a HSOG in connection with § 20 para. 7 in connection with § 13 para. 2 No. 1.

242 *Brühl* Süddeutsche Zeitung of 18.10.2018, accessible at https://perma.cc/6QDL-GD5X, last accessed 1.1.2022.

case with all predictive policing systems, are probabilistic, i.e. they include a certain probability of error.[243]

Hessen uses information from police databases that is automatically merged with communication traffic data, e.g. from telecommunications surveillance.[244] It is also possible to add information from social networks.[245] This includes data from social media, some of which are not publicly available, for example, data obtained from Facebook through requests for legal assistance made to the US.[246]

Furthermore, an additional module named Ava enables the software to offer predictive skills through machine learning and dynamic scoring.[247]

From 2012 to 2018, the 'link analysis' function used in Hessen was also used in New Orleans in the US for person-based predictive policing.[248] These points as well as the use of the software to prevent the attack in Eschwege show that the hessenDATA project certainly has potential for person-based predictive policing. Even if risk scores are not currently being generated for individual cases, the software paves the way for subsequent predictive policing through automated data merging. Moreover, its unspoken aim is to be used as a person-based predictive policing system in the future.[249] It can therefore be considered a precursor to predictive policing.

3. DyRiAS (Dynamic Risk Analysis System)

DyRiAS consists of a group of web-based prognosis tools for violent crime, including high-school shootings (DyRiAS-Schule),[250] domestic violence (DyRiAS-Intimpartner)[251] and violence at work (DyRiAS-Arbeitsplatz).[252] DyRiAS further offers an Islamism-Screener tool in cooperation with the

---

243 *Gesellschaft für Informatik* 2018a.

244 *Hessischer Landtag* 2019, 18.

245 Legal basis § 13 Abs. 1 Nr. 2 HSOG ('allgemein zugängliche Quellen'), *Hessischer Landtag* 2019, 19; see also *Martini* Verwaltungsarchiv 2016, 307, 307 et seq. m. w. N.

246 *Brühl* Süddeutsche Zeitung of 18.10.2018, accessible at https://perma.cc/6QDL-GD5X, last accessed 1.1.2022.

247 See https://perma.cc/T88L-VNQA (last accessed on 1.1.2022).

248 See *Richardson et al.* N.Y.U. L. Rev. 2019, 192, 211 ff; *Winston* The Verge of 27.2.2018, accessible at https://perma.cc/84ZW-S7HN, last accessed 1.1.2022.

249 *Löffelmann* 2018, 21.

250 *Hoffmann et al.* Polizei & Wissenschaft 2013, 49.

251 *Hoffmann/Glaz-Ocik* Polizei & Wissenschaft 2012, 45.

252 Cf. *Hoffmann* SafetyPlus 2014, 41.

extremism researcher Andreas Zick from the University of Bielefeld.[253] The tools have been developed since 2009 by the Darmstadt-based private company Institut Psychologie & Bedrohungsmanagement. The tools are currently used by the Swiss police.[254]

a) Prognosis tool development

Instead of developing the tools with a training dataset, predictors were derived from the relevant literature.[255] The first three DyRiAS instruments do not merely add up the presence of individual risk factors, and the manufacturer stresses that the tools neither use a checklist nor a psychological test.[256] Instead, they apply a 'multi-layered set of rules with more than 50 interlocking and interrelated individual rules'. Certain combinations of risk factors cause the overall risk to 'jump up' according to patterns defined in the algorithm.[257] The statistical calculations behind the results are described as 'so extensive and complex' that manual evaluation would be impossible.[258]

The weighting of the individual variables, the algorithm itself and even the statistical methods underlying the algorithm have not bene made public, and the literary basis from which the predictors were derived is also unclear.[259]

While the Islamism-Screener tool is based on less complex rules, its inner workings, too, have yet to be revealed to outsiders.

No information is available about the number of people who have been wrongly classified as high risk (false-positives). In the case of domestic violence, the developers merely state that its error performance is 'satisfactory'.[260] With regard to the Islamism-Screener, they state that false-positi-

253 *Böckler et al.* Kriminalistik 2017, 491.

254 *Basel-Stadt* 2016, 4.

255 An analysis of over 250 studies is said to have been included in DyRiAS-Schule, *Hoffmann et al.* Polizei & Wissenschaft 2013, 49.

256 *Hoffmann/Glaz-Ocik* Polizei & Wissenschaft 2012, 45, 49.

257 Referred to as 'Booster' rules *Hoffmann/Glaz-Ocik* Polizei & Wissenschaft 2012, 45, 50 et seq.

258 *Hoffmann/Glaz-Ocik* Polizei & Wissenschaft 2012, 45, 49; *Hoffmann et al.* Polizei & Wissenschaft 2013, 49, 54.

259 DyRiAS for highschool shootings *Paulus* 2016, 134.

260 *Hoffmann/Glaz-Ocik* Polizei & Wissenschaft 2012, 45, 54.

ve cannot be ruled out.[261] An independent study in Switzerland of the DyRiAS tool for domestic violence revealed that two-thirds of the people evaluated were wrongly labelled as high risk.[262]

b) Prognosis tool application

When assessing individual cases, operators click through between 13 and 40 questions depending on the tool. In the case of binary 'yes/no' questions, operators have the opportunity to use a text field to briefly explain the information used to answer the question.[263] This serves as both documentation and *ex post* verification, but is also intended to encourage operators to view cases from all possible angles.

Operators are also provided with background information that is optionally available at a mouse click. This takes the form of case vignettes that illustrate the dynamics of the queried risk factor, provide hints about which information sources could be used to answer a question, video interviews with experts about the queried risk factor, a list of literature and a short summary of it.[264]

Finally, the computer calculates a risk score of 0 to 5.[265] The statistical probabilities behind these risk categories are 'deliberately omitted'.[266] In addition to the risk score, the most important risk factors ('red flags') for each case are listed[267] and the functionality of the instrument is roughly described.[268]

In Switzerland, the follow-up measures linked to high risk scores with DyRiAS for domestic violence range from decisions on whether to keep a person in pre-trial detention to no-contact orders. Regarding the Islamism-Screener, the manufacturer emphasizes that it is not a crime investigation

---

261 *Böckler et al.* Kriminalistik 2017, 491, 502.

262 *Frei* Zeitschrift für Polizeiwissenschaft und Polizeipraxis; *Gerth et al.* Archives of Forensic Psychology 2015, 1; on the DyRiAS domestic violence tool see *Gerth* 2015, 44 ('strong overestimation of the relapse risk based on the DyRiAS result').

263 *Hoffmann et al.* Polizei & Wissenschaft 2013, 49, 54.

264 *Hoffmann et al.* Polizei & Wissenschaft 2013, 49, 54.

265 *Hoffmann/Glaz-Ocik* Polizei & Wissenschaft 2012, 45, 49.

266 *Hoffmann et al.* Polizei & Wissenschaft 2013, 49, 54; *Hoffmann/Glaz-Ocik* Polizei & Wissenschaft 2012, 45, 50

267 *Hoffmann et al.* Polizei & Wissenschaft 2013, 49, 56.

268 *Hoffmann et al.* Polizei & Wissenschaft 2013, 49, 56.

tool that should be used to track down suspects after a crime has been committed.[269] The need for this emphasis suggests that such 'off-label' use of prognosis tools by the police is a real possibility.[270]

aa) Prognosis tool operators

After brief online training,[271] the tool is intended to be used by people involved in crime prevention but without expert knowledge of prognostics. In addition to the police, judiciary, psychiatry, schools, refugee shelters and companies are mentioned as potential users.[272] It is clear that the tool is being used to break the monopoly held by prognosis experts with extensive backgrounds in psychology and criminology.

bb) People affected by crime prognoses

The DyRiAS instruments are intended for use with people who have already demonstrated 'alarming behaviour'.[273] However, no definition of 'alarming' is provided. Once a risk score has been created, it is stored in Switzerland for ten years.[274]

In summary, DyRiAS is a rule-based algorithm in which a theory is initially developed by people and the correlations found are only written into the algorithm in a second step. The algorithm does not 'discover' new connections, as in machine learning, but only applies rules that have been developed by people. Further, DyRiAS automates data processing, but not data input. However, if the system is used by the police to make decisions on follow-up measures that restrict fundamental rights, DyRiAS can certainly be described as predictive policing.

---

269 *Böckler et al.* Kriminalistik 2017, 491, 502.

270 For this procedure in the USA in the Strategic Subject List see above p. 66 et seq.

271 See about *DyRiAS*.

272 *Böckler et al.* Kriminalistik 2017, 491, 502; *Hoffmann et al.* Polizei & Wissenschaft 2013, 49, 54.

273 See *Böckler et al.* Kriminalistik 2017, 491, 499; see also https://perma.cc/UYQ2-34WD (last accessed on 1.1.2022).

274 *Grossenbacher* SRF of 5.4.2018, accessible at https://perma.cc/7ZY8-6HCS, last accessed 1.1.2022.

4. Flight Data Pattern Recognition

To prevent terrorist offences, § 4 of the German Passenger Name Record Act (Fluggastdatengesetz – FlugDaG) has allowed the Federal Criminal Police Office (Bundeskriminalamt – BKA) to carry out automated pattern recognition of air passenger data since 2017.

§ 4 (1) FlugDaG states: 'The Passenger Information Unit [...] compares it [passenger data] with databases and patterns [...] in order to identify persons for whom there are actual indications that they have committed [...] criminal offences or will do so within the foreseeable future'.[275]

Passenger data encompasses 20 data points, stretching from contact details, email address, payment information, hotel reservations and fellow travellers to flights missed in the past.[276] The aim of pattern recognition is to identify individuals with a high crime risk who were previously unknown to the police: it is thus a form of suspicion-generating predictive policing. In this case, pattern recognition is being used to predict terrorist offences and other serious criminal offences.[277] It is important to note, however, that in the FlugDaG the concept of 'serious crimes' includes crimes that are much less serious than terrorism, e.g. fraud, product piracy, car smuggling and serious bodily injury.[278] As pattern recognition results are kept for five years,[279] the process can be described as a cross-over between dragnet investigation[280] and preventive data retention.[281] Given the frequency of air travel in almost all sections of the population, it can be said that almost the entire population is exposed to predictive policing.[282]

The patterns with which passenger data are compared are drawn up by the BKA with the involvement of a data protection officer.[283] It is not clear which data flow into pattern creation. However, § 4 (4) FlugDaG provides the legal basis for obtaining patterns by analysing passenger data itself. According to BKA president Münch, possible elements of a pattern could

275 Translation by author.
276 See list in § 2 FlugDaG.
277 BT-Drs. 18/11501, p. 26, 28.
278 § 4 Para. 1 No. 6 FlugDaG.
279 On the concerns about the long storage period, *Wendt/Rasche* ZD-Aktuell 2016, 05205; *Arzt* DÖV 2017, 1023, 1029.
280 Cf. on dragnet investigations BVerfGE 115, 320; see also BVerfGE 141, 220 (1794, mn. 207).
281 *Arzt* DÖV 2017, 1023, 1023 et seq.
282 *Arzt* 2017, 11.
283 § 4 (3) FlugDaG.

include details such as the fact that a person who usually travels in a group suddenly travels alone, or that a booking was made at short notice and via cash payment.[284]

Although the Federal Criminal Police Office announced at the end of 2018 that the flight data pattern recognition system was still under construction[285] and that it was not using machine learning or big data analysis at the time,[286] machine learning and big data analysis are the ultimate goals of the FlugDaG.[287] The term 'pattern recognition' refers to the automatic detection of if-this-then-that relationships from large amounts of data.[288] The fact that a pattern may also be obtained by analysing passenger data itself opens up the possibility of using self-learning algorithms. The FlugDaG not only permits machine learning analyses in particularly 'justified individual cases', such as in the hessenDATA project, but the mass automatic reading and processing of data from all air passengers. The internationally promoted data mining and machine learning software available for the analysis of passenger data provides the technical possibility to do so.[289] The fact that the term 'pattern' does not only refer to static and immutable checklists created individually by humans is enforced by the fact that the patterns can be derived by automated processing of the passenger data themselves, i.e. 'learned' by a machine learning algorithm. The official justification given for the FlugDaG states that the aim of the act is to allow 'different, new ways of combating criminal offences'.[290]

The same document states that pattern recognition will likely result in an annual 'hit rate' of 0.07 per cent. This means that 0.07 per cent (about 100,000 persons) of all air travellers are marked as dangerous and in need of follow-up measures in Germany annually.[291]

The FlugDaG provides the most comprehensive legal basis available at the current time to use algorithmic crime prognoses. § 4 (3) FlugDaG sta-

284 Protokoll-Nr. 18/114, BT-Innenausschuss, 26rotocol No 18/114, BT Committee on Internal Affairs, p. 26.
285 See *Bundesministerium des Innern* 2018.
286 BT-Drs. 19/5874, p. 11; see also BT-Drs. 19/1556, p. 21; for a list of all software systems which are already in use today for passenger data processing, see also BT-Drs. 19/1556, p. 21. BT-Drs. 19/4755, p. 5 et seq.
287 Only with this technology is it possible to evaluate passenger data, cf. *Ulbricht et al.* 2018, 182 et seq.
288 See above p. 52 et seq.
289 For 'risk-based profiling' of passenger data, see for example https://perma.cc/DG6W-GRJU (last accessed 1.1.2022).
290 BT-Drs. 18/11501, 28.
291 BT-Drs. 19/4755, 9.

tes that the pattern recognition must contain features that give rise to suspicion and features that lower suspicion. Sensitive characteristics such as ethnic origin, sexual orientation, religion and health are not permissible. At the same time, the number of individuals covered, i.e. the false-positive rate, should be kept as low as possible.

The FlugDaG thus creates the basis for the application of fully automated suspicion-generating, person-based predictive policing. Although the law lays down some requirements for pattern development, there is no control mechanism in place other than the involvement of a data protection officer.

5. Summary Germany

This overview shows that in Germany the path has already been paved for person-based predictive policing in several areas using various approaches. The approaches fall on different points of the spectrum between suspicion confirming and suspicion generating predictive policing.

Flight data pattern recognition has the widest scope (all passengers without individual suspicion) and the closest proximity to the extensive predictive policing approaches that are applied in the US.

Although § 25a HSOG and the hessenData project merely apply algorithmic analyses to individual cases, the project still has a far-reaching impact. This is due to new machine learning technologies that connect various online and offline data sources and the fact that the software has already been used in the US for extensive person-based predictive policing.

While flight data pattern recognition and hessenData fall into the category of big data analysis and machine learning, DyRiAS, in contrast, is a rule-based predictive policing system and RADAR-iTE constitutes a preliminary stage of predictive policing implemented with even simpler technical means. Despite the rule-based nature of these systems, they lack transparency. And although DyRiAS and RADAR-iTE are limited to people already previously suspected of posing a risk, DyRiAS, in particular, fails to precisely define what a previous suspicion of danger actually means.

One aspect that must be lauded in DyRiAS, however, is that it allows its operators to use text fields to provide information about individual predictors; thus, encouraging operators to justify, document and think through their individual decisions. However, filling out the text field is not mandatory, so its benefits can easily be bypassed.

Ultimately, these tools have been developed to be used by people without special psychological-criminological training.

Finally, it is worth noting that these tools could also be used by the police for crime prediction among people with mental illnesses. In Germany (as with the Beware programme in the US)[292] there have already been efforts to use data on mental illnesses to predict future crimes. A 2018 draft amendment to the Bavarian Law on Helping the Mentally Ill (Psychisch-Kranken-Hilfe-Gesetz) would have enabled data on people with mental illnesses to be stored for at least five years and for the data to be used for crime prevention.[293] However, criticism led the plans to be abandoned.

It has now not only become clear how current the issue of automated prognoses in police work is. In addition, it has become clear that – contrary to public opinion – predictive policing is not *one* monolithic process but there are many different versions of predictive policing. Each version has to be looked at individually when assessing the legal limits of predictive policing and the tensions arising in many places between individual freedoms and the pursuit of security (see Chapter II).

G. Factual limits of person-based predictive policing

For years, algorithmic decision-making processes, big data and machine learning have been referred to only in superlatives in the media and academia. Everyone is talking about the 'disruptive potential' of the new technologies.[294] Many places refer to the changes associated with algorithms as a 'revolution'[295] that will radically change our society,[296] our legal system[297] and our way of conducting science. In the context of police work, the new technologies are often marketed as miracle weapons.[298] The 'marketing slogans' of big data and machine learning[299] claim that their new algorithmic tools will help us better understand and control the world.

292 See above fn. 185.
293 See above fn. 185.
294 See *Wischmeyer* 2020, mn. 6; *Wills* IBM Big Data & Analytics Hub 2016.
295 *Mayer-Schönberger/Cukier* 2013; *Kitchin* 2014; *Dean et al.* IEEE Micro 2018.
296 *Mayer-Schönberger/Cukier* 2013, 30, 67, 71; pessimistic also *Anderson* Wired of 23.6.2008, accessible at https://perma.cc/CE9Y-3ZYR, last accessed 1.1.2022.
297 See *Hildebrandt* Mod. L. Rev. 2016, 1, 1 ff; *Lessig* 2006.
298 *Beck/McCue* The Police Chief 2009/11, 18; critical, *Ferguson* 2017.
299 *Creemers/Guagnin* KrimJ 2014, 134, 136.

To put these superlatives into perspective, the following section describes three important limitations of the technology: (I) algorithmic decision-making is neither in a position to make an overall assessment of all circumstances in an individual case, (II) nor is it able to provide information on causation. (III) Further, contrary to popular belief, algorithms do not per se make decisions that are more neutral or objective than those made by people.

I. No overall assessment – big data does not mean all data

Andrian Kreye describes the code behind the algorithms as our 'new world language'.[300] If we entertain this metaphor, it is important to note that Wittgenstein's saying that 'the limits of my language are the limits of my world' also applies to algorithms: everything that is unquantifiable in code and that is not inscribed into it does not exist in the world of the algorithm.

If an algorithm-based decision-making system is used to make predictions in individual cases, it is important to be aware that algorithms cannot undertake comprehensive assessments of all circumstances.

The algorithm can only 'see' what it has been trained to see by people. In the examples of algorithmic predictions explored above, operators always predefine a limited number of certain input variables, i.e. the characteristics according to whose existence, absence or interaction an algorithm assesses a situation.

Algorithms cannot independently identify new relevant categories outside the given input variables or its training dataset.

Even with a large number of input variables, it is impossible for people to predict exhaustively *all* potentially relevant influences on every conceivable future individual case and to write them into a computer-readable algorithm.

Unlike human beings, who can spontaneously respond to new circumstances, algorithms are incapable of gaining a true overall picture. The inability of algorithms to process new situations spontaneously was shown, for example, during a fatal accident involving an autonomously driven vehicle in the US in 2018. The vehicle's object recognition system failed to identify a person pushing a bicycle loaded with plastic bags across a

300 *Kreye* Süddeutsche Zeitung of 22.7.2014, accessible at https://perma.cc/8FMT-B2Q8, last accessed 1.1.2022.

road at night as an 'obstacle'. This mistake probably happened because this particular pattern 'a bicycle loaded with plastic bags' had not been considered by humans beforehand. Thus, the system was not sufficiently prepared for the situation with appropriate pictures during its training phase.[301]

Algorithmic predictions are only as good as the data they are based on. If the selection and quality of the data are poor, the best machine learning algorithm will also produce poor results. This is summed up by the saying 'garbage in, garbage out', which is widely used among experts in machine learning.[302] For example, incorrect or outdated data in police databases can lead to errors in risk scores. The fact that there are also concerns in Germany about the inaccuracy of data stored by the police is clear from the reactions to the recent reports that journalists had been falsely included on the 'Gewalttäter Links' watchlist.[303]

The fact that training data limitations can also lead to problematic results is also shown by the oft-cited example of faulty object recognition by Flickr and Google, which identified photographs of people with dark skin as 'monkeys'. This, too, was because the training datasets lacked sufficient photos of people with dark skin.[304]

II. No causality

Machine learning algorithms can provide insights into *what* will happen, but not *why* something will happen.[305] They only work with statistical correlations, not with causal explanatory models. Importantly, correlations may even be completely random (spurious correlations). For example, the US suicide rate by hanging correlates with the US government's spending on science, space and technology, just as the annual number of people drowning in a swimming pool in the US correlates with the annual number of films in which the actor Nicolas Cage appears.[306]

---

301 *Marshall/Davies* Wired of 24.5.2018, accessible at https://perma.cc/F2T9-Q2DY, last accessed 1.1.2022.

302 See *Richardson et al.* N.Y.U. L. Rev. 2019, 192.

303 See above fn. 233.

304 *Kasperkevic* The Guardian of 1.7.2015, accessible at https://perma.cc/P2KT-8GEV, last accessed 1.1.2022.

305 *Mayer-Schönberger/Cukier* 2013, 70–92.

306 For more bizarre spurious correlations see https://perma.cc/4A55-4YGQ (last accessed 1.1.2022).

Spurious correlations may lead to faulty results when using neural networks. One example is that a machine learning algorithm had been trained to distinguish enemy tanks from those belonging to a country's own military. The algorithm was trained using many different pictures of tanks. In the laboratory the algorithm performed very well; however, it failed to do so when deployed in the field under reald world conditions. When researchers tried to find out exactly what the algorithm was using to determine whether an object was an enemy tank, among other things, cloudy skies led the algorithm to identify tanks as enemy vehicles. This was because the training database contained photographs of enemy tanks in cloudy weather, whereas a country's won tanks were usually photographed under blue skies.[307] This is an example of a random correlation that has nothing to do with the actual characteristics of a 'friendly' or enemy tank. Researchers demonstrated that adding clouds to pictures of tanks belonging to one's own military significantly increased the probability that the algorithm would mistakenly identify the vehicle as hostile. This example of tank misclassification can be transferred to crime predictions. Just as an algorithm interpreted the random presence of clouds as an indication of an 'enemy', an algorithm could associate the random presence of belonging to an ethnic minority or eye colour with a higher probability of committing crimes.

The following provides a further – albeit hypothetical – example:[308] a machine learning algorithm is trained to predict recidivism among people released from prison. The data set is taken from prison files from the last five years on all inmates from several prisons. The algorithm identifies a high correlation between a large shoe size and recidivism. Although algorithms cannot provide causal models that explain such connections, decision-makers in the judiciary and police are now willing to link negative consequences (no probation, police surveillance) to the characteristic 'large feet' – on the basis of an 'objective truth': the correlation identified by the algorithm. The system's developers insist that the numbers speak for themselves.[309] Nevertheless, in this situation it would be crucial to understand *why* the data set suggests that large feet have been associated with recidivism over the last five years. For example, a particularly high

307 *Freitas* ACM SIGKDD explorations newsletter 2014, 1; see similar results for the distinction between wolves and dogs, *Ribeiro et al.* ACM SIGKDD 2016, 1135; and pans and woks *Carter et al.* Distill 2019.

308 Example from *Chan/Bennett Moses* Theoretical Criminology 2016, 21, 34.

309 See *Mayer-Schönberger/Cukier* 2013, 14.

concentration of growth hormones might have caused aggression and thus crime. Or people with larger feet may have been released from prison early, because of a shortage of larger sized shoes.

In this case, it would be up to criminologists to determine the deeper causal reason for recidivism and to develop an explanatory theory. Only then can the characteristic of large feet be adequately dealt with in order to derive the correct intervention strategy from it.

However, since a functional, operational prognosis system already exists (that lacks a basis in criminological theory), it is very likely that further, cost- and time-intensive criminological investigations will be dispensed with and that decisions will be made by in the judiciary and police solely on the basis of correlations. This is one of the scenarios that many authors have in mind when they associate big data and machine learning with an impending loss of relevance[310] and even the 'methodological genocide'[311] of the social sciences, especially criminology. This lack of causal explainability is one aspect of the criticized systemic lack of transparency within algorithmic systems.[312]

III. No neutrality

'Do algorithms have politics?'
– based on Langdon Winner[313]
or
'If it is neutral, it is not technology.'
– Lance Strate[314]

The widespread representation of algorithms as neutral, objective alternatives to human decision-making processes must be met with misgiving at closer inspection: as with any other technology,[315] algorithms are human-

310 *Chan/Bennett Moses* Theoretical Criminology 2016, 21 see also *Anderson* Wired of 23.6.2008, accessible at https://perma.cc/CE9Y-3ZYR, last accessed 1.1.2022; *Mayer-Schönberger/Cukier* 2013, 30, 67; *Zedner* Theoretical Criminology 2007, 261.

311 *Uprichard* Discover Society. Focus 2013, 3, 4.

312 See in detail p. 127 et seq.

313 *Winner* Daedalus 1980, 121, 122 ('Do artifacts have politics').

314 *Strate* Educational Technology 2012, 6; see also *Winner* Daedalus 1980, 121, 122 already in the 1980s.

315 See on the eminently political nature of any technical artifact the work of the Science & Technology Studies, e.g. *Simon* 2010.

created artefacts based on value judgements. Therefore, *by definition*, they cannot work purely objectively and without the influence of prior human value judgements. To put it bluntly, Strate is correct to claim that 'If it's neutral, it's not technology'.

At each stage of the algorithm design process,[316] programmers make value judgements that reflect their individual preferences and can perpetuate existing social inequalities. In view of the numerous decisions that have to be made during algorithm design, if different developers are given the same task of designing a predictive policing algorithm, they may well arrive at very different solutions that produce diverging risk scores even when the same person is assessed.

It is difficult to draw up a final catalogue of all potential sources of error in algorithm design given the complexity of the procedure. However, the following section presents the typical problems associated with data analysis in the field of crime prevention.

1. Data selection[317]

One of the central phases of algorithm development is the compilation of the training dataset, because algorithms can only be as good as the databases on which they are developed.[318] The contents of training datasets have a direct effect on the outcomes produced by predictive algorithms. Programmers have to make decisions about finding suitable data, data quality, data representativeness and how to deal with social discrimination inscribed in the data.[319]

a) Lack of data quality

A lack of data quality means a lack of correctness, currentness and completeness of the database from which an algorithm 'learns'.[320] If, for examp-

---

316 See above p. 49 et seq.

317 Cf. *Selbst* Ga. L. Rev. 2017, 109, 137 et seq.; *Tischbirek* 2020, 103, mn. 5 et seq.

318 See *Lehr/Ohm* UCDL Rev. 2017, 653, 677.

319 Accordingly, there is no 'raw' data, i.e. data not predetermined by the human data selection process; cf. *Bowker* 2005, 184: 'Raw data is [...] an oxymoron', see also *Kunz* 2008, 16: 'the statistical material [is] not actually found, but it is created'.

320 See *O'Neil* 2016, 15-31.

le, people have been erroneously entered into a police database and if this database is used as part of a training dataset, an algorithm will learn a distorted picture of reality. It will, for example, learn that many actually 'harmless' characteristics correspond with risk and it will wrongly label 'harmless' people as 'dangerous' in the future.

In Germany, too, the quality of data stored in police files can be problematic. As natural and unavoidable as a certain error rate may be in any form of police work, examples from the recent past point to severer errors: at the G-20 Summit in Hamburg in 2017, a number of journalists were incorrectly put on the 'Gewalttäter Links' police watchlist.[321] Estimates suggest that police watchlists in Germany contain up to 10,000 incorrect or outdated entries.[322] This is a magnitude that can lead to statistically significant distortions.

b) The dark figure of crime

It is important to note that, contrary to common belief, crime statistics do not fully reflect the actual crime rate. On the one hand, only offences identified as such by the victims and brought to the attention of the police can be included in the statistics.[323] The registration of violent and property offences by the police often depends to a large extent on the tendency of victims to report them.[324] The difference between the crime rate recorded in government statistics and the actual crime rate is referred to as the dark figure of crime.[325] In this context, Hassemer speaks of the general 'enforcement deficit of modern criminal law'.[326] In criminology, the dark figure is researched primarily through interviews on self-reported criminal behaviour.[327] The dark figure of crime is quite high for many of-

321 See above fn. 233.

322 *Reuter* Netzpolitik of 30.8.2017, accessible at https://perma.cc/GR2W-MKLG, last accessed 1.1.2022.

323 Cf. *Kunz/Singelnstein* 2016, 197 et seq., 226 et seq.; *Wehrheim* 2014, 36 et seq.

324 *Lukas* Sozial Extra 2011, 44.

325 *Kunz/Singelnstein* 2016, 197 ff; *Schwind* 2010, mn. 53c; *Eisenberg/Kölbel* 2017, 804 et seq.; *Kaiser* 1996, 392 et seq.

326 *Hassemer* ZRP 1992, 382.

327 *Kunz/Singelnstein* 2016, 197 et seq., 229; on the problems of the self-reporting, *Kunz/Singelnstein* 2016, 232 ff; *Kunz/Singelnstein* 2016 as well as Zaubermann 2009.

fences[328] and it is often not evenly distributed among all strata of the population.[329] Rather, the selective perception of the police, for example, leads crimes committed by immigrants and their descendants to be detected and prosecuted more frequently than crimes committed by other population groups.[330] This leads to an overrepresentation of persons with a migration background in crime statistics that does not correspond to the actual crime rate. Such overrepresentation will lead to distortions in algorithms that are trained using such data.

Furthermore, it is important to note that police crime statistics contain data on people only suspected of having a committed a crime. The police statistics on which predictive policing algorithms are often trained do, however, not take into account whether the suspected individuals were actually convicted of a crime in court later on.[331] This is known as the 'funnel phenomenon' of crime statistics.[332] At the same time, crime statistics also regularly contain inaccuracies and errors[333] which can distort algorithmic learning.

If the police rely in their future police work solely on the predictions of algorithms based on such a distorted data basis, the police work will continue to be limited to only a small part of the actual crime rate. Ultimately, police crime statistics are activity reports about police work, and not accurate depictions of crime in society: the 'new crime statistics', which would arise after the police follow the recommendations of algorithms, would mathematically justify ever more selective policing – possibly at the expense of minorities being overrepresented in the statistics. The longer policing is based on algorithms with faulty training data, the more distorted that policing will become (so-called 'feedback loop').[334]

---

328 *Baier et al.* 2009, 94; *Liebl* 2010, 83 ff; *Ruch* 2011, 75.

329 Cf. *Polllähne* 2011, 234 et seq.

330 *Baier et al.* 2009, 11; see also *Geißler* Zeitschrift für Migration und soziale Arbeit 2000, 20; for an early discussion, *Albrecht/Lamnek* 1979; cf. on the different reporting behaviour of shoplifting by young people with a migration background *Köllisch* 2004, 228 et seq.

331 On the limits of crime statistics, *Eisenberg/Kölbel* 2017, 178 ff; *Kaiser* 1996, 388, 392; see also *Gundlach/Menzel* Schriftenreihe Polizei-Führungskademie 1992, 60; critical also *Singelnstein/Stolle* 2012, 55.

332 On the funnel phenomenon, *Heinz* 2004, 385; *Göppinger* 2008, 556 et seq., mn. 25.

333 See overview at *Göppinger* 2008, 357 et seq., mn. 30 et seq.; see also the detailed discussion at *Heinz* 2004, 365 et seq., 381 et seq.

334 Cf. the so-called 'Feedback Loop' *Tischbirek* 2020, 103, mn. 5, *Lum/Isaac* Significance 2016, 14.

c) Lack of training data representativity

Another aspect of the training dataset that is dependent on human decisions and can lead to distortions is the question of how representative a training dataset is with regard to the total population.[335] If a training dataset contains a higher or lower proportion of people from a particular social group compared to their actual representation within the population, e.g. an ethnic minority, this may distort the results of the algorithm for that social group.[336]

An illustrative example from outside the context of crime control of how the limitations of training datasets can directly impact certain population groups can be seen in the case of incorrect algorithmic object recognition by Flickr and Google cited above. Photographs of people with dark skin colour were identified as 'monkeys', because the training data of the algorithms did not contain sufficient photographs of people with dark skin.[337] Similar problems have been observed with autonomous cars: algorithmic object recognition for road traffic less often correctly identifies pedestrians with dark skin colour as 'obstacles' than it does for people with light skin.[338]

d) Perpetuation of societal discrimination

Finally, even accurate and representative data can reflect and reinforce social prejudices (if the data accurately reflect real-life societal discrimination).[339] Training data that do not contain prejudices against certain population groups are very difficult to come by.[340] Perpetuation of societal discrimination by algorithms can be illustrated with the example of an algorithm used in the UK as early as the 1980s to help select applicants for medical school: only the candidates pre-selected by an algorithm were invited to an interview. The algorithm was trained on past data on success-

---

335 See *Tischbirek* 2020, 103, mn. 5; *Barocas/Selbst* Calif. L. Rev. 2016, 671, 684-87.

336 *Barocas/Selbst* Calif. L. Rev. 2016, 671, 684-87.

337 See above fn. 304.

338 *Wilson et al.* arXiv 2019.

339 *Tischbirek* 2020, 103, mn. 7 ff; *Barocas/Selbst* Calif. L. Rev. 2016, 671, 681-84; *Citron/Pasquale* Wash. L. Rev. 2014, 1, 13-16; *Perry et al.* 2013, 116, 112 ('biases in the inputs will skew the predictions','it is important to understand how the data are collected because they may have systematic biases').

340 So also *Hacker* Common Market L. Rev. 2018, 1143, 1160 et seq.

ful applicants. Since the past data contained mainly men of Caucasian descent, the algorithm learned that women and people of colour, regardless of their professional qualifications, were less apt as applicants, and so they were less likely to get invited to interviews by the algorithm.[341] Historical human discrimination against women and people of colour was taken up by the supposedly neutral algorithm and transformed into a mathematical rule. This shows that an algorithm can have a discriminatory effect even if a programmer has 'done everything right' in terms of mathematical standards and the training dataset has been compiled representatively as a 'mirror of reality'. These effects can, of course, also be seen in the area of crime control.[342] For example, if in the past the police did not distribute their activities evenly across all strata of society or all parts of a city, but, for example, in the case of drug-related crime, concentrated on people of colour or on a particular part of the city where predominantly people of colour live, this would lead to a statistically higher rate of detection of drug-related crime among people of colour than among other groups of people.[343] If an algorithm were trained using this historical data, it would learn that people of colour have a higher risk of drug-related crime. The discriminatory focus of human police work is continued and reinforced in algorithm-based police work[344] (see above 'feedback loop').[345] Legal proof that a certain algorithm's training data does not correctly reflect reality but discriminates against certain social groups is, however, often extremely difficult to provide. It may require extensive and costly social science studies.

e) Conclusion on data selection and possible solutions

It should be noted that algorithms cannot automatically overcome human prejudices in the data. If programmers refrain from searching for and actively compensating for discrimination in the data, it will appear in the results of an algorithm. Prejudices that have been identified, however, can be addressed in the algorithm design phase.[346] This can be done using

---

341 *Lowry/Macpherson* BMJ 1988, 657.
342 See above fn. 350.
343 See *Tischbirek* 2020, 103, mn. 5.
344 Cf. for the use of algorithms to select applicants on the basis of sexist data *Fröhlich/Spiecker* Verfassungsblog of 26.12.2018, accessible at https://perma.cc/9GVX-X564, last accessed 1.1.2022.
345 See above fn. 334.
346 Cf. e.g. beyond crime control *Zhao et al.* arXiv 2017.

the methods associated with 'non-discrimination by design'. These include the process of regularization proposed by Toshihiro and Kamishima,[347] the proposals by Hardt et al. on 'equalized odds and equal opportunity',[348] Feldman's approach to adding random data points,[349] and the research by Gummadi et al. at the Max Planck Institute for Software Systems.[350] The deliberate integration of these approaches as standard procedure in the design phase of crime algorithms is certainly possible. A widespread use is, however, currently still pending.

2. Definition of target variables

Value judgements are made not only in the data collection phase, but also in the subsequent data analysis stage. Discrimination can also result from the determination of target variables, i.e. the determination of which event an algorithm should learn to predict on the basis of the training data, for example, a crime prognosis algorithm could be trained using police arrest data, rather than judicial conviction data, which would more accurately correspond with criminally relevant behaviour. It may well be that the police more frequently wrongly arrest certain population groups, such as people of colour,[351] without subsequent judicial convictions. If an algorithm is then based solely on arrest data, it will ascribe a disproportionately high crime risk to persons of colour.

Training datasets may be selected out of pure convenience, since it is easier to collect data on arrests than on convictions. We see this, for example, in the case of the Chicago Strategic Subject List, as well as in prognosis tools such as VRAG.[352]

---

347 See *Kamishima et al.* Joint European Conference on Machine Learning and Knowledge Discovery in Databases 2012, 35 et seq.

348 See *Hardt et al.* NIPS 2016.

349 *Feldman et al.* ACM SIGKDD 2015, 259, 11-15.

350 *Grgic-Hlaca et al.* NIPS Symposium on Machine Learning and the Law 2016; *Zafar et al.* arXiv 2016.

351 See above fn. 330.

352 See above fn. 79 and accompanying text.

3. Selection of input variables

The selection of input variables is also a value judgement. How suitable certain input variables are for predicting behaviour can vary for different groups in society.[353] By choosing a certain input variable, programmers often (unconsciously) decide that the algorithm will make more mistakes for certain social groups.[354]

4. Calibration and monitoring of the learning process

Programmers also have to make numerous value judgements when monitoring the learning process.

a) Error rate

What is considered to be an error that an algorithm must avoid also boils down to decisions made by people. It is in fact a highly political decision how to adjust the false-positive and false-negative error rates of a predictive policing system. Programmers involved in the design phase can determine that an algorithm should commit more false-positive errors ('harmless' people classified as 'dangerous') or false-negative errors ('dangerous' people classified as 'harmless'). This is known as adjustment of the 'asymmetric cost ratio'.[355] As explained above, both error types are connected and a reduction in one error rate leads to an increase in the other.[356] For example, if the programmer specifies an asymmetric cost ratio of 5:1, this means that an algorithm will make five false-positive errors for each false-negative error.[357] With the HART algorithm, for example, the developers deliberately calibrated the algorithm to make more false-positive errors.[358] This was done because: 'The worst error would be if the model forecasts

353 *Barocas/Selbst* Calif. L. Rev. 2016, 671, 688-90.
354 *Barocas/Selbst* Calif. L. Rev. 2016, 671, 688-90.
355 Cf. the so-called problem of the 'Asymmetric Cost Ratio', *Lehr/Ohm* UCDL Rev. 2017, 653, 691 et seq.
356 See above fn. 88 and accompanying text.
357 *Lehr/Ohm* UCDL Rev. 2017, 653, 692.
358 *Oswald et al.* Information & Communications Technology Law 2018, 223, 236.

low [risk] and the offender turned out high [risk]'.[359] The decisionistic nature of definitions such as 'worst error' is obvious, and with it the need for critical examination of decisions made in the design phase. For it is by no means obvious that such errors are indeed 'the worst' and that they are not just as bad or even worse than a 'harmless' person being wrongly classified as dangerous. Assigning the security of society more importance than individual freedom and equality is not a mathematical, objective decision but a value judgement that should be disclosed and put forward for democratic debate. The question of how many people in crime control must be wrongly labelled highly dangerous in order for an algorithm to actually identify *one* highly dangerous person correctly is ultimately a question that should not be left to programmers but to society as a whole. The more far-reaching the consequences of such errors, the more important critical monitoring becomes.

b) Overfitting and spurious correlations

Finally, each dataset contains spurious correlations.[360] For example, as mentioned above, the rate of suicide by hanging in the US corresponds with the level of spending by the US government on science, space and technology. Further, the annual number of people who drown in a swimming pool in the US corresponds with the number of films in which Nicolas Cage appears.[361] Spurious correlations are also found in police records. Certain types of algorithms are more likely to pick up spurious correlations and turn them into a rule for decision-making[362] ('overfitting'). The more input variables used in an algorithm, the greater the risk of overfitting. Studies have shown that datasets for minority groups may be especially likely to contain spurious correlations.[363] This may cause algorithms to make less precise predictions for members of a minority.[364] Whether programmers choose models that are particularly susceptible to overfitting is again a value judgement.[365]

---

359 Sheena Urwin, Head of Criminal Justice at Durham Constabulary *University of Cambridge* 2018.
360 *Lehr/Ohm* UCDL Rev. 2017, 653, 684, 693 et seq.
361 See above fn. 306.
362 *Lehr/Ohm* UCDL Rev. 2017, 653, 693 et seq.
363 *Lehr/Ohm* UCDL Rev. 2017, 653, 704.
364 *Lehr/Ohm* UCDL Rev. 2017, 653, 704.
365 *Lehr/Ohm* UCDL Rev. 2017, 653, 693.

5. Summary of no neutrality

Algorithmic models do not simply emerge spontaneously from databases, but from multi-stage, human-controlled processes.[366] In the context of any such process, numerous value judgements and discretionary decisions must be taken. These decisions demonstrate that data scientists are directly involved as political actors in the normative construction of society.[367] Algorithms – as mentioned in the introductory quotation – are by no means guarantors of neutrality and objectivity. Because of the political dimension of many decisions, social scientists and humanities scholars should also be involved in algorithm design. Moreover, it is especially important to include people from minority populations in the process.

H. Conclusion on Chapter I.

Person-based predictive policing in Germany is no longer a purely hypothetical scenario. Flight data pattern recognition, RADAR-iTE and hessenDATA have directly paved the way for automated, algorithmic crime prediction.[368] The previous sections have shown that the promises associated with the new technology should be treated with caution. The following provides critical analysis from the legal (Chapter II) and criminological perspective (Chapter III).

---

366 See *Lehr/Ohm* UCDL Rev. 2017, 653, 668.

367 *Green* arXiv 2018, 9 et seq.

368 See above 82.

Chapter II. Legal limits of person-based predictive policing

The following assesses the legal limits of predictive policing from the point of view of constitutional law. The analysis focuses on guarantees found in the German Constitution but readers from other countries around the world will likely find similar or the same fundamental guarantees in their own country's legal system.

Some may think that the attempt to give a legal framework to new technologies is an idle undertaking, since technology often relativizes law itself. Lessig expressed this concern at the turn of the millennium in his much-quoted expression 'Code *is* Law'.[369] To adhere to old requirements such as the predictability of causal relationships and individual decisions in policing may seem a hopeless undertaking in view of technology that easily surpasses human capabilities without meeting these requirements. Some may even think of the Persian king Xerxes, who, according to legend, had the sea whipped because his troops were held up at the Dardanelles.[370]

The algorithmic turn in crime control certainly has the potential to fundamentally transform the legal system through the logic of algorithms (see Chapter III). This does not, however, mean that attempts at legal containment should be abandoned from the outset. A legal classification of the challenges posed by person-based predictive policing must also be the starting point of this book, before criminological, sociological and legal-theoretical implications will be discussed in Chapter III.

A. *Constitutional framework*

The following begins by examining the constitutional dimensions of person-based predictive policing regarding privacy, non-discrimination, rule of law, democracy and the presumption of innocence.

---

369 *Lessig* Harvard Magazine of 1.1.2000, accessible at https://perma.cc/59RX-P6VK, last accessed 1.1.2022; *Lessig* 2006, 1 et seq.

370 Metaphor in *Darnstädt et al.* Der Spiegel 2009, 68.

I. Privacy

'nam scientia potestas est.' – 'Knowledge is power.'
– Francis Bacon[371]

Like so many successful aphorisms, Francis Bacon's notorious utterance about knowledge and power is above all an abbreviation. Knowledge may represent latent opportunities for power, but the connection between 'empire and empiricism'[372] is not self-evident: it is based on targeted processes of appropriation, processing and application.

One of the aims of the fundamental right to privacy is the regulation of the state's informational power indicated in the opening quotation. Such informational power can also result from algorithmically generated crime correlations. Algorithmic decision-making processes use personal data in training databases.[373] In addition, the calculation of risk scores creates new personal data, i.e. a person-based probabilities of committing a crime. In view of the central role that personal data plays in algorithmic decision-making systems, the following examines the compatibility of person-based predictive policing with the right to privacy, which restricts the state's processing of personal data. First, the scope of privacy is determined. The next step involves addressing the limits of privacy. Subsequently, the specific requirements of privacy in person-based predictive policing are derived.

1. Scope

The right to privacy in the form of informational self-determination (Article 2 (1) in conjunction with Article 1 (1) of the German Constitution) was first elaborated on by the German Constitutional Court (Bundesverfassungsgericht – BverfG) in its 1983 census judgment.[374] The right guarantees protection to people's personal sphere in the form of self-determination and self-portrayal; the BVerfG speaks, among other things, of a 'right to

371 *Bacon* 1863, 59, 79.
372 *Brendecke* 2009.
373 See above p. 49 et seq.
374 BVerfGE 65, 1 .

be left alone'. In academic literature this is described as a basic norm that guarantees individual autonomy.[375]

a) Autonomous decisions about the disclosure and use of personal data

The right to informational self-determination is a response to the threats posed by the vast data processing capabilities of the information society.[376] Eifert calls it the 'core fundamental right in the digital world'.[377] It protects individual's personal data from inspection by the state and specifies the conditions and limitations of government data processing. The collection, processing, use and transmission of personal data constitute separate infringements and all fall within the scope of protection of this fundamental right.[378] The right to informational self-determination guarantees the 'right of the individual to decide on the disclosure and use of his or her personal data'.[379]

b) Protected data

The right to informational self-determination covers all data that contain information about the personal or factual circumstances of an identified or identifiable person.[380] Data do not have to be particularly sensitive,[381] because even personal data that contains only a small amount of information, can, for example through 'processing and linking possibilities, have substantial effects on the privacy and freedom of conduct of the data subject'.[382] According to the BVerfG census ruling, no data are legally 'ir-

---

375 *Schöndorf-Haubold* 2018, 4; similar to *Hofmann*, in: Schmidt-Bleibtreu/Hofmann/Henneke, GG, Art. 2 mn. 14; *Britz* 2007, 37 et seq., 65 et seq. *Schöndorf-Haubold* 2018, 4.

376 BVerfGE 65, 1 (LS 1) ('Under the conditions of modern data processing, the protection of individuals against unlimited collection, storage, use and disclosure of their personal data is covered by the fundamental rights of Art. 2(1) in conjunction with Art. 1 (1) oft he German Constitution'); *Schöndorf-Haubold* 2018, 1.

377 *Eifert* JURA 2015, 1181, 1181.

378 SeeBVerfGE 65, 1 (LS 1); BVerfGE 120, 274 (mn. 198).

379 See BVerfGE 65, 1 (419 LS 1, 421); BVerfGE 120, 274 (mn. 198).

380 BVerfGE 65, 1 (422).

381 BVerfGE 65, 1 (422).

382 BVerfGE 120, 274 (mn. 198).

relevant'.[383] The analysis of publicly accessible data from online social networks also falls within this scope, especially when it is connected to other data sources in order to obtain additional informative value.[384]

c) Prohibition of personality profiling

The fundamental right particularly protects against the new capabilities of personality profiling, which result from the possibility of accessing and combining constantly growing state and private data stocks.[385] The term 'personality profile' refers to the systematic, computer-aided collection of information about a large number of areas of a person's life.[386] According to the BVerfG, the term also covers the creation of 'partial profiles' (travel profile, profiles of political behaviour, etc.)[387] of only parts of a person's life.[388] In such cases, privacy (in the form of informational self-determination) is 'above all threatened because in modern decision-making processes it is no longer necessary to rely on manually compiled files, but rather today, with the help of automatic data processing, individual data [...] can technically be stored indefinitely and retrieved at any time in a matter of seconds without regard to physical distances'.[389]

d) Public interest dimension and chilling effects

The right to informational self-determination is also intended to protect people from the intimidating 'chilling effects'[390] of extensive data processing.[391] If large numbers of people are included in the scope of a data

---

383 See BVerfGE 65, 1 (422); lately BVerfGE 150, 244 = NJW 2019, 827 (829).
384 BVerfGE 142, 234 (252) with reference to BVerfGE 120, 274 (836, mn. 309); BVerfGE 100, 313 (Art. 2 mn. 88); last confirmed in BVerfGE 150, 244 = NJW 2019, 827 (829),
385 BVerfGE 65, 1 (421) 'complete personality profile'; cf. also *Eifert* JURA 2015, 1181, 1182; cf. on the criticism of an exaggerated concern of the court about profile formation *Trute* Die Verwaltung 2009, 85, 100 et seq.; *Zöller* 2002, 43.
386 *Denninger* KJ 1985, 227.
387 See examples at *Denninger* KJ 1985, 227.
388 BVerfGE 65, 1 (424).
389 BVerfGE 65, 1 (421).
390 BVerfGE 65, 1 (422)-
391 Cf. in detail on the chilling effect, *Knierim* Zeitschrift für Datenschutz 2011, 7, 17 et seq.

processing measure, fear may prevent citizens from exercising their fundamental rights freely. This may particularly occur when the large scope of investigative measures contributes to 'risks of abuse and a sense of being monitored'.[392] Chilling effects have been investigated, for example, in the light of Edward Snowden's revelations about surveillance measures by the US Foreign Intelligence Agency (NSA) in 2013. A decline in visits to Wikipedia pages on privacy and surveillance topics was measured following the revelations,[393] as well as a reduction in searches on Google for personally sensitive subjects.[394] Chilling effects are not evenly distributed among the population, but it is assumed that marginalized groups are increasingly affected by them.[395] The intimidation-free ability of citizens to exercise their fundamental rights is, however, indispensable in a free and democratic society. The BVerfG has thus stressed that privacy and the right to informational self-determination do not just protect mere individualistic interests, but also public interests.[396]

2. Limits and proportionality

Under which circumstances can privacy in the form of the right to informational self-determination be restricted? The right to informational self-determination has limits: 'The individual does not have a right in the sense of an absolute, unrestrictable monopoly of their data'.[397] Restrictions may result from overriding public interest as well as from conflicting fundamental rights of third parties. Data connected to a person's inviolable human dignity is, however, exempt from justifiable infringements. The BVerfG stated that 'even serious public interest cannot justify interventions in this core area; a weighing of interest according to the principle of

---

392 BVerfGE 115, 320 (535) with reference to BVerfGE 107, 299 .

393 *Penney* Berkeley Tech. LJ 2016, 117.

394 *Marthews/Tucker* SSRN 2017; the studies measure less the reactions to the phenomenon of state surveillance per se than the effects of such surveillance activities that become known and scandalized. See also the further empirical study on chilling effects at *Kaminski/Witnov* U. Rich. L. Rev. 2014, 465.

395 See *Brennan-Marquez* U. Kan. L. Rev. 2018, 485 495.

396 BVerfGE 100, 313 (63).

397 BVerfGE 65, 1 (422); there is also no right to be represented *only* as oneself wishes; *Murswiek/Rixen*, in: Sachs, GG, Art. 2 mn. 72 fn. 126.

proportionality does not take place in this respect'.[398] The inviolable human dignity rooted in Article 1 (1) of the German Constitution includes, for example, non-public communication with intimate partners conducted with the legitimate assumption that it is not being monitored; this includes conversations at home.[399] Further, Article 1 (1) may also come into play when the totality of a person's life are affected (German: 'Totalerfassung').[400] Article 1 (1) prohibits 'reconstruct[ing] practically all the activities of citizens'.[401] However, it can be difficult to determine when the threshold of 'Totalerfassung' has been crossed, and no German courts have yet determined that the government has done so.[402] The statement of the BVerfG therefore rather guides the proportionality test in individual cases than representing a categorical prohibition of a clearly defined, delimitable phenomenon.[403]

Any restriction to the right to informational self-determination must be based on a statutory authorization and comply with the principles of proportionality.[404] The BVerfG has further elaborated on these requirements *inter alia* in its judgements on automated licence plate recognition (2008 and 2018),[405] the Federal Criminal Police Act (2016),[406] dragnet investigations (2006)[407] and data retention (2010).[408] Person-based predictive policing shows extensive parallels to dragnet investigations, since both procedures attempt to identify the 'most dangerous' people from a group of individuals who are not suspected of having committed a crime. If, as in case of flight data pattern recognition, the input data (i.e. the flight data) are stored over a long period of time, this also represents a form of data

398 Cf. BVerfG GesR 2018, 459 (260, mn. 27) with reference to BVerfGE 6, 32 (41); 34, 238 (245); 54, 143 (146); BVerfGE 141, 220 (276 mn. 120) with reference to BVerfGE 109, 279 (313).

399 BVerfGE 141, 220 (1786, mn. 121).

400 BVerfGE 125, 260 (322; 324) – data retention ('The fact that the citizens' perception of freedom may not be totally recorded and registered is part of the constitutional identity of the Federal Republic of Germany'); see also BVerfGE 112, 304 (319) – GPS.

401 BVerfGE 125, 260 (mn. 218).

402 See *Schöndorf-Haubold* 2018, 21.

403 See *Schöndorf-Haubold* 2018, 21.

404 See BVerfGE 65, 1 (44, 46).

405 BVerfGE 150, 244 = NJW 2019, 827 .

406 *Rusteberg* KritV 2017, 24 24 ff; *Darnstädt* DVBL 2017, 88 88 ff; *Kießling* Verwaltungsarchiv 2017, 282, 282 et seq.

407 BVerfGE 115, 320.

408 BVerfGE 125, 260.

retention (e.g. flight data are kept in a data pool for at least five years for subsequent access by law enforcement authorities).

The BVerfG has stated that high-intensity infringements of people's private lives are only permitted in these contexts to protect 'sufficiently important legal interests',[409] and that a threat to these legal interests must be 'concretely foreseeable'[410] (investigations are not permitted unless they have specific objectives, *Germ.* 'ins Blaue hinein').[411] Moreover, special provisions must be made to protect the core area of people's private lives and organizational and procedural requirements such as transparency, individual legal protections, external controls,[412] notification, rectification, inspection, obligations to delete data and documentation[413] must be guaranteed by statutory law.[414] The intensity of infringements is determined by their degree of secrecy[415] and scope[416] as well as the sensitivity of the collected data.[417]

3. Specific limits placed on person-based predictive policing by the right to privacy

The next section elaborates on the specific consequences for person-based predictive policing that follow from the right to privacy.

a) Presence of high-intensity infringements

In order to determine the limits of the right to informational self-determination on person-based predictive policing, it is important to assess the infringement intensity of each planned predictive policing system. Decisive factors are whether the system is suspicion confirming or suspicion

---

409 See lately BVerfGE 150, 244 = NJW 2019, 827 (LS 5, 833).
410 BVerfGE 115, 320 (LS 1 and 2).
411 BVerfGE 115, 320 (536); lately BVerfGE 150, 244 = NJW 2019, 827 (834).
412 See lately BVerfGE 150, 244 = NJW 2019, 827 (835).
413 Lately BVerfGE 150, 244 = NJW 2019, 827 (840)
414 Cf. §§ 73 et seq. BKAG, see BVerfGE 141, 220 (LS 1b); *Eifert* JURA 2015, 1181, 186.
415 Cf. BVerfGE 141, 220 (mn. 113); BVerfGE 115, 320 (534); *Tanneberger* 2014, 246 ff; *Schwabenbauer* 2013, 165 et seq.
416 Cf. BVerfGE 115, 320 (535).
417 Cf. *Eifert* JURA 2015, 1181, 186 et seq.

generating and the type of input data that are used (e.g. data from social networks such as in hessenDATA,[418] or health data as in Beware).[419] The storage period of input data and risk scores are also relevant.

Suspicion-generating predictive policing can generally be said to have a high-intensity impact for four reasons: it involves a high level of secrecy, has a large scope, involves automated data processing and is similar to the process of creating personality profiles, which the BVerfG barred in its census decision.[420] Suspicion-confirming predictive policing may also have a high-intensity impact due to the secrecy and automation involved, and its similarity to the development of personality profiles.

aa) Secrecy and lack of transparency

The secrecy of predictive policing measures is problematic in two regards: on the one hand, people are neither informed that a risk score has been generated nor what that risk score is. On the other hand, the composition of the patterns with which predictive policing compares an individual's behaviour is unclear. The BVerfG has repeatedly stressed that secrecy[421] and a lack of transparency[422] increase the infringement intensity of governmental measures. It has elaborated that informational self-determination is particularly impacted when 'personal data are used and linked by public authorities in a way that the persons concerned cannot oversee or control'.[423] Person-based predictive policing provides the people affected with no possibility to oversee or control their data.

bb) Scope

Suspicion-generating predictive policing has a particularly wide scope for impact, i.e. it infringes on a large number of people's right to privacy. It is characteristic of this kind of predictive policing that a large amount of data on 'harmless' people must be processed in order to filter out

418 See above p. 75 et seq.
419 See above p. 64 et seq.
420 BVerfGE 65, 1 (424).
421 See BVerfGE 115, 320 (534).
422 Cf. BVerfGE 125, 260 (mn. 242) 'The legislator must counteract the threats of data storage with effective transparency rules'.
423 BVerfGE 130, 151 (mn. 122).

the 'dangerous' ones.[424] The BVerfG has explicitly stated: 'Data processing of persons who did nothing to initiate a suspicion through their behaviour are generally of a higher infringement intensity than those related to a specific occasion or behaviour'.[425]

cc) Automation

Finally, the automation of data processing also adds to an increased intensity of infringement.[426] In the context of dragnet investigations, the BVerfG has stated that automated data processing 'has the advantages that automated, computer-aided operations generally bring with them, i.e. it enables the processing of almost unlimited amounts and complexities of data at great speed. The investigative process [...] is thus provided with a previously unknown penetrating power and effectiveness. From the point of view of fundamental rights, the new quality of the police investigation leads to an increased infringement intensity.'[427]

dd) Proximity to personality profiles

The more individual data points that are used in person-based predictive policing, the greater the risk of creating personality profiles. However, it is argued in the literature that the BVerfG is wrong to warn against the creation of personality profiles for dragnet investigations[428] (authors posit that neither dragnet investigations nor person-based predictive policing come close to creating personality profiles).[429] However, when the behavioural patterns of people who have committed crimes (such as their travel movements, methods of payment, criminal history, drug use, social network data, etc.) are identified and compared to similar patterns among new groups of individuals, people are associated with existing personality profiles. There is therefore a real danger in dragnet investigations as well as in person-based predictive policing of systematically sounding out nu-

424 See fn. 40 and accompanying text.
425 BVerfGE 120, 378 (1507).
426 Cf. *Arzt* 2017, 10.
427 Cf. on dragnet investigations BVerfGE 115, 320 (535).
428 *Trute* Die Verwaltung 2009, 85, 100.
429 *Rademacher* AöR 2017, 366, 380.

merous aspects of a person's life. Personality profiles are created when algorithms are used to discover patterns associated with people who have committed a crime which are then assigned to specific individuals. This can impair a person's right to self-expression as significantly as collecting and evaluating individual details about them.[430]

Moreover, a closer look reveals a paradox: person-based predictive policing is accompanied by a 'hunger' for more and more data and for ever more precise profiling in order to further refine predictions. This hunger is logically fuelled by literature that frames person-based predictive policing as constitutional if it would only provide sufficiently precise predictions.[431]

ee) Stigmatization

Finally, it is true for all forms of person-based predictive policing that the infringement intensity – as stated by the BVerfG in its dragnet judgment[432] – increases with the stigmatization of specific population groups. The BVerfG expressly noted that the dragnet investigations carried out after the September 11 attacks involved a heightened intensity of infringement because they were particularly directed against Muslim minorities.[433] The same intensification of infringement can also occur in the context of person-based predictive policing used in counterterrorism, if, for example, people of Arab descent fall into a particular 'pattern'.

Person-based predictive policing systems generally show a high infringement intensity regarding the right to informational self-determination. Furthermore, the greater complexity and opacity of the methods used, mean that person-based predictive policing is even more infringement-intensive than standard dragnet investigations.

b) Consequences of a high infringement intensity

Because of the high infringement intensity described above, person-based predictive policing systems – in line with BVerfG case law on inter alia

---

430 *Fröhlich/Spiecker* Verfassungsblog of 26.12.2018, accessible at https://perma.cc/9GVX-X564, last accessed 1.1.2022.

431 See *Rademacher* AöR 2017, 366, 397.

432 BVerfGE 115, 320 (534) with reference to *Limbach* 2002, 10.

433 BVerfGE 115, 320 (534).

dragnet investigations – must meet the following requirements in order to be constitutional.

aa) Sufficiently serious offences

The aim of the system must not be to prevent all and any kind of offences, but rather only sufficiently serious offences, i.e. offences against the continued existence or security of the state or a person's life, limb or freedom.[434] Moreover, the offences that a predictive policing system is aimed at preventing must be explicitly listed in a statutory authorization.

bb) Concretely foreseeable danger

(1) Requirements of the BVerfG for dragnet investigations

Predictive policing is only permitted to counter concretely foreseeable dangers. The BVerfG has stated: 'The use of dragnet investigations is prohibited prior to the existence of concrete danger. A general threat situation, as it has existed since the September 11 terrorist attacks, [...] is not sufficient to trigger the use of dragnet investigations. Rather, the existence of *additional* facts from which a concrete danger arises of further terrorist attacks is derived are required to justify the use of dragnet investigation technology.'[435]

This means that a specific threat must have existed *before* a dragnet investigation can be used. As such, a specific threat must also have existed *before* the more infringement-intensive person-based predictive policing can be used. BVerfG case law thus calls into question the constitutionality of suspicion-generating predictive policing, when it is applied before specific threats have arisen. It therefore also questions the constitutionality of the suspicion-generating flight data pattern recognition permitted by § 4 FlugDaG.[436]

---

434 BVerfGE 115, 320 (LS 1 and 2); see also BVerfGE 125, 260 (LS 5).

435 BVerfGE 115, 320 (LS 1 and 2).

436 On constitutional concerns, also *Gless* 2016, 165, 169; *Arzt* 2017, 9, 11, 13, 14, 17.

(2) No lowering of the intervention threshold below a concrete danger

The literature argues that a concrete danger would not be needed to justify predictive policing if it were to deliver precise enough predictions.[437] This, it is argued, would significantly reduce the number of people who are wrongly placed into a pattern compared to dragnet investigations. Such reasoning is not convincing, however. First, it is hard to clearly define the threshold at which algorithmic predictions could be considered 'sufficiently precise'. Precision alone does not suffice to constitutionally justify technological surveillance. If it were to do so, we would end up living in a surveillance state, based on the highly problematic mantra of 'more data equals more precision'.

It is unclear why a lower threshold should apply to the more infringement-intensive, opaque and complex person-based predictive policing than to dragnet investigations.

Finally, the argument that person-based predictive policing cannot be used at all if the application threshold is not lowered beyond a specific level of threat is unconvincing. The advantages of any government action may only be enjoyed within its constitutional limits. This also applies to new policing technologies.

This book, therefore, argues that a specific threat is necessary for the application of person-based predictive policing.

This limits the scope for person-based predictive policing. It also carries the risk that the concept of a specific threat could be overstretched in practice in order to permit the use of person-based predictive policing as often as possible. Still, this restriction is necessary in order to protect the right to privacy (informational self-determination), to prevent the total surveillance of the population and to avoid chilling effects.

c) Organizational and procedural safeguards

Finally, the constitutional right to privacy requires a statutory authorization for person-based predictive policing that includes organizational and procedural safeguards. These must cover transparency, individual legal rights, external controls, notification, rectification, testing and deletion ob-

437 *Rademacher* AöR 2017, 366, 394, 396 et seq. ('This already shows that the court is not going in the right direction if it ties measures of risk assessment to the threshold of concrete danger').

ligations as well as documentation[438] (see also Chapter IV on transparency requirements).[439]

4. Summary of privacy

In summary, person-based predictive policing is lawful only if it is used to defend against a sufficiently serious criminal offence, only if there is a concrete danger of such an offence, and only when it is undertaken in compliance with organizational and procedural safeguards. Person-based predictive policing in the form of the Chicago Strategic Subject List[440] would not be constitutional in Germany, nor would California's Beware system.[441] The constitutionality of the flight data pattern recognition set out in § 4 FlugDaG is also questionable. Its restriction to people using air travel does not dispel these concerns, since almost all sections of the population use air travel and therefore almost the entire population will at some point in their lives be subject to predictive policing.[442]

Person-based predictive policing may therefore only be used in the face of a specific threat to identify currently unknown perpetrators. Person-based predictive policing could also be used to allocate resources if, from the police's point of view, certain known individuals are assumed to pose a specific threat (e.g. they are on a watchlist), but resources only suffice to conduct surveillance on a limited number of people.

II. Non-discrimination

Discriminatory effects of predictive algorithms in crime control have been reported repeatedly in the US.[443] The next step of this book will therefore be to examine the compatibility of person-based predictive policing in Ger-

---

438 See BVerfGE 141, 220 (LS 1b); *Eifert* JURA 2015, 1181, 186; concerns about the FlugDaG in this regard, *Ruthig*, in: Schenke/Graulich/Ruthig, Vorbem. FlugDaG mn. 6 with further references.

439 See above p. 120 et seq.

440 See above p. 66 et seq.

441 See above p. 64 et seq.

442 *Arzt* 2017, 11.

443 *Angwin et al.* ProPublica of 23.05.2016, accessible at https://perma.cc/LAE9-A656, last accessed 1.1.2022; *Starr* Stan. L. Rev. 2014, 803; *Ferguson* U. Pa. L. Rev. 2015, 327, 389 f; *Ferguson* 2017, 49 et seq.; see also generally on discrimination

many with the constitutional ban on discrimination. Unequal treatment is not in itself illegitimate. In the field of crime control, legislators and police practitioners have to make differentiating decisions all the time.[444] The question is which differentiations are justified and which are not. Only unjustified differentiations constitute discrimination. Before this question can be answered for person-based predictive policing, the next section begins with an introduction to the possible sources of algorithmic discrimination that were mentioned in Chapter I.

1. Introduction

'Technology is neither good or bad, nor is it neutral.'
Melvin Kranzberg's First Law of Technology[445]

Human decision-makers are not free from prejudices or subjective preferences:[446] quite the contrary. Psychologists have shown with the so-called "Implicit Association Test" that we can suffer from racist prejudices of which we are not even aware.[447] Studies on the criminal justice system have shown that judges tend to be more reluctant to grant early releases before lunch than afterwards.[448] Algorithmic decision-making systems are not subject to such preferences or fluctuations. Unlike a human brain, an algorithm can be programmed to ignore certain sensitive data such as skin colour or religious affiliation as input variables.[449] At first glance, algorithms thus have the potential to be more neutral and less discriminatory than humans in their decision-making.[450] But this appearance of neutrality is deceptive. As *Kranzberg's* First Law of Technology states, there is no

---

by algorithms *Kroll et al.* U. Pa. L. Rev. 2017, 633, 679 ff; *Pasquale* 2015, 38 et seq.

444 Cf. *Nußberger*, in: Sachs, GG, Art. 3 mn. 2 ('insofar all law is differentiation').

445 *Kranzberg* Technology and Culture 1986, 544, 545.

446 Cf. the cognitive distortions in *Kahneman/Tversky* Cognitive Psychology 1972, 430; see for the reception in Germany e.g. *Gigerenzer* Eur. Rev. Soc. Psychol. 1991, 83.

447 Cf. https://implicit.harvard.edu; see also *Martini/Nink* NVwZ - Extra 10/2017, 1, 1; *Krieger* Stan. L. Rev. 1995, 1161 ff; *Jolls/Sunstein* Calif. L. Rev. 2006, 969.

448 *Danziger et al.* PNAS 2011, 6889

449 *Rademacher* AöR 2017, 366, 374 et seq., 384 et seq.

450 See *Wischmeyer* AöR 2018, 1, 26; *Martini/Nink* NVwZ - Extra 10/2017, 1; *Chander* Mich. L. Rev. 2017, 1023.

truly neutral technology,[451] and this also applies to prediction algorithms. The use of algorithms cannot prevent discrimination, but merely replaces unequal treatment by humans with unequal treatment by algorithms.[452] Subjective, human preferences, rather than being eliminated, are hidden behind supposed neutrality and mathematical justifications.[453] However, it is not just scholars who are sceptical of the algorithm industry's promises of neutrality.[454] A survey conducted by the Bertelsmann Stiftung in 2018 showed that only 6 per cent of interviewees agreed with the following statement: 'I think it's better if algorithms judge me instead of people. They make factual decisions that are equal for everyone.'[455]

Discriminations can enter an algorithm in different ways.[456] In order to avoid discrimination, it is not sufficient for a human decision-maker to be given the opportunity to deviate from the algorithmic, discriminatory risk score *after* it has been calculated. Due to "automation bias", humans will often follow the algorithmic score, even if they could theoretically deviate from it.[457] People's decision-making corridors are thus pre-set as discriminatory.[458]

Once the idea of neutral, non-discriminatory algorithms has been refuted, advocates of the use of algorithms often argue that discrimination by an algorithm is still preferable to unequal treatment by humans.[459] They stress that discrimination can be detected and eliminated more easily

451 See above p. 87 et seq.

452 *Eaglin* Emory L.J. 2017, 59, 97 et seq., *Wischmeyer* AöR 2018, 1, 26; *Macnish* Ethics and Information Technology 2012, 151, 151 ff; *Bozdag* Ethics and Information Technology 2013, 209, 209 et seq.; *Barocas/Selbst* Calif. L. Rev. 2016, 671, 671 et seq.; for the police context for example *Lum/Isaac* Significance 2016, 14.

453 See above p. 87 et seq.

454 Cf. *Wischmeyer* AöR 2018, 1, 26; see especially *Barocas/Selbst* Calif. L. Rev. 2016, 671, 673; see also *Hannah-Moffat* Fed. Sent'g Rep. 2014, 244, 244 ff; *Harcourt* Fed. Sent'g Rep. 2014, 237, 240; *Klingele* Notre Dame L. Rev. 2016, 537, 538 ff; *Starr* Fed. Sent'g Rep. 2015, 229, 229 et seq.

455 *Fischer/Petersen* 2018, 25; cf. however *Center for the Governance of Change* 2019, 10 ('25 per cent of Europeans are somewhat or totally in favor of letting an artificial intelligence make important decisions about the running of their country').

456 See above p. 87 set seq. and p. 113 et seq.

457 Cf. the precedence of a decision corridor in the relationship between judge and expert in criminal proceedings such as *Jordan/Gresser* Der Sachverständige 2014, 71, 76; *Barton* 2018, 216.

458 *Wischmeyer* 2020, mn. 43.

459 Cf. also already in the 1960s 'There are no rational reasons to prefer human performance to machine performance' *Luhmann* 1966, 60 mit fn. 24.

in algorithms than among people.[460] But this conclusion is false: firstly, unequal treatment by an algorithm is extremely difficult to detect and prove;[461] and secondly, algorithms threaten to act as a mathematical justification for existing discrimination[462] instead of eliminating it. The Austrian Labour Office provides a good example: they used an algorithm to allocate financial support to help people re-enter the labour force. The algorithm generally allocated less financial support to women, and mothers in particular, than to men.[463] It has been argued that the algorithm does not discriminate because it only reflects statistical realities in society: women are less successful in re-entering the workforce than men. With this argument, existing inequalities in society are consolidated by algorithms instead of eliminated.[464]

Further, once an algorithm contains a discriminatory preference, it can be much more far-reaching and affect more citizens than the subjective preference of a single police officer. An algorithm is often designed for the mass production of predictions: this will cause existing algorithmic discriminations to be applied *en masse*.[465]

Finally, some proponents of algorithms argue that discrimination is primarily a problem of data scarcity. In this view, if algorithms simply have enough personal data, they no longer need to assign group characteristics on a flat-rate basis. Instead, each person could be judged according to their individual circumstances.[466] According to this view the only way out of discrimination is to limit data protection and the right to privacy. The view, which corresponds to the interests of the big data industry, wants to derive from the principle of non-discrimination a support for the view that "more data is better data".[467] This implies that if, as a society, we were not prepared to accept this restriction on privacy, we would have to tolerate the unavoidable side effect of algorithms discriminating.[468] This

---

460 *Capers* N.C. L. Rev. 2017, 1241; cf. also *Rademacher* 2020, 103, mn. 35.
461 For more details see p. 117 et seq.
462 Cf. *Starr* Stan. L. Rev. 2014, 803 ('Scientific Rationalization of Discrimination').
463 Example at *Fröhlich/Spiecker* Verfassungsblog of 26.12.2018, accessible at https://perma.cc/9GVX-X564, last accessed 1.1.2022.
464 See above p. 87 et seq.
465 See *Wischmeyer* AöR 2018, 1, 26.
466 Cf. *Strahilevitz* U. Chi. L. Rev. 2008, 363, 364 ('by increasing the availability of information about individuals, we can reduce decision-makers' reliance on information about groups'); cf. discussion at *Wischmeyer* AöR 2018, 1, 30.
467 See above fn. 141 and accompanying text.
468 Cf. *Cofone* SMU L. Rev. 2019, 139, 11 et seq.

is, however, clearly not the case. Permitting the widespread use of private data would not lead to a 'non-discriminatory' society. Quite the contrary: the more data about a person that are disclosed, the more potential there is for discrimination.

2. Sources of algorithmic discrimination

Discriminatory patterns can enter algorithmic systems in many ways. They can originate in all phases of the algorithm design already described in Chapter I:[469] when compiling the training database, defining the target variables, defining the input variables, and calibrating and monitoring the learning process. The following provides an overview of the detailed discussion set out in Chapter I.

a) Compiling the training database

During data selection for the case database, discrimination can result from a lack of data quality, a lack of representativeness and the fact that social prejudices are inscribed in the data.[470] Contrary to widespread opinion, the use of an algorithm cannot automatically overcome social prejudices. Rather, this requires conscious human intervention. For example, computer science methods can be used to compensate for inequalities in a dataset.[471] However, this is often difficult to do without reducing the predictive accuracy of an algorithm. Research into 'non-discrimination by design' methods is still in its infancy.[472]

b) Defining target variables

Discrimination can also occur when the target variables are being defined.[473] This is the case when, for reasons of convenience, arrests rather

469 See above p. 87 et seq.
470 See *Selbst* Ga. L. Rev. 2017, 109, 137 ff; *Tischbirek* 2020, 103, mn. 5 et seq.
471 Cf. e.g. beyond crime control *Zhao et al.* arXiv 2017.
472 *Zafar et al.* arXiv 2015; *Zafar et al.* arXiv 2016; *Grgic-Hlaca et al.* NIPS Symposium on Machine Learning and the Law 2016.
473 See *Barocas/Selbst* Calif. L. Rev. 2016, 671, 677-80.

than court convictions are used as an indicator of delinquency. For example, if people from certain ethnic minorities are more likely to be arrested than others, and if people from one ethnic minority are arrested more frequently without being sentenced by a court, the choice of arrest as a target variable will distort the prognosis to the detriment of that ethnic minority.

c) Defining predictive input variables

First, a programmer can deliberately use a discriminatory input variable such as ethnic origin as a differentiating feature. However, input variables can also lead to discrimination in other ways. How suitable certain input variables are for predicting behaviour can vary from one social group to another.[474] By choosing a particular input variable, programmers often (unconsciously) lead an algorithm to make more mistakes for a certain social group.[475]

d) Calibration and monitoring of the learning process

Programmers also need to make numerous value judgements during the calibration and monitoring phase of the learning process and these can lead to discrimination. This includes determining which type of error (false-positive or false-negative) the algorithm should prioritize avoiding. It also includes decisions that can increase the likelihood of overfitting (deriving a generally valid if-this-then-that relationship from a random, spurious correlation). Studies have shown that datasets for minority groups often contain an increased amount of such spurious correlations. This leads to the danger that an algorithm will overfit members of a minority to a greater extent and thus make less precise predictions for them.[476]

All these value judgements described can be consciously used by programmers to discriminate against certain social groups and to conceal their own discriminatory intentions behind the supposed objectivity of the figures ('masked discrimination').[477] However, programmers are more likely to *unconsciously* inscribe discriminations into an algorithm. Since an

---

474 *Barocas/Selbst* Calif. L. Rev. 2016, 671, 688-90.
475 *Barocas/Selbst* Calif. L. Rev. 2016, 671, 688-90.
476 *Lehr/Ohm* UCDL Rev. 2017, 653, 704.
477 See *Tischbirek* 2020, 103, mn. 4.

inscription of discrimination in the algorithm design process can never be avoided 100 per cent *ex ante*,[478] it is even more important to ensure that algorithm manufacturers actively search for discrimination in their systems and have them reviewed by third parties.[479]

3. Constitutional law view on algorithmic discrimination

Article 3 (3) of the German Constitution places an *absolute ban* on differentiation by 'gender, descent, race, language, nationality, origin, religious or political beliefs and disability'.[480] Article 3 (1) provides for a *general principle* of equality, which makes it illegal for people 'to treat basically equal [...] something that is unequal or to treat basically unequal [...] something that is equal without sufficient justification'.[481] What is required by the constitution is not blind and obstinate *identical* treatment,[482] but rather the application of 'just' differentiation standards that respect the commonalities as well as the uniqueness of all people.[483]

The following provides an overview of the peculiarities of the application of non-discriminatory principles to predictive policing.

In accordance with Article 3 (3) of the German Constitution, *Direct* discrimination may occur in predictive policing if a programmer explicitly chooses one of the protected categories set out in Article 3 (3) as an input variable (e.g. religion or ethnic origin). It is more likely, however, that Article 3 (3) is violated *indirectly*.[484] In the case of *indirect* discrimination, a decision is based on a seemingly neutral characteristic such as place of

---

478 *Wischmeyer* AöR 2018, 1, 28.

479 Cf. also the transparency requirement on p. 135 et seq.

480 *Sachs*, in: Handbuch Staatsrecht, § 182 mn. 55 et seq., 68 ff; *Sachs* 2017, 315; *Nußberger*, in: Sachs, GG, Art. 3 mn. 249 et seq. with further references; different, however, is *Boysen*, in: Münch/Kunig, GG, Art. 3 mn. 132, 165 (justification by conflicting constitutional law possible); see also (BVerfGE 89, 276 (288 et seq.)).

481 BVerfGE 1, 14 (52) (Südweststaat)

482 *Nußberger*, in: Sachs, GG, Art. 3 mn. 3.

483 *Nußberger*, in: Sachs, GG, Art. 3 mn. 3.

484 Cf. *Tischbirek* 2020, 103, 12; see also *Barocas/Selbst* Calif. L. Rev. 2016, 671, 673; *Hardt* Moody Rd 2016 ('Historically, the naive approach to fairness has been to assert that the algorithm simply doesn't look at protected attributes such as race, color, religion, gender, disability, or family status. [But] there are almost always ways of predicting unknown protected attributes from other seemingly innocuous features.'); see also *Hannah-Moffat* Fed. Sent'g Rep. 2014, 244, 244 ff;

residence. However, place of residence may correlate statistically with a protected characteristic such as ethnic origin, if a certain part of the city is inhabited predominantly by people with a certain ethnic origin. If an algorithm automatically attributes a higher risk to people living in this city district, it will discriminate indirectly because of ethnic origin. Indirect discrimination follows from the fact that people of a specific ethnic origin are *disproportionately* affected by the application of a certain neutral characteristic. In German constitutional law, an exact statistical percentage from which a measure can be definitively said to 'disproportionately' affect, for example, an ethnic minority, has yet to be established.[485] In a case of indirect discrimination against women, however, which concerned lower pay for part-time employment, the BVerfG concluded that the fact that 70 per cent of the affected individuals were women was sufficient to establish a 'disproportionate' effect and therefore to establish the presence of indirect discrimination.[486]

All the sources of algorithmic discrimination described above can lead to discrimination (and therefore a violation of Article 3 (3) of the German Constitution). This could occur if they consolidate existing unjustified unequal treatment in society or introduce new forms of unequal treatment (e.g. different error rates) such as during the calibration phase of the algorithm.

In addition, discrimination pursuant to Article 3 (1) of the German Constitution can also be expected if an algorithm differentiates in an unjustified manner based on a feature that is not covered by Article 3 (3). This may occur, for example, through incomprehensible or erroneous calculations (e.g. overfitting).[487]

Predictive policing thus displays two factual and legal peculiarities when it comes to the constitutional ban on discrimination. Firstly, the mere factual identification of unequal treatment is made difficult because algorithmic systems lack transparency; secondly, algorithmically generated statistical justifications pose new challenges to constitutional law doctrine.

Harcourt Fed. Sent'g Rep. 2014, 237, 240; *Klingele* Notre Dame L. Rev. 2016, 537, 538 ff; *Starr* Fed. Sent'g Rep. 2015, 229, 229 et seq.

485 *Tischbirek/Wihl* JZ 2013, 219, 223.

486 See BVerfGE 121, 241 (254 et seq.); *Sachs* 2017, 317.

487 See above fn. 362 and accompanying text.

a) Detection of unequal treatment

The first problem for those affected[488] by a person-based predictive policing system is to recognise unequal treatment as such. In order to prove direct discrimination, it is necessary to gain insight into the input data. In order to prove indirect discrimination, i.e. a disproportionate impact on certain groups of people, it is necessary either to examine the algorithm itself or to carry out a systematic analysis of the algorithm's output (all the risk scores produced). However, the asymmetry of knowledge between government and citizens about the exact functioning of a person-based predictive policing system makes it almost impossible for individuals to obtain this necessary information. Even if a person were to have access to the relevant data of an algorithm, for example by introducing transparency standards for predictive policing[489], this data would still have to be analysed. For the average citizen this is practically impossible without the help of pricey experts.[490] Tischbirek warns that this cost-intensiveness of data analyses to prove discrimination could have a deterrence effect on citizen's exercise of their constitutional rights.[491]

b) Statistical justifications

A second novelty that person-based predictive policing brings to the prohibition of discrimination is those of statistical justifications. As stated above, unequal treatment[492] only constitutes discrimination, if it is unjustified. Statistical, algorithmic calculations may, in this context, provide the state with an easy, almost automatic, first attempt to justify unequal treatment, which might be hard to refute for the average citizen. The State might argue in this context that the unequal treatment is justified, because – as indicated by the objective algorithm's calculations – it merely represents

488 What is meant here are first and foremost the citizens. However, a person-based predictive policing system can also be intransparent for the users, i.e. the police themselves. This may make it difficult for the police themselves to identify discriminatory patterns, especially if an algorithm was developed by a private manufacturing company.
489 See also p. 158.
490 *Tischbirek* 2020, 103, mn. 41.
491 *Tischbirek* 2020, 103, mn. 41.
492 Beyond the specially protected categories of Art. 3 (3) German Constitution, race, gender etc.

a statistical reality ('rational racism'). Fruther, the State may argue that an algorithmic discrimination is justified if it is statistically less discriminatory than human decisions ('lesser evil'). The following will illustrate the challenges of both strings of argument.

aa) Argument of 'rational racism'

The state may argue that it is justified that a person-based predictive policing system generally assigns a higher risk score to, for example, a certain minority, because such a risk score corresponds to the crime reality identified by the algorithm in the case database. If the case database shows that people from a certain minority are more likely to commit certain crimes, it could be argued that this is not discrimination, but a reflection of reality.[493] Moreover, if the aspect of belonging to a certain minority were not taken into account, an algorithm would lose its predictive power.[494] This argument reflects the view expressed in the *obiter dictum* of the Higher Regional Court of North Rhine-Westphalia in Germany.[495] It states that a distinction based on 'race' may be constitutional if it relies on scientifically sound crime statistics.

However, this argument, also known as 'rational racism', must be rejected. Of course, all policing is based on the principle of effectiveness, but police work is at the same time value-based and derives its values from the Constitution.[496] The conflict between individual rights and effectiveness constitutes one of the fundamental conflicts in policing. A balance between individual rights and effectiveness must be constantly negotiated. However, in other areas of policing, efficiency arguments take a back seat compared to constitutional values.[497] This is the case for the ban on constant, total surveillance of the entire population ('Totalerfassung') and on the use of private diary entries in police investigations, regardless of how effective these measures could be in preventing and fighting crime.

493 Cf. *Tischbirek* 2020, 103, 10 with further references calls this pattern of argumentation 'Normative Unresponsiveness'.

494 See *Tischbirek* 2020, 103, 10.

495 OVG NRW, NVwZ 2018, 1497 (1500, mn. 43 et seq.).

496 So *Tischbirek* DPolBl 3/2019, 17, 6.

497 E.g. no reading of diaries, no eavesdropping on clergy and lawyers, no torture in interrogation practice, examples at *Tischbirek* DPolBl 3/2019, 17, 6.

Certain constitutional values cannot be overwritten by utilitarian considerations.[498]

Further, it must be noted that statistics are not linked to individual actions, but abstract general likelihoods.[499] If, however, someone were to be ascribed a higher probability of crime because of, for example, their ethnic origin, this leads to the very stigmatization that Article 3 of the German Constitution is intended to prevent.[500]

In short: the principle of non-discrimination is so fundamental within constitutional tectonics that it cannot be overridden by efficiency considerations.[501]

bb) Argument of 'lesser evil'

In the discussion on algorithms, it has also been argued that discrimination should, by way of exception, be justified if an algorithm discriminates a little less, i.e. in fewer cases, than human decisions have done so in the past.[502] This argument of the 'lesser evil' must, however, be rejected. First, reliable evidence that humans discriminate more than algorithms is difficult to present. Second, one act of unconstitutional conduct cannot be justified by reference to another act of unconstitutional conduct. Discriminatory behaviour on the part of police officers is unconstitutional. This does not mean, however, that a slightly less discriminatory algorithm is constitutional. The question of constitutionality must be answered in isolation for each situation – human and algorithm. Third, by deliberately and knowingly inscribing discrimination into an algorithm, it will become part of the state apparatus and 'officially' endorsed. Discrimination as part of official government policy can by no means be considered the 'lesser' evil. The argument of the lesser evil therefore cannot cancel out the ban on discrimination in Article 3 of the German Constitution. Any other position would send the wrong signal regarding the innovations taking place in the realm of algorithmic non-discrimination. There would no lon-

---

498 Cf. *Baer* ZRP 2002, 290, 292 et seq.

499 *Tischbirek* DPolBl 3/2019, 17 et seq.

500 *Tischbirek* DPolBl 3/2019, 17 et seq.

501 Cf. *Baer* ZRP 2002, 290, 292 et seq.

502 Cf. *Hacker* Common Market L. Rev. 2018, 1143, 1164 ('If this is the case [algorithmic decision making reduces bias vis-à-vis other types of (non-algorithmic) decision making], the use of the discriminating classifier should be considered appropriate as it maximizes the position of the marginalized group.').

ger be any incentive to develop computer science methods that eliminate prejudices in databases as much as possible.

4. Conclusion on non-discrimination

A refutation of algorithmic justification is possible, but usually only at great costs and effort. Therefore, a de facto reversal of the burden of proof could occur within the framework of algorithmic prediction. In principle, in anti-discrimination law, the burden of proof to refute discrimination lies with the state[503] as soon as unequal treatment is demonstrated. In the case of algorithmic discrimination, however, it seems to be *the citizens* who carry a twofold burden of proof: firstly, to prove the presence of unequal treatment and, second to refute automatic, algorithmic justifications.[504]

Such erosion of the ban on discrimination by non-transparent algorithms must be counteracted in two steps: firstly, the judiciary must be made more aware of the inner workings of algorithms and lawyers need to foster a basic understanding of statistical and computer science knowledge.[505] Secondly, reviewing algorithms for discrimination must not be left up to costly and time-intensive court proceedings initiated by private individuals. Instead, it must be carried out systematically[506] and preventively by an independent government body. If these steps are omitted, algorithms will – through a facade of mathematical certainty and neutrality[507] – perpetuate and consolidate existing prejudices.

III. Transparency

'Scientific truth does not have to be eternal; it does not even have to be understandable anymore, or be accessible to human reason as such.' Hannah Arendt wrote these words as early as in 1958 in the context of the traditional natural sciences.[508] Given the increasing use of algorithmic systems that are inherently opaque to humans – commonly referred to

---

503 See *Tischbirek* 2020, 103, mn. 20.
504 *Fröhlich/Spiecker* Verfassungsblog of 26.12.2018, accessible at https://perma.cc/9GVX-X564, last accessed 1.1.2022.
505 Cf. *Tischbirek* 2020, 103, mn. 44 et seq. ('paradigm of knowledge creation').
506 See *Tischbirek* 2020, 103, mn. 45.
507 *Creemers/Guagnin* KrimJ 2014, 134, 136.
508 *Arendt* 1994 [1958], 283 (translation by author).

as 'black box algorithms' – Hannah Arendt's statement also applies to scientific truths in crime control today. How such a truth, which is no longer accessible to human reason, is to be legally evaluated is examined in the following. On a factual level, three different layers of non-transparency in algorithms are presented (2). This is followed by a discussion of mechanisms that could be used to foster transparency (3) and the three arguments most frequently put forward against the need for transparency are refuted (4). Finally, the foundations of transparency in constitutional law are explored (5). Prior to this, the term 'black box', often used without reflection as an antonym for transparency, is critically challenged (1).

1. Janus-headedness of the black box terminology

'Language is never innocent: words possess a secondary memory, which in the midst of new meanings mysteriously persists.'
Roland Barthes[509]

The societal as well as the scholarly discussion about new technologies is often characterized by the use of metaphors and analogies. When it comes to the legal classification of new technologies, Crootof even speaks of a 'battle of analogies'.[510] Metaphors and analogies offer islands of familiarity, when legally navigating through the floods of complex technological evolution. Metaphors often begin where the intuitive understanding of new technologies ends.[511] The less familiar we feel with a technology, the greater our need for visual language as a set of epistemic crutches. The words that we choose to describe our world, however, have a direct influence on how we perceive the world.[512] Wittgenstein even argues that they represent the boundaries of our world.[513] Metaphors and analogies are never neutral or 'innocent', as Barthes puts it, but come with 'baggage',[514] i.e. metaphors in the digital realm are loaded with the assumptions of

509 *Roland* 1968, 16.
510 *Thomson-DeVeaux* FiveThirtyEight of 29.5.2018, accessible at https://perma.cc/YG65-JAXA, last accessed 1.1.2022.
511 So-called cognitive metaphor, cf. *Drewer* 2003.
512 *Lakoff/Johnson* 2003; *Jäkel* 2003.
513 *Wittgenstein* 1963, Satz 5.6.
514 *Lakoff/Wehling* 2016, 1 et seq. speak of the so-called 'Issue Defining Frame'.

the analogue world from which the imagery is borrowed.[515] This can be illustrated by one of the most widespread metaphors on the subject of algorithms, the black box.[516] Consider the following question:

> What do you see before your inner eye,
> when you hear the term 'black box'?

Some people may think of a monolithic, robust, opaque, dark and square figure. What few people will see is *humans*. This demonstrates both the strengths and the weaknesses of the black box narrative and thus its Janus-headedness.

In the discussion about algorithms, the black box narrative was originally intended as a 'wake-up call'[517] to direct our attention – through memorable visual language – towards certain risks of algorithmic automation; namely towards the risks of a loss of (human) control. The black box terminology successfully fulfils this task. But it also threatens to obscure our view of the people *behind* algorithmic systems and their value judgements. The terminology conceals an opportunity to control algorithms and falsely suggests that algorithms are independent of human prejudices. By drawing attention to one problem area of the use of algorithms (non-transparency), the black box narrative threatens to distract from others (controllability, value judgements, the lack of neutrality). The term 'black box' hides the fact that algorithms are complex socio-technical systems[518] that are based on a multitude of different human decisions.[519] Further, by presenting algorithmic technology as a monolithic, unchangeable and incomprehensible black box, connotations such as 'magical' and 'oracular'

515 See for example how metaphors differently relate to the data we unconsciously leave behind on the Internet: data as the 'new oil' (*Mayer-Schönberger/Cukier* 2013, 20), 'data waste' (*Harford* Significance 2014, 14, 15) or 'data extortion' (*Singer/Maheshwari* The New York Times of 25.4.2017, accessible at https://perma.cc/9VF8-J7F7, last accessed 1.1.2022). A metaphor's starting point has great significance for the outcome of a discussion, as Behavioral Economics Research under the heading of 'Anchoring' has shown, see *Kahneman* 2011, 119 et seq.

516 See *Tischbirek* 2020, 103, mn. 27; *Wischmeyer* AöR 2018, 1, 8; *Pasquale* 2015; *Citron/Pasquale* Wash. L. Rev. 2014, 1, 6; *Price* BUJ Sci. & Tech. L. 2015, 347, 21; *Rich* U. Pa. L. Rev. 2016, 871, 886; *Roth* Yale L.J. 2017, 1972, 1977.

517 In this sense, *Pasquale* 2015.

518 Cf. *Simon*, in: Floridi 2015, 145 et seq., 146; for the corresponding work of the Science & Technology Studies see *Simon* 2010, 61 et seq. with further references.

519 See *Lehr/Ohm* UCDL Rev. 2017, 653, 668 ('Out of the ether apparently springs a fully formed "algorithm"').

often arise.[520] Instead of provoking criticism, such terms often lead to awe and ultimately surrender to the opacity of the black box. Our options for dealing with algorithms are reduced to 'use vs. do not use'. Opportunities that would allow for nuances in the human design process of the black box go unnoticed. The inner processes of the black box as a system are sealed off from humans and attributed an inevitability that strongly resembles the inevitability of the forces of nature; forces that can be 'tamed' but never systematically controlled.[521] The black box narrative also ascribes such problematic inevitability to negative side effects such as the discriminatory effects of an algorithm. This view diverts attention away from the very *human-made* sources of algorithmic discriminatory behaviour listed above.[522] The black box narrative in its most widespread form – namely as an unreflected catchphrase – paradoxically achieves the opposite of what it is intended to do; namely, to protect us from a loss of control over algorithms.

As will be explained in detail below,[523] however, it is possible to disclose the numerous human value judgements that stand behind a supposed black box algorithm, for example, through logging requirements in the design phase or output testing.[524] The challenge posed by the regulation of algorithms, therefore, is more appropriately described as an 'algorithmic veil' than a black box; 'an algorithmic veil' that is placed over human decisions and values. One advantage of the metaphor of the veil is that it almost inherently invites to be lifted. A black box, on the other hand, does not contain such prompt. Quite the opposite: a black box indicates that an attempt to gain insights is unlikely to succeed. The metaphors we use in the discussion about algorithms, therefore, can directly influence what we think is possible in terms of algorithm regulation. By conjuring up the image of the flowing fabric of an algorithmic veil, which only has to be

---

520 *Elish/boyd* Communication Monographs 2017, 1, 6 et seq.;*Garzcarek/Steuer* arXiv 2019, 6 ('algorithms act very similar to ancient oracles'); science fiction framing and a reference to the book/film *Minority Report*, in which human oracles predict murders with the help of technology, are also frequently found; see *Brühl/Steinke* Süddeutsche Zeitung of 4.3.2019, accessible at https://perma.cc/6J55-VGCX, last accessed 1.1.2022; *Stroud* Verge of 19.2.2014, accessible at http://perma.cc/T678-AA68, last accessed 1.1.2022

521 Similarly, as early as 20 years ago, *Nissenbaum* Science and Engineering Ethics 1996, 25, 34.

522 Cf. p. 113 et seq.

523 Cf. p. 139 et seq.

524 Cf. p. 140 et seq.

lifted, instead of a massive black box, which has to be broken open, the intention is not to minimize the challenges of algorithm regulation. Rather, the veil should be understood as an invitation to society, programmers and scholars: instead of talking about what algorithms 'do' (as if they were independent actors), we should talk about what the human programmers, statisticians,[525] and data scientists *behind* the algorithm do. Only when this perspective is adopted can algorithms be more than just 'tamed', i.e., systematically controlled by regulation. If the term black box is used in this book, it is to be understood only in conjunction with the described reservations.

2. Three layers of non-transparency

a) Terminology

In order to facilitate a differentiated discussion, the various aspects under which an algorithm can be described as 'non-transparent' must first be described. Transparency is demanded in almost every scholarly publication on algorithms. It is hoped that this will help uncover errors in computer code and training data,[526] disclose infringements of the law, for example, with regard to privacy and non-discrimination,[527] and put the value judgements behind an algorithm made by programmers up for democratic debate, thereby preventing chilling effects.[528] However, the exact meaning of 'transparency' is rarely explained;[529] often only isolated aspects of transparency are elaborated upon, while an overall picture of the concept is missing. The scholarly discussion on transparency is thus difficult to keep track of.[530] To clarify the concept and make its numerous facets systema-

525 See *Lehr/Ohm* UCDL Rev. 2017, 653, 660.

526 *Datenethikkommission* 2018, 2; see references in *Wischmeyer* 2020, fn. 1; *Mayer-Schönberger/Cukier* 2013, 176; *Zarsky* U. Ill. L. Rev. 2013, 1503 et seq.; *Pasquale* 2015; *Burrell* Big Data & Society 2016, 1; *Zweig* AlgorithmWatch 2016; *Ananny/Crawford* New Media & Society 2018, 973; *Maas* Press release 2018.

527 E.g. see different audit possibilities at *Sandvig et al.* Data and Discrimination: Converting Critical Concerns into Productive Inquiry - ACM preconference 2014, 8 et seq.

528 For example, to uncover the 'illusion of neutrality' *Wischmeyer* 2020, mn. 51.

529 *Eichenhofer* Forschungsjournal Soziale Bewegungen 2017, 133, 138; see, also *Wischmeyer* 2020, 75, *Wischmeyer* 2020, mn. 51 et seq.

530 *Wischmeyer* 2020, mn. 53.

tically visible the following sections break down transparency into three subgroups.

Algorithmic systems are usually criticized as lacking transparency because certain information about an algorithmic process (e.g. training data, input and target variables, prediction accuracy, error rates, source code, reason for a correlation, etc.) is inaccessible or incomprehensible to certain people. Three cumulative or individual 'layers' of the inaccessibility of information can be distinguished: non-transparency qua intentional secrecy (intentional lack of transparency), non-transparency qua lack of expertise (illiterate lack of transparency) and non-transparency qua inherent system complexity (intrinsic lack of transparency) (Fig. 3).

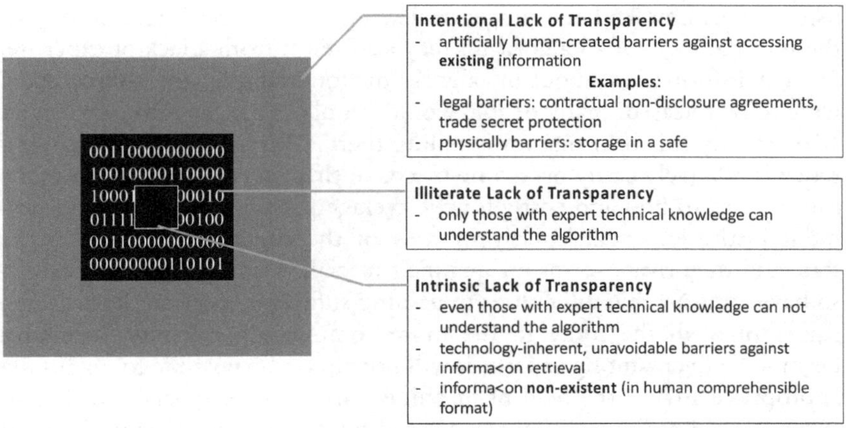

Fig. 3. Three layers of algorithmic non-transparency[531]

aa) Intentional lack of transparency

The outermost layer of non-transparency consists of the inaccessibility of information qua secrecy.[532] This occurs when information about an algorithm exists in a human-understandable format (with the algorithm manufacturer or the state), but this information is simply not disclosed to third parties. In this context, artificial human-made obstacles to transparency are present. This layer can consist of both legal and factual obstacles. Legal obstacles include situations in which a private manufacturing com-

531 Based on *Burrell* Big Data & Society 2016, 1; see also *Wischmeyer* 2020, mn. 53.
532 Cf. *Wischmeyer* 2020, 75, mn. 16 et seq.

pany claims trade secret protection.[533] Factual obstacles include situations in which information on decisions in the algorithm design phase is not recorded or subsequently destroyed. Under this aspect, an algorithm is a 'black box' only for third parties. This layer of non-transparency is often driven by the economic interests of the manufacturers or security interests, for example to prevent spying on a system.[534]

bb) Illiterate lack of transparency

For the majority of the population without computer science training – which includes people affected by algorithmic decisions, the police officers using algorithms and the judges reviewing them – the inaccessibility of the internal logic of an algorithm may also result from a lack of expertise. Even if information about an algorithm, for example, the source code, were to be released, many people would simply not be able to understand what exactly this information is telling them. This aspect of non-transparency is relatively easily overcome by consulting experts. However, experts can be hard to find and costly for the average person and even for government institutions. Particularly in view of the competition between the state and the private sector for qualified specialists, the government can also have considerable difficulties in gaining sufficient specialist knowledge; this applies all the more to the more complex algorithmic procedures become.[535] Even among experts, it will not always be possible to obtain the appropriate advice: the field of machine learning is so specialized that an expert specialized in decision tree algorithms may be unable to understand other types of algorithm, such as neural networks.[536]

Interestingly, this lack of expertise among the general population is often cited as an argument against publishing the source code of an algorithm: the average person would simply not be able to understand it. However, this argument is unconvincing. In a democratic constitutional state, the possibility of examining the legality of any state measure, including algorithms, should rightly be open to the entire population – with

---

533 See details below p. 149 et seq.; cf. on the situation in the USA *Wexler* Stan. L. Rev. 2018, 1343, 1343 et seq.

534 See details below p. 151 et seq.

535 Cf. *Wischmeyer* 2020, 75, mn. 10 with further references.

536 Cf. *Wischmeyer* 2020, 75, mn. 10 with further references.

or without expert advice.[537] Whether the majority of the population will make use of this opportunity is irrelevant.

cc) Intrinsic lack of transparency

The innermost layer of algorithmic inaccessibility is epistemic non-transparency in the form of system-immanent complexity.[538] This lack of transparency can even exist for the programmers of an algorithm.[539] It can occur especially with machine learning algorithms,[540] but also with rule-based algorithms.[541]

(1) Machine learning algorithms

First, system-inherent non-transparency can occur regarding the explainability of the if-this-then-that relationships 'learned' by a machine learning algorithm from the training dataset. For example, a programmer may find that an algorithm has been trained in such a way that it can predict an event with great certainty using a certain number of input variables, but it is not possible to see which of the input variables, or more precisely which combination of variables, is decisive in the occurrence of an event. The output of a system can no longer be assigned with certainty to a specific input.[542] In this situation, not only can no statement be made about the causality of an event (this is never the case with machine learning algorithms),[543] but it is not even possible to understand the exact correlation. Such non-transparency particularly occurs in neural networks, a subgroup of machine learning which is particularly difficult to explain. It can also occur, however, in what at their core are explainable forms of machine learning such as decision trees, if a large number of decision trees are used

---

537 See p. 137 et seq.
538 *Redemacher* calls this layer lacking 'plausibility' *Rademacher* AöR 2017, 366, 388.
539 See *Kroll et al.* U. Pa. L. Rev. 2017, 633, 638; *Rich* U. Pa. L. Rev. 2016, 871, 886 ('machine learning tends to create models that are so complex that they become "black boxes", where even the original programmers of the algorithm have little idea exactly how or why the generated model creates accurate predictions').
540 See on the term above p. 50.
541 See on the term above p. 52.
542 Cf. e.g. *Hildebrandt* Philos. Technol. 2011, 371, 375 et seq.
543 See above p. 85.

(random forest approach). In this case, even programmers may no longer comprehend the exact connections made within the decision trees.[544]

(2) Rule-based algorithms

Finally, inherent system non-transparency can also occur with rule-based algorithms if software consists of hundreds of lines of code, so that the relationships between individual variables are hidden in a mass of code.[545] Even after investing ample amounts of time and resources, the exact internal processes of a rule-based algorithm may remain hidden from experts.

(3) Examples

In the case of the first two non-transparency layers, only certain groups of people are denied access to an algorithm's information. While the readers of this book may not have any insight into the source code of, say the Chicago Strategic Subject List,[546] *someone* (such as the algorithm's programmers) has de facto access to the algorithm's information and the necessary expertise to read it. However, with regard to the innermost non-transparency layer, there may not be *anyone* in the world who understands the exact connections within the Chicago algorithm. There may not be *anyone* who can explain exactly why person A received a high-risk score and person B a low-risk score.[547] Having access to the source code of an algorithm does not automatically mean – even for experts – being able to understand and explain the connections within an algorithm.

---

544 *Burrell* Big Data & Society 2016, 1, 1 (Algorithms 'are opaque in the sense that if one is a recipient of the output of the algorithm (the classification decision), rarely does one have any concrete sense of how or why a particular classification has been arrived at from inputs').

545 Cf. *Van Otterlo*, in: Hildebrandt/de Vries 2013, 41, 57 ('hundreds of rules are very hard to inspect visually, especially when their predictions are combined probabilistically in complex ways'); see also *Wischmeyer* 2020, mn. 4.

546 See Strategic Subject for details above p. 66 et seq.

547 *Matthias* Ethics and Information Technology 2004, 175, 179 ('the human trainer himself is unable to provide an algorithmic representation'), *Kroll et al.* U. Pa. L. Rev. 2017, 633, 638 ('even experts often struggle to understand what software code will do, as inspecting source code is a very limited way of predicting how a computer program will behave').

There are many examples of how system-inherent complexity can cause even experts to struggle to find the exact cause of algorithmic behaviour. This can be seen, for example, in cases where software malfunctions occurred at IBM and Tesla without it being possible to discover which part of the algorithm exactly led to the erroneous result.[548] Another example is a malfunction in a rule-based Toyota automotive software that led to the sudden acceleration of a car and the death of a driver in 2007. Even NASA investigators were unable to uncover the cause. Instead, it required a multi-headed, external team of experts, which discovered the error only after nearly two years (!) of analysing the innumerable lines of vehicle code.[549]

It is this form of inaccessibility of information in human-readable format that represents the greatest novelty for society and the legal system. It is also this innermost layer of non-transparency that most strongly drives the narratives describing algorithms as 'black boxes' and opaque oracles.[550]

(4) Attempt at a solution: Explainable AI

For some years now, efforts in the computer sciences under the headline of 'XAI' (short for 'Explainable AI') have been directed against this system-inherent lack of transparency.[551] The aim is to design algorithms from the outset as 'white boxes' or 'glass boxes' instead of 'black boxes' (transparency by design) and at the same time to develop algorithmic procedures that make existing black box systems subsequently explainable.[552] Research in this field is still in its infancy, i.e. it is not currently being used across the board. It enables experts, albeit to a limited extent, to gain a better under-

---

548 *Tutt* Admin. L. Rev. 2017, 83, 89 et seq. with further references

549 *Barr* Embedded Gurus 2013.

550 See for the criticism of this view as black box above p. 121 et seq.

551 *DARPA* 2016; *Doshi-Velez et al.* arXiv 2017; *Datta et al.* 2016 IEEE symposium on security and privacy (SP) 2016, 598; *Fong/Vedaldi* Proceedings of the IEEE International Conference on Computer Vision 2017, 3429; see also *Russell et al.* AI Magazine 2015, 105; *Montavon et al.* Digital Signal Processing 2018, 1; *Palacio et al.* Proceedings of the IEEE Conference on Computer Vision and Pattern Recognition 2018, 3108.

552 Zu Deep Dream *Levy* Wired of 11.12.2015, accessible at https://perma.cc/HTY5-Y299, last accessed 1.1.2022;*Carter et al.* Distill 2019 ('With activation atlases humans can discover unanticipated issues in neural networks — for example, places where the network is relying on spurious correlations to classify images'); *Olah et al.* Distill 2018; zu Feature Visualization in Neural Networks *Olah et al.* Distill 2017; see also *Doshi-Velez/Kim* arXiv 2017.

standing of how complex algorithms work. At the same time, however, in view of its own complexity, it does not contribute to comprehensibility for laypersons. Nor does explainable AI enable a clear assignment of input A to output B. It should also be noted that the algorithm-supported methods of making an algorithm explainable often exhibit internal complexity to such a degree themselves that, to put it pointedly, one 'black box' is explained with the help of another 'black box'.[553]

b) Conclusion on transparency layers

The three layers of intransparency must be clearly distinguished in the discussion about algorithms, since they must be each tackled with a different mechanism (see following section).

Often the fact of system-immanent intransparency is used as a pretext to argue for the general futility of disclosing any information about an algorithm. What is hidden behind such argument is, however, in many cases the secrecy interests of the first intransparency layer. In many cases when this argument is made, if we look closely, there is actually a vast amount of information about an algorithm (e.g. about its design phase) that could be disclosed, if the manufacturer and the state would only be willing.

Even for algorithms with system-immanent intransparency, there is usually a lot of information from the design phase or information that can be obtained through so-called output testing. This information can at least help to better understand an algorithm and to uncover the value judgements inscribed in it. The fact that system inherent intransparency exists should not make us give up bringing light to the areas of algorithms outside of this innermost intransparency layer.

The following will give a systematic overview of various conceivable transparency mechanisms aimed at each of the three intransparency layers.

553 Cf. *Pedreschi et al.* arXiv 2018.

3. Transparency fostering mechanisms

Various ways of tackling non-transparency have been proposed in the literature and in politics. They range from algorithmic 'quality labels'[554] and an individual's right to explanation[555] to the use of open-source software.[556] A systematization of these various proposals can be undertaken along the three dimensions of transparency: the moment of transparency, the group of persons entitled to access transparency and the scope of transparency (Fig. 4).

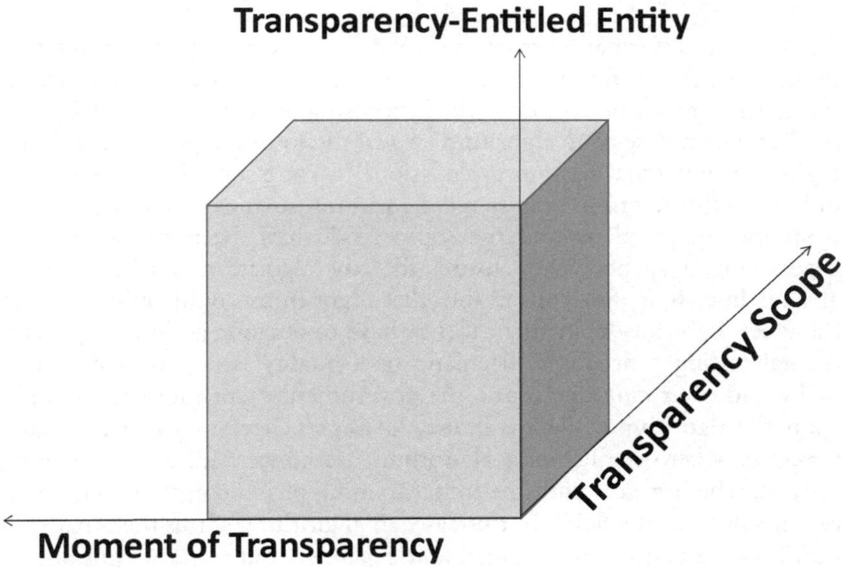

Fig. 4. Three dimensions of transparency

---

554 In Germany discussed under the term 'Algorithmen TÜV'. TÜV is short for 'Technischer Überwachungsverein'. In Germany it stands for the seal of approval awarded by a private technical inspection company which performs security controls required by state laws or regulations; see *Dräger* Handelsblatt of 21.8.2017, accessible at https://perma.cc/6M6X-GXTT, last accessed 1.1.2022; *Martini* DÖV 2017, 443 453; *Beuth* Zeit Online of 3.7.2017, accessible at https://perma.cc/Y64R-77TK, last accessed 1.1.2022; see for USA *Tutt* Admin. L. Rev. 2017, 83

555 See *Goodman/Flaxman* AI Magazine 2017, 50.

556 See *Hildebrandt* UTLJ 2018, 12, 29; *Hildebrandt* Mod. L. Rev. 2016, 1, 30.

a) First dimension of transparency: moment of transparency

moment of transparency	*ex ante* - registration regime - licensing regime
	ex post - auditing regime - individual right to explanation

Tbl. 4. Moment of transparency

Disclosure of information from the algorithm may be required at different moments: either before the first use of an algorithm (*ex ante* disclosure regime, e.g. registration requirement,[557] licensing regime or quality labels)[558] or after the first use of an algorithm (*ex post* disclosure regime, e.g. auditing regime or individual right to explanation[559]). For example, the police may only be permitted to use registered algorithms: such as when information from the design phase and the source code have been deposited with a government agency. This ensures that the algorithm can be reviewed at any time. It is also conceivable that algorithms could only be given the green light for deployment if they have undergone additional governmental testing procedures (licencing or a quality label). In addition to or instead of *ex ante* disclosure, the government or private parties could study the algorithm while it is in use. An *ex post* check may be particularly necessary where self-learning algorithms are concerned, as the learning process, which begins with the initial training phase, continues with each case it solves 'in the field'. In this case, an algorithm's if-this-then-that relationships are constantly modified and expanded and warrant constant review. Another argument in favour of *ex post* reviewing as a supplement to *ex ante* reviewing is that certain negative effects, such as indirect discrimination, may only become apparent under real-life conditions. Algorithmic

557 Cf. *Hildebrandt* 2018; e.g. registration with the Open Science Framework an online platform to document design and research processes, see https://osf.io (last accessed 1.1.2022).

558 See *Tutt* Admin. L. Rev. 2017, 83, 83 ff; *Citron/Pasquale* Wash. L. Rev. 2014, 1, 18 ff; *Roth* Geo. L.J. 2017, 1245, 1298 et seq. ('front-end regulatory safeguard'); see also *Scherer* Harv. JL & Tech. 2015, 353 353 et seq.

559 See different audit option at *Sandvig et al.* Data and Discrimination: Converting Critical Concerns into Productive Inquiry - ACM preconference 2014, 8 ff; *Gesellschaft für Informatik* 2018b, 64 ff; *Citron/Pasquale* Wash. L. Rev. 2014, 1, 21-24.

systems in an area sensitive to fundamental rights such as crime control, must be actively monitored during their operation, as this is the only way to determine whether a system achieves its intended objectives without violating the law.

b) Second transparency dimension: transparency-entitled entity

transparency-entitled entity	government control body
	individually affected citizens
	general public

Tbl. 5. Transparency-entitled entity

Three different groups could be eligible to inspect the information disclosed about an algorithm: the people individually affected by the algorithm, governmental control bodies or the general public, including private data experts. All three groups pursue different interests as illustrated below.

aa) Affected citizens

(1) Single individuals

An individual affected by an algorithmic risk score will want to gain insights primarily into specific aspects of the algorithm that concern them. The aim could be to prove the faultiness or illegality of the risk score they have been assigned. People have a legitimate interest in understanding an algorithm's workings, especially when they are directly involved. Any transparency regime for person-based predictive policing needs to take this into account if it is to provide effective legal protection. However, controlling police algorithms *solely* through the enforcement of individual rights leads to gaps. The detection of legally problematic algorithms, for example, regularly requires the use of considerable resources: time, the costly expertise of algorithm and data experts, and possibly even extensive criminological studies to prove statistical distortions in training data. A long time span may lie between the first use of a legally questionable algorithm, the discovery of the problem and its judicial evaluation. Finally, individual success before the courts does not guarantee that a person-based predictive policing system will no longer be used in the same manner with regard to people who are not covered by the court decision. A transparency regime based solely on the enforcement of individual rights also threatens to neglect the societal and systematic (such as discriminatory) effects of algorithms. These effects are difficult to identify from the perspective of one affected person and their risk score. They can often only be discerned from an analysis of the totality of all risk scores. Focusing a transparency regime on individual law enforcement before the courts will inevitably provide only incomplete, random insights into any algorithm. Individualized legal protection can therefore not sufficiently offset the collective risk posed by the use of person-based predictive policing.[560]

(2) Collaborative crowdsourcing

The results of an algorithm can also be systematically reviewed using collaborative crowdsource audits.[561] This approach involves a large group of affected individuals collecting the information that they have received about their risk score and having it systematically analysed by experts. This approach is used by the German NGO Open Knowledge Foundation to analyse Schufa credit scores;[562] it was also used by the NGO ProPublica which demonstrated discrimination in the COMPAS algorithm in the US.[563] However, this approach is very costly and time-consuming, and depends on whether private organizations take up the initiative. In addition, it can only provide a snapshot of an algorithm, and does not provide a realistic possibility of systematically monitoring the development of an algorithm over time. This is particularly true of some types of machine learning algorithms that use learning processes that are not limited to one-off training phases, but that continue to learn from each case presented during their use.[564] In addition, it can be difficult to find people who are willing and able to share their predictive policing score by crowdsourcing – partly because of the sensitivity of the information and partly because not everyone for whom a score has been created may know about it. This

560 See also *Fröhlich/Spiecker* Verfassungsblog of 26.12.2018, accessible at https://perma.cc/9GVX-X564, last accessed 1.1.2022.

561 *Sandvig et al.* Data and Discrimination: Converting Critical Concerns into Productive Inquiry - ACM preconference 2014, 14 et seq.

562 See https://perma.cc/HC9H-PP4M, last accessed 1.1.2022.

563 *Angwin et al.* ProPublica of 23.05.2016, accessible at https://perma.cc/LAE9-A656, last accessed 1.1.2022.

564 Cf. *Ananny/Crawford* New Media & Society 2018, 973, 982.

suggests that an individual right of explanation can be an important, but that it is not the only building block within an effective transparency regime.

bb) Government control body

Voluntary self-regulation by algorithm developers is also conceivable. In March 2019, for example, the German Federal AI Association (Bundesverband KI) developed quality standards for AI. These are relatively general requirements which are based on compliance with basic ethical values as well as secure and data protection-compliant, unbiased transparent data handling.[565] In an area sensitive to fundamental rights such as crime control, however, the state must not, from the outset, discharge itself of the obligation to set standards by outsourcing to the private sector. The gaps left by an individual right of explanation can only be closed by direct state control of predictive policing algorithms. The interests of government control bodies are markedly different from those of an individual person's right to explanation. State control must be concerned with reviewing the effects of an algorithm over long periods and with a view to all citizens. For example, unlike individuals, state control institutions can develop clear, generally binding standards for predictive policing algorithms, and compliance can be verified by disclosure to a government control body.

(1) Possible configurations

Within a governmental framework, predictive policing controls can either be attached to an existing or a new government agency.[566] Finally, an inspection could also be carried out by a private testing organization such as the TÜV[567] in Germany. However, these organizations are typically an instrument of administrative law, which is used to regulate mass phenomena in the relationship between the state and its citizens, for example,

---

565 *KI Bundesverband* 2019.

566 Cf. *Wischmeyer* 2020, 75, mn. 44 et seq.; *Sachverständigenrat für Verbraucherfragen* 2018, 30; for the USA see also *Tutt* Admin. L. Rev. 2017, 83; *Citron/Pasquale* Wash. L. Rev. 2014, 1, 20 f; *Selbst* Ga. L. Rev. 2017, 109, 168 ff; *Podesta et al.* 2014, 65 et seq.

567 See for the term above fn. 554.

by overseeing the periodic safety inspection of people's cars.[568] The externalization of government controls is hardly applicable to the control of complex value judgements in person-based predictive policing algorithms used by the state. The form of state control that will ultimately be chosen for algorithms, however, needs to be decided democratically.

(2) Personnel resources

A government control body must undoubtedly be able to develop uniform legal and technical (statistical and computer science) standards for person-based predictive policing to verify compliance by means of inspection and to sanction shortcomings. This would require diverse expertise (computer scientists, statisticians, lawyers, criminologists, possibly supplemented by civil society) and sufficient resources to keep pace with the constant developments in the field of machine learning. Given the salaries paid in the private sector to computer experts, the government would have to be willing to invest.[569] However, if this were the case, it would be relatively easy to develop standards and carry out a standardized evaluation of an algorithm.[570] The fact that government agencies are able to recruit computer science expertise in specialist fields is clear from the expertise found at the German Federal Financial Supervisory Authority (BaFin) for the control of algorithms in the financial sector.[571]

(3) Organizational-structural considerations

In addition, the independence of a government control body must be ensured in order to prevent it from coming under pressure, for example within official police hierarchies. A control body must therefore always be located outside the police organisation. In order to achieve uniform standards and a concentration of the best possible expertise, a uniform federal control body would be better than several control bodies at state

568 *Ibler*, in: Maunz/Dürig, GG, Art. 86, mn. 75 et seq.
569 Problem of lack of transparency primarily due to a lack of institutions to create transparency, *Wischmeyer* 2020, 75, mn. 8.
570 See for private-sector 'scoring' *Gigerenzer et al.* Wirtschaftsdienst 2018, 860, 863; *Gesellschaft für Informatik* 2018b, 155 et seq.
571 So also *Gigerenzer et al.* Wirtschaftsdienst 2018, 860, 866.

or district level. Further, it would also be possible to transfer algorithmic control to existing data protection authorities. However, doing so would be associated with several problems. In the case of simpler information technology systems such as anti-terror watchlists, involvement of the data protection officers may suffice for control. But this does not apply to complex person-based predictive policing systems. It is not enough to primarily consider person-based predictive policing under the heading of data protection. Setting standards for and controlling predictive policing algorithms is about more than just data protection. The issues of non-discrimination and the asymmetric cost ratio,[572] for example, involve far more than the compliance of algorithms with data protection regulations. The data protection authorities still lack specialized expertise in computer science. In addition, the data protection authorities could become overburdened if they are made responsible for person-based predictive policing particularly due to existing deficits with regard to the GDPR.[573] Ideally, control bodies for person-based predictive policing should also be independent of the data protection authorities.

(4) Conclusion on a government control body

No institutions currently exist that could use inspection to effectively control person-based predictive policing algorithms in Germany. A control body needs to be established as it is an indispensable component of any transparency regime for person-based predictive policing. The development and operation of person-based predictive policing systems prior to the establishment of such a body would be highly problematic.

cc) General public

Finally, all or certain information about person-based predictive policing algorithms could also be made available to the general public. The interests with regard to a general public right of inspection are again different from those of the two previous groups. Enabling the general public to access this information ultimately enables democratic control and public discussion, not only with regard to illegal, but also with regard to legal yet

572 See above for the Asymmetric Cost Ratio, fn. 355 and accompanying text.
573 Cf. already *Jöns* 2016, 44 et seq.; *Schütz* 2018, 251, 265 et seq.

socially undesirable, aspects of algorithms. For example, the information stored in an *ex ante* registration regime could be made publicly accessible. If an algorithm's source code is made available to the public, it is referred to as 'open source'. One example of a successful open-source approach is the location-based predictive policing system HunchLab in the US.[574]

dd) Summary of the people authorized to access information

As it is not enough to leave the task of controlling algorithms to the general population, an independent government control body with sufficient resources and expertise needs to be established specifically for person-based predictive policing systems. The control body should be located outside the police organizational structure instead of being merely attached to existing data protection officers. While the general public should be denied insight into police algorithms, the burden of control of algorithms should also not be imposed solely on the public However, it should be possible for individuals to consult experts in order to examine person-based predictive policing algorithms. For this reason, in addition to an individual right of explanation about algorithms, and the establishment of a state control body, as much as possible of the information listed below should be made public.

574 Cf. https://perma.cc/A7YN-S3MN (last accessed 1.1.2022).

c) Third dimension of transparency: scope of transparency

scope of transparency	abstract information - existence and use - abstract principles of action - source code - output testing - logging obligations in design phase
	explanation in individual cases - generally intelligible - computer science details - counterfactual explanations

Tbl. 6. Scope of transparency

The third dimension of transparency, the scope of transparency, is determined by the exact information provided about an algorithm. This can range from the narrowest form of disclosure, i.e. the abstract design principles of an algorithm, to demands for the exclusive use of open-source algorithms. Roughly speaking, the different scopes of information can be divided into abstract information about a person-based predictive policing system and the explanation of an algorithmic result in individual cases.

aa) Abstract information

(1) Existence and use

As far as abstract information is concerned, the public could demand to be informed whether a person-based predictive policing system actually exists at all.[575] It is also possible to inform individuals targeted by a police measure *that* a risk score was produced for them and *what* the result was.[576]

575 Cf. also *Wischmeyer* 2020, 75, mn. 44 et seq.
576 Cf. *Arbeitsgruppe 'Digitaler Neustart'* 2018, 7.

(2) General principles of action

As a next step, it would be possible to explain the general principles that a person-based predictive policing system is based on in a concise and generally understandable way, and to provide separate information for computer science experts.[577] This would include an abstract description of the training data, target and input variables and the prediction accuracy and error rates.[578]

(3) Source code

Further, the source code of an algorithm could also be disclosed.[579] Source code is the set of human-readable instructions that a programmer writes when they create an algorithm. In the case of complex systems, the source code can consist of hundreds or thousands of lines of code. In rule-based AI systems, programmers write all the if-this-then-that relationships into the source code. In machine learning AI systems, the source code prescribes the algorithm's learning function, without defining if-this-then-that relationships. With machine learning AI, the disclosure and isolated analysis of the source code usually provides only limited information.

(4) Output testing

In addition to or instead of source code disclosure, insight can be given into the risk scores created and the corresponding (possibly anonymized) input data. Systematic analysis of all previous input-output pairs (called

577 *Ferguson* 2017, 137 et seq. ('citizens do not necessarily need information about the mathematical formula underlying the algorithm but do need explanation about why the algorithm is being used … The issue is explaining not the mathematical formula but the reasons why a mathematical risk assessment is necessary'); cf. for France *Wischmeyer* 2020, 75, mn. 16 with further references.

578 See for the USA the proposal of a discrimination impact assessment based on known environmental impact assessments, *Selbst* Ga. L. Rev. 2017, 109, 47-59.

579 Cf. Bill No. 1696, N.Y.C. Council (2017) = Local Law 49 (2018) - Automated Decision Systems Used By Agencies.

black box testing, output testing or reverse engineering),[580] also enables discrimination in prediction patterns to be identified.[581]

Further, disclosure may also consist of allowing access to the person-based predictive policing system's input and output masks without disclosing the source code, so that controllers can enter various hypothetical data into the system and systematically observe how risk scores change.[582] Systematic analysis undertaken in this manner can also reveal discriminatory behaviour.

(5) Logging obligations in the design phase

In the case of algorithms used by the state, output testing is not enough: control measures are needed as early as the algorithm development phase.[583] Another source of transparency – often overlooked in the discussion – is the design and training phase.[584]

Information can be provided about a number of value judgements that have a decisive influence on the results of the algorithm, such as the selection of the training database[585] or the calibration of the error rate in favour of false-positive or false-negative errors.[586] This is particularly the case with machine learning. Information about the logging obligations in place during the design phase can be used to ensure that the value judgements made were recorded in a comprehensible manner and are available for review.[587] No completely new standards would have to be

580 See *Diakopoulos* Tow Center for Digital Journalism 2014; *Kroll et al.* U. Pa. L. Rev. 2017, 633, 650 et seq.; see also *Wachter et al.* Harv. J.L. & Tech. 2018, 841, 841

581 Cf. *Larson et al.* ProPublica 2016

582 Cf. for private-sector scoring so-called 'hypothetical alterations' *Citron/Pasquale* Wash. L. Rev. 2014, 1, 28; *Gigerenzer et al.* Wirtschaftsdienst 2018, 860, 863

583 *Krafft/Zweig* 2018, 471, 471.

584 The so-called 'playing with the data stage', *Lehr/Ohm* UCDL Rev. 2017, 653, 655; *Konferenz der Informationsfreiheitsbeauftragten* 2018, 4.

585 Called 'Black Data' by *Ferguson* 2017, 131 if tainted with discrimination.

586 See above on Asymmetric Cost Ratio p. 94; see also *Lehr/Ohm* UCDL Rev. 2017, 653, 657, 691-692 ('Different kinds of errors are often viewed by stakeholders as having different normative valences; it is very rare for a stakeholder to view being wrong in one way as equally harmful as being wrong in the opposite way').

587 *Lehr/Ohm* UCDL Rev. 2017, 653, 657; no whole new standards have to be developed for this, but existing ISO standards could be referred to. Logging obli-

developed to implement this, but reference could be made to, for example, existing ISO standards.[588]

This general information is useful for individuals and experts as it helps them gain a better understanding of the algorithm; however, it is difficult to use it to explain individual risk scores. The source code or the training data do not provide enough information (especially not for lay people) to explain why a certain individual received a high risk score. In order to develop an explanation of an individual case, therefore, other paths must be taken.

bb) Explanation in individual cases

Justification for individual cases should be understandable enough for a person concerned to take administrative steps against a risk score[589] and to correct errors in the input data; if necessary, after legal advice. At the same time, individuals should receive a detailed computer-based scientific explanation that can be further analysed with the help of experts.

The abstract information should already show which input variables are generally used in a system.[590] Individual explanations should begin by disclosing the values of the input variables used in the specific individual case. Weighting should be used to indicate which key variables had the strongest influence on the result. In addition, 'counterfactual explanations' can be used:[591] this means that not all input variables would have to be disclosed to those affected, but only the key variables that would have to be changed in order to arrive at a different result. An example would be: 'Had you not travelled to Iraq or had you no access to firearms, the algorithm would not have led to a lower risk score.' Counterfactual explanations help

---

gations are addressed in ISO 14721:2012 (electronic records archiving); as well as ISO 16363:2012 (organizational, infrastructure, digital object management and technologies, technical infrastructure & security); see on 'preregistration' requirements, *Hildebrandt* 2018

588 Logging obligations are addressed, for example, in ISO 14721:2012 (electronic records archiving) and ISO 16363:2012 (organizational, infrastructure, digital object management and technologies, technical infrastructure & security).

589 See on affected persons entitled to transparency above p. 133 ff; *Wischmeyer* AöR 2018, 1, 54 with further references, *Wischmeyer* 2020, mn. 56.

590 See above p. 140.

591 *Wachter et al.* Harv. J.L. & Tech. 2018, 841; on the concept of counterfactuals *Lewis* 1973.

provide an initial understanding of an algorithm, but do not allow more in-depth examinations of a system. Such explanations help individuals to understand what they have to address in court proceedings, but are not sufficient to provide transparency. For example, isolated explanations will not provide enough evidence to uncover widespread discrimination by an algorithm or reveal the value judgements on which it is based.[592]

It follows from this that a transparency regime for person-based predictive policing must contain a combination of abstract information and explanations in individual cases.

cc) Conclusion on transparency mechanisms

An effective transparency regime thus consists of various building blocks from all of the dimensions of transparency (Fig. 4). Ideally, an effective transparency regime should record the logging obligations that apply even before the algorithm is used for the first time, i.e. during the development phase. On the one hand, transparency is ensured *ex ante* by publishing the decisions taken during the design phase and the abstract working principles of the algorithm; possibly supplemented by the need for a licence. Compliance with these *ex ante* requirements must be ensured by a governmental control body, which can gain detailed insight into source codes and training data before a system is used and can prohibit its use if necessary. In addition, the control authority should conduct regular audits of the algorithm. Finally, the people directly affected by a person-based predictive policing algorithm should be provided with an individual explanation of their score beyond the publicly accessible abstract information on the algorithm that was used. Only through the interaction of these different approaches to transparency can the risks associated with algorithmic crime prediction be steered in a direction that is acceptable under the law. The following overview lists the most important points.

592 *Wachter et al.* Harv. J.L. & Tech. 2018, 841, 883.

moment of transparency	*ex ante* - registration regime - licensing regime
	ex post - auditing regime - individual right to explanation
transparency-entitled entity	government control body
	individually affected citizens
	general public
scope of transparency	abstract information - existence and use - abstract principles of action - source code - output testing - logging obligations in design phase
	explanation in individual cases - generally intelligible - computer science details - counterfactual explanations

Tbl. 7. Overview of transparency mechanisms in relation to the three dimensions of transparency

4. Arguments against transparency

Now that the concept of transparency has been examined at a factual level, the arguments most frequently put forward against transparency will presented and disproven.

The arguments put forward against transparency can be divided into three categories:

- Impossibility of transparency (a)
- Unnecessity of transparency (b)
- Preponderance of competing interests (c)

a) Impossibility of transparency

The very fundamental criticism that transparency is impossible is based on the argument that people can never fully understand algorithms[593] due to system inherent intransparency.[594] It is claimed that the striving for transparency is destined to fail from the outset. Any attempt at transparency is said to be mere "window-dressing".[595] Measures to create transparency could only pretend the possibility of a fully transparent algorithm that could infact never be achieved. It would be better to openly admit that we are unable to understand algorithms down to the last detail and on the basis of this admission to decide for or against the use of algorithms.

The argument that the average person cannot understand a detailed explanation of algorithms because they lack specialist knowledge also falls under the heading of 'impossibility'; namely the impossibility of fostering trust in algorithms through transparency. Annany and Crawford call this phenomenon 'seeing without understanding'.[596] A detailed description of the algorithm would merely unsettle citizens, as they would never understand it, and this would sow distrust of the technology.[597] Overloading people with information would reduce their confidence in the technology. In this view, transparency contributes nothing to people's agency.[598]

Neither of these views stand up to scrutiny. The first point of criticism relates only to system-inherent complexity. It thus only relates to one out of three possible layers of non-transparency. With regard to the other two layers of non-transparency, a great deal of information can be disclosed about an algorithm, this includes the value judgements made during the design phase and systematic analyses of the output data. Finally, there are efforts to explain even system-inherent complexities with new computer scientific methods. The inherent complexity of new procedures is not a valid reason to avoid tackling transparency. Ultimately, the reasoning presented above would mean that we are generally released from the obligation to monitor algorithms every time a system is constructed in a complicated enough manner; this, of course, would provide great potential for abuse.

593 See *Ferguson* 2017, 138-139.
594 See p. 127.
595 See *Ananny/Crawford* New Media & Society 2018, 973, 983.
596 *Ananny* Science, Technology & Human Values 2016, 93.
597 *Mnookin/West* Yale JL & Human. 2001, 329, 357.
598 *Mnookin/West* Yale JL & Human. 2001, 329, 357.

The view that too much information could 'confuse' people is also untenable. Such a patronizing view, which deprives people of information for their own good, is to be rejected on principle. After all, people can always resort to experts and, with their help, initiate a debate about person-based predictive policing.[599] If the information provided about an algorithm is difficult to understand, the information needs to be supplemented with better explanations, not omitted completely.

b) Unnecessity of transparency

aa) Human in the loop

Under the headline of the unnecessity of transparency, it is argued that other mechanisms are enough to ensure error-free and legally compliant algorithms. In this view, if a human has the last say on whether an algorithm's recommendations should be followed ('human in the loop'),[600] full transparency vis-à-vis third parties may be unnecessary. This is the case, it is argued, when a system does not automatically lead to adverse legal consequences, but only prepares and supports human decisions. This argument was also put forward by the Wisconsin Supreme Court when deciding on whether the use of the non-transparent COMPAS recidivism prediction algorithm to assist judges in sentencing was lawful.[601] It stated that it is sufficient that judges are permitted to decide how much weight they want to attach to the algorithm and that they can obtain information beyond an algorithmic risk score from the defendant themselves. The psychological mechanism of 'automation bias', however, weakens the human in the loop argument. The psychological pressure of having to justify any deviation from the result of an algorithm often leads people to implement the result without thoroughly questioning it.[602] Police officers who receive a person-based predictive policing score are hardly in a position to check the score for errors. Even algorithms that support human decisions thus

599 Cf. *Wischmeyer* 2020, mn. 55; on the need to also structure the available information and not just increase its quantity in order to create more transparency. *Bröhmer* 2004, 18 et seq.

600 Cf. *Wischmeyer* 2020, mn. 47 ('If necessary – as in analogous administrative law – a normative correction of the forecast must then be made at later stages of decision-making').

601 See State v. Loomis, 881 N.W.2d 749 (WI 2016) (mn. 56).

602 See automation bias on p. 60 for more details.

narrow the corridor for humans to such a degree that it is no longer possible to make completely free decisions.[603] Ensuring that a process has a 'human in the loop' is just not effective enough to protect the interests of the people affected by an adverse risk score.

bb) Comparison with existing non-transparencies

A perceived lack of necessity leads to the argument that there is no need for complete transparency in algorithmic decision-making processes, since true transparency is not expected elsewhere in crime control. Comparisons are often made with the lack of transparency of the human brain, which is described as an 'organic black box'.[604] People are non-transparent because, as Kahneman and Tversky famously pointed out, their decision-making suffers from numerous cognitive biases,[605] making it almost impossible to reveal the true reasons behind a human decision. Even neuroscientists have yet to fully decipher the exact functions of the human brain in decision-making processes. Therefore, the argument goes, as there is already a high degree of non-transparency in human decisions in crime control, non-transparency (in this case of an algorithmic system) is nothing new in itself. Rather, algorithmic non-transparency would correspond to our *status quo* of decision-making today. If we demanded disclosure of training data and source code, we would in fact be demanding more from the algorithm than we would expect from humans. If the level of transparency required of algorithms were applied to police officers, so the argument goes, it would lead to grotesque scenarios: police officers would be obliged to wear EEG hoods to measure brain activity. A police officer's entire educational history and every case ever dealt with would also have to be disclosed, so that the actual causal processes in the police officer's life and

---

603 *Wischmeyer* 2020, mn. 43.

604 See *Wischmeyer* AöR 2018, 1, 54; *Rademacher* AöR 2017, 366, 399; *Tutt* Admin. L. Rev. 2017, 83, 103 cf. also *Lem* 2013, 98; but see also comparisons with committee decisions *Wischmeyer* AöR 2018, 1, 54; with explosive detection dogs *Rich* U. Pa. L. Rev. 2016, 871, 911; and with police informants *Rich* U. Pa. L. Rev. 2016, 871, 907.

605 See above fn. 446 and accompanying text; see also *Tutt* Admin. L. Rev. 2017, 83, 103, especially for cognitive biases of the police *Rademacher* AöR 2017, 366, 399; *Taslitz* Ohio St. J. Crim. L. 2010, 7, 27-29; cf. on the lack of transparency of judges *Slobogin* U. Ill. L. Rev. 1999, 363, 403 et seq., see also *Rachlinski/Wistrich* Annu. Rev. Law. Soc. Sci. 2017, 203.

body that led to a particular decision could be uncovered. The fact that we do not expect such things from police officers, shows that we should also not expect them from algorithms.

However, these points do not hold up to scrutiny and must be rejected: The rejection does not have to be limited to providing reasons why an algorithm should be subjected to a higher transparency standard than a human being. Already the premise that human and algorithmic non-transparency are at all comparable is faulty. Algorithmic decisions differ in several key points from human decisions. Algorithmic non-transparency does not correspond to the current *status quo* of human non-transparency. Human non-transparency is nothing new for the legal system. Over centuries, the legal system has adapted to human non-transparency and designed mechanisms to counteract it. One of these mechanisms is the constitutional obligation to justify administrative and judicial action.[606] The obligation to give reason makes it possible to subsequently check any reason given (even if a person's exact motives remain hidden) by asking a person in a conversation to explain their motives further or to defend them against criticism. Human decision-makers can articulate themselves in detail when questioned and the answers they provide can be understood directly.[607] The statement of reasons is also a central mechanism for individual legal protection, since it is only through giving reason that it becomes clear to the person concerned what arguments he or she has to put forward against a certain measure.[608] Since algorithms cannot be directly questioned in the same way and since they cannot explain themselves to the same extent,[609] this deficit has to be compensated for. It has to be compensated namely by an insight right into the algorithms' design process. As long as this compensation is not guaranteed algorithms will fall far behind the current *status quo* of transparency in crime control.

---

606 See *Wischmeyer* AöR 2018, 1, 55 with further references; generally on the requirement to state reasons in state actions, *Lücke* 1987, 37 ff; *Kischel* 2003, 63 BVerwG, DVBl 1982, 198/199 ('the citizen [...], in whose rights the administration interferes, have a right [...] to know the relevant reasons because only then are they in a position to defend their rights properly').

607 . *Mittelstadt et al.* Big Data & Society 2016, 1, 7

608 See *Hornung* 2018, 79, 88.

609 Cf. illustration of the lack of transparency on p. 124 et seq.

c) Preponderance of competing interests

This last form of criticism treats transparency as a legitimate interest in crime control. However, in this view, other values protected by the law outweigh the need for transparency. Three competing interests that are often put forward are (aa) the protection of trade secrets belonging to private algorithm manufacturers,[610] (bb) the protection of algorithms against spying by criminals (cc) and the protection of personal data in algorithm databases.[611]

aa) Trade secrets

Information on algorithms may constitute trade secrets, the protection of which is constitutionally enshrined in Germany in Articles 12 and 14 of the Constitution.[612] Trade secrets may apply to information connected with a business enterprise. Such information must be known only to a limited circle of individuals, must be kept secret by the business enterprise, and there must be a legitimate economic interest in such secrecy.[613] In 2014, the German Federal Court of Justice (Bundesgerichtshof – BGH) ruled on the protection of the Schufa algorithm used to assess creditworthiness. It stated that the 'abstract method of calculating credit scores does not have to be made public'. Schufa's trade secrets also included 'the general calculation variables used in the first step of the score formula, such as the statistical values used, the weighting of individual calculation elements in determining the probability value and the formation of any comparison groups as the basis for the scorecards'.[614] It is precisely these data, however, that would need to be examined to reveal the presence of potential discrimination. Trade secrets are also expressly mentioned in the EU's GDPR as interests that are to be considered in relation to claims for information.[615] The decision by the BGH, and the scope of the GDPR, however, primarily concern algorithms developed by private individuals for use in the private

610 Cf. generally *Kugelmann* 2001, 70 et seq.
611 Cf. generally *Kugelmann* 2001, 64 et seq.
612 *Kugelmann* 2001, 70 et seq.; BVerfG, Urt. v. 7. 12.2017, 2 BvE 2/11, mn. 234 et seq.; in detail on all relevant fundamental rights *Wolf* 2015, 72 et seq.; see also in principle *Beyerbach* 2012; *Schnabel* Computer und Recht 2016, 342.
613 *Kugelmann* 2001, 70, cf. also *Prinz* 2015, 192 et seq.
614 BGH, ZD 2014, 306 (308).
615 See recital 63 GDPR.

sector. However, if private algorithms are used by the state in an area sensitive to fundamental rights such as crime control, different standards must apply.[616] In Germany, for example, the DyRiAS[617] and Palantir Gotham[618] systems have been developed by private companies. In the area of location-based predictive policing, the Precobs[619] and SKALA[620] systems are also being co-developed by private companies. The need to protect private individuals' trade secrets has often been used in the past to prevent the disclosure of administrative information under the German Freedom of Information Act.[621] For person-based predictive policing, however, such arguments would be particularly problematic: it would enable the state to consciously place an additional layer of non-transparency over its decisions by outsourcing decision-supporting algorithms to the private sector. It should be stressed that person-based predictive policing systems are not mere 'tools', such as a police officer's gun is a tool. Whereas it may be justified to argue that the exact design of a firearm used by the police is a trade secret, this does not apply to a person-based predictive policing system that centrally shapes an official decision-making process. Moreover, a firearm can hardly directly discriminate against people, whereas a person-based predictive policing system can do so by attributing risk. When developing person-based predictive policing software for the state, private companies must be aware that government action, especially in the area of policing, must be subject to greater transparency than algorithms used for purely private purposes. In state crime control, the financial interests of private individuals rightly do not have priority. There are concerns that the police could not benefit from private sector innovation if trade secrets were not protected, as private companies would refuse to cooperate with the police. However, the examples of the US software companies CivicScape and Azavea,[622] which voluntarily disclose the source code of their location-based predictive policing software, show that companies can also be economically successful with an open-source approach. If the police in Germany were to insist on a similar level of openness in privately developed person-based predictive policing software, they could promote innova-

616 Similarly *Hoffmann-Riem* 2018, 12, 60.
617 See above p. 76 et seq.
618 See above p. 75 et seq.
619 See *Knobloch* 2018, 13.
620 See *Knobloch* 2018, 10.
621 *Wischmeyer* Die Verwaltung 2018, 393, 423; *Schoch* IFG, § 6 mn. 122 m. w. N.
622 *Gershgorn* Quarz of 22.3.2017, accessible at https://perma.cc/QJ6P-WB8N, last accessed 1.1.2022; see also https://perma.cc/A7YN-S3MN (last accessed 1.1.2022).

tion in open-source software, because this is a typical way of providing incentives for innovation in this area. Finally, the open-source approach can be particularly conducive to innovation, as other software vendors are able to examine existing systems and use their findings to improve their own. An open source approach could be additionally supported by the state through research funding.[623] As a result, the police would benefit because they would be able to choose from more sophisticated systems. The use of open source algorithms also makes it possible to advance the scientific discourse on crime forecasting.[624]

In summary, trade secrets are certainly not a general knock-out argument against disclosing information about person-based predictive policing algorithms.

bb) Spying on the algorithm

Concerns about criminals spying on an algorithm used by the state are often put forward as an argument against transparency.[625] It is said that publishing information about an algorithm jeopardizes the security of the system. Proponents of this view argue that secrecy is necessary to secure the future functioning of an algorithm.[626] Asymmetry of knowledge between state and citizen, therefore, is essential. Moreover, publishing information would enable people to consciously adapt their behaviour to avoid detection. However, using the possibility of spying as a blanket argument is problematic: it threatens to thwart disclosure of virtually any kind of police technology.[627] Moreover, the blanket argument about spying is still of a highly hypothetical nature – there are no known cases where a predictive policing system has been spied upon to facilitate criminal activities. The argument that predictive policing requires secrecy, therefore, is

623 *Wischmeyer* AöR 2018, 1, 25.

624 See *Glover et al.* Law and Human Behavior 2017, 507.

625 See for in credit scoring algorithms *Citron/Pasquale* Wash. L. Rev. 2014, 1, 30 with further references

626 See *Wischmeyer* Die Verwaltung 2018, 393, 398 et seq.; see § 88 para. 5 sentence 4 AO ('Details of the risk management systems may not be published if this could jeopardize the uniformity and legality of taxation'); see also §§ 32a para. 2 no. 2 and 32b para. 1 sentence 2 AO; § 155 para. 4 AO.

627 Criticism of this argument at *Wischmeyer* 2020, 75, mn. 20; *Citron/Pasquale* Wash. L. Rev. 2014, 1, 30 et seq.s. also *Kugelmann* 2001, 329.

unsound.[628] Moreover, concerns about spying can be used as an unreflected blanket justification to deny transparency vis-à-vis the public as a whole or the people directly affected. The social costs of a lack of transparency are higher than the uncertain security gains associated with secrecy.

Further, in the past, detailed catalogues of the input criteria used with traditional prognosis tools (HCR-20,[629] VRAG,[630] etc.) were and still are publicly available. This has not led criminals to adapt their behaviour to avoid being classed as high risk. The argument of spying on algorithms should therefore not be accepted to generally trump transparency.

cc) Third-party data protection

In addition to trade secrets and concerns about the security of the system, another interest that competes with transparency is the protection of the personal data processed in the predictive policing system. The need for data protection with regard to the personal data in the training database, and with regard to people for whom a new risk score is generated, does, however, not generally speak against transparency.

First, as explained above,[631] personal data are only a small subset of the data that could be disclosed. Refusal to disclose personal data does not mean that other information (such as input variables or asymmetric cost ratio) cannot be published. Second, information containing personal data can be made available to the public anonymously, or the data can be made available to a government control body which is bound to confidentiality. In any case, data protection does not fundamentally speak against transparency, and a balance between transparency and data protection can be achieved.

dd) Summary: Preponderance of competing interests

None of the competing interests mentioned outweighs transparency *per se*. In general, private economic interests (trade secrets) should not be conside-

628 Cf. *Wischmeyer* Die Verwaltung 2018, 393, 398 et seq.
629 *Douglas/Webster* Criminal Justice and Behaviour 1999.
630 *Rettenberger et al.* 2017; *Rice et al.* Psychological Assessment 2013, 951; *Quinsey et al.* 2006.
631 See above p. 139 et seq.

red when assessing person-based predictive policing. It is important that concerns about spying are not used as pretexts to block transparency. The interests of third parties in data protection do not rule out transparency; rather, these interests can be effectively protected within a transparency regime.

Even if concerns about trade secrets and spying are viewed as preventing information from being made available to the general public, this does not preclude the implementation of a transparency model that enables a government control body to inspect algorithms while maintaining confidentiality.

d) Conclusion on arguments against transparency

In short, none of the arguments against transparency are convincing. In a next step this book will examine where transparency is anchored within a constitutional law framework.

5. The foundations of transparency in constitutional law

Transparency obligations in the form of having to disclose certain information are anchored in various parts of constitutional law: in the principle of human dignity, which is at the core of the right to informational self-determination, in the principles of democracy and in the rule of law principle.[632]

a) Human dignity as the core of the right to informational self-determination

The fact that privacy in the form of the constitutional right to informational self-determination (Art. 2 (1) in connection with Art. 1 (1) of the German Constitution)[633] gives rise to certain limits for person-based predictive policing (e.g. their use only for the protection of high-ranking legal interests) has been discussed above.[634] Therefore, the following specifically

---

632 See also *Gusy* 2012; *Scherzberg* 2013, 665.
633 See generally *Gusy/Eichenhofer* 2017.
634 See above p. 107.

examines the extent to which the principle of human dignity, which is at the core of transparency, (Art. 1 (1) German Constitution) can serve as an anchor of transparency.

It follows from human dignity that people may not be made the mere object of a machine.[635] According to the 'recognition theory' human dignity is constituted among other things by *social* recognition, i.e. 'by positive evaluation of social claims to respect'.[636] Part of this is also the 'mutual recognition of the other in their idiosyncrasies and individual peculiarities'.[637] This in turn demands that people be evaluated not merely according to general group characteristics but their individual circumstances.

Human dignity may be infringed upon if people who share traits with a group of people who have committed crimes in the past are assigned high risk scores, as this endangers the recognition of each individual's own 'idiosyncrasies and peculiarities'. When a person's subjectivity is called into question during data processing, human dignity may be affected.[638] Human dignity demands the maintenance of a minimum of self-determination and traceability during the processing of personal data.[639] One may argue that human objectification occurs particularly when algorithms that lack transparency and are no longer understood even by experts are used to create risk scores. As shown above, police officers will often lack the training to review the results and recognize errors. Moreover, 'automation bias' leads police officers to follow the algorithm's prognosis without questioning it. However, as human dignity is at the core of the right to informational self-determination, in areas as sensitive to fundamental rights as crime control, the state should not use any algorithms that lack transparency qua system-inherent complexity. It is simply not good enough to know *that* a prognosis tool works in most cases if we do not understand *how* it works. Based on the current state of research, this excludes the application of algorithmic decision systems in the form of particularly intransparent neural networks for crime control.

635 Cf. *Botha* Stellenbosch L. Rev. 2009, 171; *Zöller* 2002, 44.

636 Basic *Hofmann* AöR 1993, 353 et seq.

637 *Hofmann* AöR 1993, 370.

638 *Duwell* 2014, 28; cf. the worries of 'degrading' people to an 'information object' through prognostic data processing already at *Graulich*, in: Schenke/Graulich/Ruthig, § 18 mn. 11; *Zöller* 2002, 163; cf. on the prohibition of the reduction to an 'information object' already BVerfGE 65, 1 (423).

639 *Zöller* 2002, 44.

b) Democracy principle

The principle of democracy, Article 20 (2) of the German Constitution, imposes an obligation to make administrative decisions, including police decisions, public.[640] Decisions must be made in a way that informs the general public. This is important because every government decision must be ultimately traced back to an official appointed in a democratic process (uninterrupted chain of democratic legitimation) (aa).[641] Further, public decisions are necessary so that people have a chance to form an opinion about what the government is doing and whether they support it and want to vote accordingly (democratic formation of opinions) (bb). Finally, public decisions also enable democratic control (cc).[642]

This is an integral aspect of democracy, and it comes under threat when decisions are no longer made by accountable police officers, but by private company programmers behind closed doors, without explanation or insight.

aa) Chain of democratic legitimation

The chain of democratic legitimation means that administrative decisions must be traceable back to a public official. Decisions that are merely traceable to autonomous algorithms or private programmers, therefore, lack democratic legitimacy. If police officers make decisions using algorithms that are incomprehensible even to experts, these decisions may formally be attributable to a police officer, but actually predetermined by an algorithm, which, in turn, reflects the decisions made by private programmers. In this scenario, the chain of democratic legitimation may be interrupted. Algorithms with system-inherent non-transparency, such as neural networks, are particularly problematic in this regard.

bb) Democratic formation of opinion

Democratic opinion formation means that people must be able to form a political opinion about government action in order to decide whether

640 *Scherzberg* 2000, 291 et seq.; *Kugelmann* 2001, 64; *Bröhmer* 2004, 38 et seq.
641 BVerfGE 47, 253 (LS 2, 275).
642 *Gusy*, in: Hoffmann-Riem et al. 2012, § 23 mn. 21.

they support or oppose the action it takes (e.g. via voting). According to this functional understanding of the public and its role in the realization of democracy, the population can, however, only form a political will[643] if information about administrative decisions are made public in the first place.[644] This includes decisions on the use of algorithms and the general working principles behind them.

cc) Democratic control

Finally, in a democratic state, the public should to some extent guarantee the correctness of administrative decisions and act as a limit to the exercise of executive power.[645] While primary control of the executive is the responsibility of the legislative and judicial branches of government, the general public provides additional control.[646] Their control function becomes all the more important if parliament and the courts do not exercise their control function properly, as has been the case with person-based predictive policing to date. However, the public can only exercise their control function if they have information about the actions of the administration.[647] This is the only way of ensuring that the advantages and risks of certain algorithmic technology can be discussed in public (possibly after consulting experts).[648]

In its ruling on the Federal Criminal Police Office Act, the German BVerfG also stressed the importance of the democratic principle for the control of police activities: in particular, the regular reporting obligations of the police to parliament and the public serve 'to facilitate public discussion and democratic control'.[649] As early as 2013, the BVerfG stated that the central function of transparency was that 'trust and legal certainty can arise and the handling of data remains part of a democratic discourse'.[650]

---

643 *Kugelmann* 2001, 77.

644 *Gusy*, in: Hoffmann-Riem et al. 2012, § 23 mn. 21; *Kugelmann* 2001, 77 with further references

645 *Pieroth* JuS 1981, 625, 628; *Krebs* 1984, 7 ff; *Kugelmann* 2001, 78 with further references see also *Bröhmer* 2004, 40.

646 *Kugelmann* 2001, 79.

647 *Pieroth* JuS 1981, 625, 626.

648 *Diakopoulos* Tow Center for Digital Journalism 2014, 2.

649 BVerfGE 141, 220 (mn. 143, 268); see also BVerfGE 133, 277 (mn. 221 et seq.), see also BVerfGE 118, 277 = NVwZ 2007, 916 (926).

650 BVerfGE 133, 277 (mn. 206).

It follows from this that – at least on request, for example, by members of parliament – there is an obligation to disclose the fundamental mechanisms behind any predictive policing system to parliament. Further information obligations vis-à-vis the public are equally desirable from a democratic perspective.

c) Rule of law

Finally, the rule of law also entails transparency dimensions. The principle of the rule of law[651] is enshrined in Article 20 (3) of the German Constitution. It leads to a requirement that administrative actions be transparent and understandable to citizens *ex ante*[652] and reviewable *ex post*.[653] It also results in a need for explanation.[654] Therefore, the police are required to do more than merely state that they conducted a particular measure 'because the computer told them to'. Explanations must be more detailed and make some of the fundamental algorithmic processes underlying a decision clear.

This constitutional requirement to provide explanation consists of two elements: an explanatory aspect that is easily comprehensible to the person concerned (general information about an algorithmic system), so that they are able to seek redress; this is supplemented by a more detailed explanatory aspect that only experts can understand. Any affected citizen has the right to know why their fundamental rights have been infringed, because they need this information if they are to be able to defend themselves properly.[655] In order to be able to defend their fundamental rights effectively, for example, with regard to non-discrimination or informational self-determination, the population requires certain information from which a violation of these fundamental rights can be discerned.[656] The BVerfG explicitly stated: 'Without knowledge, the data subjects cannot assert any unlawfulness of the government use of data nor any rights to deletion, rectification or satisfaction'.[657] If the population is to be able to exercise its constitutional rights, access needs to be provided to all data sources from

651 Fundamentally *Scherzberg* 2000, 320 ff; *Bröhmer* 2004, 147.
652 *Scherzberg* 2000, 321 ff; *Bröhmer* 2004, 159.
653 *Scherzberg* 2000, 328 et seq.
654 *Wischmeyer* AöR 2018, 1, 54 et seq.
655 BVerwG, DVBl 1982, 198 (199).
656 See *Eichenhofer* Forschungsjournal Soziale Bewegungen 2017, 133, 138.
657 BVerfGE 141, 220 (mn. 134); BVerfGE 125, 260 (mn. 242).

which discrimination can arise (including training data and decisions in the design phase).

6. Summary of transparency requirements

Human dignity, the principle of democracy and the rule of law mean, on the one hand, that no algorithms that are completely non-transparent may be used within person-based predictive policing systems. On the other hand, it follows from this that sufficient information must be made available to the public so that they can take effective action against police measures based on algorithms and form their own political opinions. The aim of the transparency flowing from the constitution is, in summary, the 'self-control of the administration, enabling third-party control, generating social acceptance and trust, as well as social recognition of affected persons as procedural subjects'.[658] Technological complexity is not an excuse to withhold essential information from the public.[659] It should be noted that there are no institutions that could effectively control person-based predictive policing at the current time in Germany. However, a control body would be a central component of any transparency regime for person-based predictive policing, and should therefore be established in the future.

Person-based predictive policing systems should not be used until the control body is in place. Transparency, as some voices in the literature have already warned, is not a legal panacea capable of solving all the problems associated with algorithms. However, transparency certainly has a key role to play.

An effective transparency regime must be comprised of three pillars. It must provide transparency not only vis-à-vis the general public, but also vis-à-vis the individuals affected and vis-à-vis a government control body. This results in the 'triangle of algorithmic transparency' shown in Fig. 5.

658 *Wischmeyer* 2020, mn. 56.
659 See *Art. 29 Data Protection Working Party* 2018, 14.

Fig. 5. Triangle of algorithmic transparency for person-based predictive policing

Decisions taken during the design phase of an algorithm and the abstract principles on which an algorithm is based should be logged. This information must be deposited in a publicly accessible manner with a state registry (the 'registration side' of the triangle) before the algorithm is used. In addition to the abstract principles on which an algorithm is based, an individual affected by a predictive policing score should be provided with an explanation of their specific score. The explanation needs to contain a section that the general public can understand and a detailed part directed at computer science experts (the 'individual rights side' of the triangle). In addition to these disclosure requirements, state control of person-based predictive policing should take place prior to deployment (licence) and at regular intervals during deployment (auditing). The control body should review the algorithm for, inter alia, violations of the right to privacy and the ban on discrimination. In addition, the control authority should develop its own standards, for example, on error rates and forecasting accuracy of predictive policing systems, and check for compliance with these standards (the 'state control side' of the triangle). The government control body should not permit the police to resort to secrecy by invoking security or the protection of trade secrets.

Only through these requirements visualized in the triangle in Fig. 5 and am interlocking of personal and government as well as *ex ante* and *ex post* controls can all risks of automated crime control be addressed sufficiently: the threat to human dignity, which is at the core of the right to informational self-determination, the threat to the rule of law and effective legal protection as well as the threat to democracy.

IV. Presumption of innocence

Now that the compatibility of person-based predictive policing with informational self-determination, the principle of non-discrimination and the constitutional requirement for transparency have been investigated, the following focuses on the presumption of innocence.

The presumption of innocence means that a person must be considered innocent until proven guilty in court (ban on the presumption of guilt).[660] Any doubts are to the detriment of the prosecution, any pursuit of punitive ends before conviction is unlawful.[661] Similarly, it is also illegal to impose measures that are equivalent in their effect to a punishment (punishment-equivalent interventions) on the accused.[662] The presumption of innocence is *the* core maxim of the criminal justice system.[663]

The presumption of innocence is protected on the constitutional level. It is interpreted by the BVerfG as a special expression of the principle of the rule of law (Art. 20 (3) of the German Constitution).[664] At the same time, the presumption of innocence is expressly anchored in international law in Art. 6 (2) ECHR.[665] In political debates, the presumption of innocence regularly carries considerable weight.[666] It is also commonly referred to

---

660 BVerfGE 74, 358 'Until proven guilty by law, his/her innocence is presumed'; *Stuckenberg* 2012, 67; *Eckstein* 2013, 321 et seq.; *Gaede*, in: MüKo-StPO Bd. 2, Art. 6 EMRK, mn. 126

661 *Stuckenberg* 2012, 69 et seq.; *Gaede*, in: MüKo-StPO, Art. 6 EMRK, mn. 133.

662 *Stuckenberg* 2012, 70 et seq. with further references; for an overview of all legal consequences flowing from the presumption of innocence see *Stuckenberg* 2012, 67; for the prohibition of punishment-like interventions, *Eckstein* 2013, 326 et seq.

663 See *Lindner* AöR 2008, 235.

664 See BVerfGE 74, 358, 370; BVerfGE 82, 106; BGH JR 2017, 226 m. Anm Stuckenberg; in academic literature the presumption of innocence is also anchored in human dignity, *Stuckenberg* 2012, 48 et seq. m.w.N; *Eckstein* 2013, 321.

665 See also EU-RL 2016/343 über die Stärkung bestimmter Aspekte der Unschuldsvermutung und des Rechts auf Anwesenheit in der Verhandlung in Strafverfahren.

666 *Frister* 2016, 152.

in the media in discussions of predictive policing.[667] However, a widespread misunderstanding needs to be cleared up: although there is debate about the exact interpretation of the presumption of innocence,[668] there is agreement in jurisprudence and the literature that the presumption of innocence relates *solely* to *ex post* prosecution and thus does not apply to preventive policing.[669] The presumption of innocence therefore refers only to innocence with regard to *past* crimes, but not to innocence, or rather harmlessness, with regard to *future* crimes. A 'presumption of harmlessness' would contradict basic preventive police law, according to which the state can avert threats even in the event of uncertainty, and even if doing so encroaches on people's rights. Doubts in the area of preventive policing do not generally fall to the detriment of the state.

There is no presumption in favour of harmlessness precisely because the state is required to effectively protect itÄs citizens legal assets.[670] It is therefore impossible to apply the presumption of innocence to preventive policing.

However, this does not mean that the state may assume that its citizens are dangerous on a blanket basis without a threshold or a specific reason. Rather, the limits for state action in preventing crime are to be found in *other* constitutional guarantees such as privacy, as described above.[671]

B. Summary of Chapter II: Legal limits of person-based predictive policing

Constitutional law only restricts person-based predictive policing to a limited extent.[672] It does not provide for an absolute ban, but it offers a framework within which person-based predictive policing must operate in order to be lawful.

The constitution does not generally prevent the legislature from further developing the traditional form of police law 'on the basis of a determination of new or changed situations of danger and threat subject to its prerogatives,' as the BVerfG stated in its dragnet judgment. However, the

---

667 Cf. *Beuth* Zeit Online of 11.10.2017, accessible at https://perma.cc/T4GL-6U5A, last accessed 1.1.2022.

668 Critical *Stuckenberg* ZStW 1999, 422, 4.

669 See *Esser*, in: Löwe/Rosenberg-StPO, Art. 6 ERKR, 449; *Satzger*, in: SSW-StPO, Art. 6 EMRK mn. 110.

670 See on the effectiveness of security *Dendinger*, in: Handbuch Polizeirecht, 36.

671 See p. 98 et seq.

672 Generally on scurity legislation, *Singelnstein/Stolle* 2012, 115 et seq.

BVerfG also stresses that '[t]he balance between freedom and security [...] may be readjusted by the legislator, but the weights [...] must not be fundamentally shifted by it'.[673] This also applies to person-based predictive policing, in which a fundamental shift can take place particularly easily and go unnoticed due to its complexity and the lack of transparency in its associated procedures.

From the perspective of realpolitik, the advance of person-based predictive policing in Germany and around the world is unlikely to be stopped. The proposed minimum requirements set out in Chapter IV, are not aimed at accelerating the use of person-based predictive policing. Rather, they are aimed at steering the existing predictive policing movement into a corridor that is compatible with the rule of law. The 'adjustment' that has occurred in the balance between freedom and security must not be permitted to become a 'fundamental shift'. Before we reach the chapter on recommended minimum requirements, however, the following Chapter III presents a fundamental critique of person-based predictive policing from a criminological, sociological and legal-theoretical perspective.

673 BVerfGE 115, 320 (536).

Chapter III. The algorithmic turn in crime control – a criminological, sociological and legal theoretical analysis

'The decision-makers no longer judged [...] They calculated.'
Hannah Arendt, Crises of the Republic[674]

Does the use of crime prediction algorithms bring something genuinely new to crime control or does it merely represent a continuation of existing trends with new means in the security society[675] and the actuarial turn? The use of algorithms is often presented as a continuation of developments that have existed for decades.[676] While it is true that person-based predictive policing was born out of an existing focus on risk well in advance of actual harm,[677] person-based predictive policing is more than just a continuation of this phenomenon. Algorithmic crime predictions raise new problems, introduce new specific rationalities (i.e. ways of thinking or not thinking) into crime control and fundamentally change it. The new technological possibilities lead to changes at the institutional level, shift resources, and influence how individual police officers perform their tasks. The new technology has the potential to evolve from a mere tool of crime control to its determinant ratio, thus shaping its entire internal logic.

These manifold changes can be summarized under the heading of the 'algorithmic turn',[678] based on the 'actuarial turn' coined by Feeley and Simon[679] to describe the criminal justice system at the end of the twentieth century.

When observing the effects of the algorithmic turn in crime control, it is not necessary to wait and see whether its (questionable) promises of effectiveness and salvation (cost-saving resource allocation and reduced crime figures) come true. The philosopher of science Thomas Kuhn stated in his seminal work, *The Structure of the Scientific Revolution*, that paradigm shifts do not occur because new scientific methods *are* more effective than

674 *Arendt* 1972, 37.
675 *Singelnstein/Stolle* 2012; see below p. 175 et seq.
676 Cf. *Ostermeier*, in: Singelnstein/Puschke 2018, 101 et seq.
677 In detail below p. 181 et seq.
678 Cf. the related term 'Computational Turn' Hildebrandt/de Vries 2013.
679 *Feeley/Simon* Criminology 1992, 449, 449 et seq.; cf. *Eisenberg/Kölbel* 2017, 457.

their predecessors. Rather, paradigm shifts occur because they carry with themselves the *promise* that better solutions to existing problems can be developed in the future.[680] It is through these promises about the future that paradigm shifts gain traction. And one characteristic of the algorithmic turn is that it already influences the thinking and judgements of decision-makers irrespective of whether it has been proven successful. It entices us with its promises of imminent success, and modernised algorithms.

The following sections discuss in detail the societal and legal context under which algorithmic crime predictions have emerged and trace their development within the security society[681] and the actuarial turn (B). In a second step, the peculiarities of the algorithmic turn are laid out and critically evaluated (C). However, the following begins by examining the central concept of 'risk', which is relevant both for the emergence of the algorithmic turn as well as within the algorithmic turn (A).

A. *Risk: a definition*

> *'Nothing in itself is a risk, there is no risk in reality. But on the other hand, everything can be a risk; it all depends on how one analyses the danger, considers the event.'*
>
> – François Ewald, Der Vorsorgestaat [The Welfare State][682]

The seemingly oppositional pair 'security and risk' is omnipresent in almost all areas of society, but especially in crime control. Banse[683] even speaks of an inflationary use of the term 'risk' and of society's debate about risk as merely a ritual.[684] But what exactly does the term risk mean? Is it a contourless 'all and nothing', as the opening quotation seems to suggest? The term risk is used neither in police nor in criminal law statutes in Germany and yet, as this book demonstrates, it lies at the very heart of our legal thinking about crime.

680 *Kuhn* 1970, 159 et seq.
681 See below p. 175 et seq.
682 *Ewald* 1993, 210.
683 *Banse* 1993, 6.
684 *Banse* 1993, 19 with further references.

I. Ambiguity

Ambiguity is inherent in the term 'risk': it implies the possibility of damage if an enterprise fails, but also the chance of making a profit if it is successful.[685] Risk is thus always connected to uncertainty, but at the same time constitutes potential for action. This ambiguity is also reflected in the late medieval etymological root of the term: on the Italian peninsula, 'risco' used to refer to a 'cliff that has to be circumnavigated'.[686] In the probability theory of stochastics, in which the words risk and probability are used synonymously, 'risk' does not necessarily come with negative connotations.[687] If a certain event A occurs *k* times during *n* times of a random experiment, the expected relative frequency *k/n* is called probability *P(A)*, or the risk that a certain event will occur.[688] In this sense, economics distinguishes between a calculable risk and an uncertainty that is inaccessible to prognostic calculations. However, in society and particularly in the field of crime control, risk is primarily interpreted negatively in the sense of impending loss, an anomaly or a disruptive factor. This is accompanied by the notion that every possible effort must be made to avoid risks, or at least make them controllable.[689] The following contextualizes this general understanding of risk.

II. Negative connotations of risk in the risk society

Ulrich Beck's 'risk society' has been much quoted in the literature since the 1980s and has also been widely received outside of academia. Beck argues that society's defensive attitude towards risk is only understandable because modern society faces an objective increase in the level of risk.[690] This leads the logic of risk distribution to replace the logic of wealth production.[691] The major risks of modernity created by man himself – also

685 *König*, in: Münkler et al. 2010, 209.
686 For roots of the term also in Persian s. *Banse* 1993, 28.
687 Cf. also *Stier* 2017, 14.
688 Cf. *Schurz* 2015, 3.
689 As an alternative to the risk society, see the concept of the 'experimental society', which combines both opportunity and danger, *Krohn/Weyer* Soziale Welt 1989, 349, 370; cf. also *Krohn/Weyer* 1990, 89 et seq.
690 *Beck* 1986, 25 et seq., cf. also *König*, in: Münkler et al. 2010, 209; see also *Giddens* 1990.
691 *Beck* 1986, 13, 26.

labelled "possibilities of self-destruction" by Beck (e.g. nuclear energy) – are thus increasingly superimposing the problems of wealth distribution in industrial society.[692] The new risks are of a different nature than the traditional risks of the past: they can neither be limited nor attributed, nor can they be compensated for.[693] The risk society is characterized by 'confusion, ignorance, uncertainty, lack of predictability, long latency periods, unknown causalities' and a general increase in the population's sense of insecurity. But even if one does not want to follow *Beck's* thesis – for example with reference to the fact that major risks were part of everyday life at all times in the course of history,[694] (war, epidemics or the extinction of civilizations for example in South America and East Asia through ecological collapse[695]) – there are further interpretative approaches that explain our predominantly negative connotations associated with risk. From the point of view of media science, society's handling of risks can mainly be explained by a media 'fear industry', which serves the population's desire for 'catastrophe consumption'.[696] However, the most convincing explanation seems to be that the volume of risk has not increased overall compared to past societies. Instead, the relative share of natural risks (e.g. epidemics) has decreased and the human-created share of civilizational risks (e.g. through technology) has increased. Risk awareness in industrial society has grown[697] precisely because of our modern-day options on combating risks. The anticipation and prediction of risks remained irrelevant only as long as the consequences of the risks could not be influenced or changed by targeted measures.[698] This ability has existed for us on a large scale only since the emergence of the modern industrial society. Regardless of which explanatory approach and which periodization one follows, it becomes clear that the negative understanding of risk represents a key category of modern society and modernization narratives. Our growing attention to risk is more than just a fad. Within the framework of crime control, there are two separate areas in which one can speak of risks: on the one hand, the imminent perpetration of a crime constitutes a social risk that must be combated. However, the technologies themselves used to combat crime

692 *Beck* 1986, 17.
693 *Beck* 1988, 120.
694 *Renn* 1991, 06:1, 06-3.
695 See also *Brunhöber*, in: Singelnstein/Puschke 2018, 193, 201.
696 See *König*, in: Münkler et al. 2010, 209.
697 *Banse* 1993, 8.
698 *Häfele et al.* 1990, 373, 375; *Grymer* 1989, 137; *Banse* 1993, 12.

risks can also have unforeseen negative consequences and thus risks such as being falsely identified as a 'threat' by an algorithm.

III. Unequal distribution of risks

Risks can be unequally distributed in society and, as Beck emphasizes, sometimes adhere to a class scheme, as does the distribution of wealth.[699] For example, majority decisions on the acceptance of risks can burden certain minority groups with excessive risks.[700] Sometimes it is only superficially a matter of minimising risks, while what is actually decided upon is the distribution of risks.[701] An unequal distribution also applies to risks in crime control.[702] For example, members of lower social strata are more often victims of violent crimes.[703] Finally, by applying certain crime control technologies, certain minority groups may be at greater risk of being falsely identified as posing a risk.

IV. Social assignment of meaning

Inherent to the concept of risk is always a reference to the future and a certain call to action:[704] it describes the possibility of a future evil, along which at the same time a normative duty to act, a behavioural imperative in the present is established.[705] As the French philosopher and sociologist Ewald notes in the opening quote, almost anything can be declared a risk.[706] The justification for naming something a risk is ultimately a narrative, a coherent story that explains how and why a person has to protect themselves in a specific situation.[707] A successful risk narrative is

699 *Beck* 1986, 46; particularly dangerous risk industries are outsourced to poor countries, *ibid.* 56.
700 *Banse* 1993, 9.
701 *Banse* 1993, 20.
702 Cf. *Kunz/Singelnstein* 2016, § 18 mn. 22 et seq., § 22 mn. 42 et seq.
703 *Kunz/Singelnstein* 2016, § 18 mn. 22.
704 *Kaufmann* 2012, 258.
705 *Dollinger* 2016, 57, 61, 63.
706 *Dollinger* 2016, 57 et seq.
707 *Dollinger* 2016, 58; see specifically for the analysis of 'coherent stories' in the context of location-based predictive policing *Egbert* European Journal for Security Studies 2018, 95.

often used to justify political action, particularly in the area of crime, but also in many other areas such as health or the environment.[708] Risk cannot be considered independently of safety and normality. Dollinger correctly states that there must be stories and conceptions of a 'risk-free or safe life in order to be able to distinguish and scandalize risks as special phenomena'.[709] This means that the quality of being risky is not invariably inscribed in a situation or person. Risk is not a descriptive term,[710] in the way that people can be objectively described as having blond hair or brown eyes. Rather, situations only constitute risks once meaning has been ascribed to them.[711] This process of ascribing meaning enables situations to be experienced *as* reality, as Ewald also states in the opening quotation when he notes that there is no risk *in* reality.[712] Those who define risks thus actively produce a new reality with a claim to the truth instead of merely describing an existing one (the performative effect of the risk concept).[713] 'Truth productions,' Foucault emphasizes, 'cannot be separated from power and power mechanisms, because on the one hand power mechanisms enable and induce the production of truths, and on the other hand the production of truth also has power in the form of a binding effect for us'.[714] Those who define risks thus exercise power over social reality.[715]

V. Quantification of risks: the lure of numbers

Some methods of ascribing risk appear to be neutral, objective and free from particular interests.[716] This includes probabilistic security research, which promises to control contingent futures with the means of formal rationality. Since the 1960s in particular,[717] the probability theory of stochastics, a subfield of mathematics, has been increasingly used to assess the

708 Cf. *Stone* Political Science Quarterly 1989, 281 281; see also *Jones et al.* 2014.
709 *Dollinger* 2016, 57 et seq.
710 *Dollinger* 2016, 57 et seq.
711 *Dollinger* 2016, 57.
712 *Dollinger* 2016, 57.
713 Cf. also *Singelnstein/Stolle* 2012, 199 ('Through the compilation of risk and danger prognoses it [the police] acquires a power of definition over social reality'); see also *Wächtler* 2007, 136
714 *Foucault* 2003, 521.
715 Cf. also *Creemers/Guagnin* KrimJ 2014, 134, 137; *Fuchs* 2002, 22-36.
716 *Simon* Law & Soc'y Rev. 1988, 771, 771 ff; *Dollinger* 2016, 63 et seq.
717 *King*, in: Münkler et al. 2010, 214.

risks posed to society by new technologies.[718] The availability of methods for quantification is centrally linked to the rise of the concept of risk. The quantifying approach was originally used in insurance.[719] It demonstrated that calculations gain precision with increase numbers of past cases for analysis, i.e., the more frequently an event has already occurred in the past (law of large numbers).[720] In contrast, the more rarely an event has occurred and the higher the damage to be expected, the more difficult it is to calculate. Rapoport describes the urge to quantify risks even under these difficult circumstances, as the 'lure of numbers'. 'The temptation to express all possible values numerically is tremendously strong [...]. The lure of numbers lies in the possibility of reaching consensus with quantitative estimates.'[721] But consensus, neutrality and reliability are not identical. The definition of risks always follows moral-normative premises.[722] The psychologist and risk researcher Gigerenzer warns fundamentally against false security in dealing with risks. He attests that people have an inherent need for security and risk control.[723] But the 'self-encouragement of modern societies'[724] to manage unmanageable risks through probability mathematics is, as he states, an illusion; absolute security is an illusion.[725] False certainties can lead to blind scientism[726] and cause great damage: 'They make us believe that our future is predictable as long as the right technology is available'.[727] Bansen even posits that 'faith in divine providence is replaced by faith in science and its supposed laws, by the myth of the predictability, calculability and controllability of all events'.[728]

VI. Risk perception

Besides the problem of the exact determinability of risks, there are also problems of subjective risk perception and risk understanding. People

718 See Münkler et al. 2010, 8.
719 *Banse* 1993, 62.
720 Cf. *Schurz* 2015, 19.
721 *Rapoport* Leviathan 1988, 123 132; *Banse* 1993, 65.
722 *Dollinger* 2016, 64; see also *König*, in: Münkler et al. 2010, 215.
723 *Gigerenzer* 2015, 41.
724 See Münkler et al. 2010, 8.
725 *Gigerenzer* 2015, 38.
726 *Gigerenzer* 2015, 43.
727 *Gigerenzer* 2015, 42.
728 *Banse* 1993, 13.

are poor at correctly assessing risks and interpreting risk statistics. In his research, Gigerenzer shows that people often have problems correctly understanding statistically abstract risks.[729] People behave 'neither logically nor consistently when practising risk avoidance'.[730] Risk perception is influenced by numerous irrational factors.[731] It is much more true that 'the risk that kills people and the risk that frightens them are completely different issues'.[732] Added to this is the problem of the communication of risks between technology and society: the concept of risk is emotionally charged in society, whereas in technology it is used computationally and mechanically.[733]

VII. Tolerable risks

There is no such thing as absolute security. The German BVerfG also expressly states (in connection with the construction of a nuclear power plant) that society as a whole must tolerate certain residual risks.[734] In road traffic, we tolerate high risks and have decided to make these risks manageable with an insurance approach, instead of avoiding them altogether. Road traffic victims are to be understood as the intrinsic price of a society interested in mobility. It can also be said that victims of crime are generally to be understood as the systemic price of a society interested in liberal, democratic and constitutional values that refrains from the comprehensive scoring and total surveillance of its citizens. The issue of the threshold at which risk should no longer be tolerated can also be formulated as the question: How safe is safe enough? Importantly, this question can only be answered by a value judgement and not a stochastic calculation.[735] The objectives and values contributing to such a decision are not fixed, but depend on the situation and time. The reason given for

729 *Gigerenzer* 2013, 14 et seq.; see also *Heilmann/Urquhart* 1983, 40; *Fritzsche* 1986, 28.
730 *Heilmann/Urquhart* 1983, 40; *Prittwitz* 1993, 69.
731 *König*, in: Münkler et al. 2010, 216; *Kahneman/Tversky* Cognitive Psychology 1972, 430.
732 *Peters* 1991, 11, 11; *Prittwitz* 1993, 68.
733 *Kuhlmann* 1989, 17.
734 BVerfGE 49, 89 (137 et seq.).
735 Cf. the permitted risk in criminal law dogmatics and other contexts, *Freund* 1987, 198.

the exact determination of the threshold of tolerated risk is often hard to objectively justify.[736]

Kunz emphasizes that a risk, unlike a danger, only arises in the perception as such. He also stresses that risk is socially constructed.[737] As such, it is important to highlight the performative effect of the risk prediction itself: it is only through the possibility of prediction that a risk comes into focus. 'As knowledge of causal chains of action increases, society has the tools and institutions to anticipate negative events and their consequences and to design and implement appropriate countermeasures. At the same time, the moral claim to take risk precautions in order to exclude or limit negative events is growing.'[738] The less a risk can be predicted, the less power there is to act and this results in higher risk tolerance in practice.

VIII. Risk vs. danger

The two terms risk and danger are defined similarly in the dictionary: danger is 'the possibility that damage will occur,' whereas risk is a 'possible negative outcome of an enterprise with which damage is associated'.[739] A study by the German Federal Institute for Risk Assessment has also shown that the distinction between the terms risk and danger does not play a role in social discourse and that the two terms are largely used synonymously.[740] Even in risk research – by Beck[741] among others – no importance is attached to the distinction.[742] Finally, no clear systematic dividing line between risk and danger can be derived from the legal terminology in crime control.

Evers suggests that risk should only be understood as 'a certain form of the practice of dealing with dangers […] namely those which, by means of action techniques, methods and institutions, attempts to make danger delimitable, calculable or attributable'.[743] Similarly, Hüfner describes risk

736 *Banse* 1993, 21.

737 *Kunz* 2011, 339; *Kunz/Singelnstein* 2016, 340 et seq.

738 *Renn* 1991, 06:1, 6 et seq.

739 *Scholze-Stubenrecht* 2015.

740 *Ulbig et al.* 2009, 54

741 *Prittwitz* 1993, 55 with further references; see *Beck* 1986, 49 ('The actors of modernization themselves get emphatically and very concretely into the whirlpools of dangers that they cause and from which they profit').

742 Cf. *Luhmann* 1991, 31 with further references.

743 *Evers* Kommune 1989, 33, 34.

as a kind of measurement of danger.[744] Beck draws a distinction based on the controllability of consequences: the consequences of a danger are not controllable, but the consequences of a risk are.[745] Luhmann makes a distinction based on the source of damage. He speaks of risk when future losses are regarded as the result of a human decision. He speaks of danger when damage is regarded as being caused externally and attributed to the environment.[746] Prittwitz points out that the term 'danger' has negative connotations throughout, whereas the term 'risk' has a negative, but also a positive element of opportunity.[747] A risk can be consciously taken in order to achieve special, hard-to-gain advantages. As already mentioned, Kunz emphasizes that a risk, unlike a danger, only arises through perception as such.[748] Finally, Höffler sees risk and danger as being in a temporal relationship: whoever is in danger is always exposed to a risk; whoever is confronted with a risk, however, is not necessarily in danger.[749]

This plurality of approaches need not cause concern because there is no uniform concept of risk. Different meanings are appropriate for different situations and different perspectives.[750] The approach used to define risk in this book in the context of crime prediction technologies follows the delineation proposed by Höffler, as it is particularly suitable to promoting the systematization of person-based predictive policing. A risk only becomes a danger when it is sufficiently substantiated and intensified. A probability value calculated by a predictive policing system, therefore, is only able to indicate a risk, but not the fact that a person poses an actual, concrete danger.

IX. Conclusion on risk

The key points on the risk concept are:
- A situation becomes a risk narratively through social attribution[751]
- Any risk assessment has a performative effect[752]

744 *Hüfner* 1989, 34.
745 *Beck* 1986, 188.
746 *Luhmann* 1991, 30 et seq.
747 *Prittwitz* 1993, 33, 269.
748 See above fn. 737.
749 *Höffler* MschrKrim 2012, 252, 254.
750 See also *Krüger* 1986, 299, 300 et seq.
751 See fn. 707 and accompanying text.
752 See fn. 713 and accompanying text.

- There are tolerated risks. Decisions as to when risks should no longer be tolerated are value judgements[753]
- Risk and danger are interrelated in a gradual relationship, whereby the term risk is broader than that of danger[754]

B. Status quo: risk-based crime control

The orientation of crime control in Germany towards risk prognoses has not only emerged as a result of the new possibilities associated with algorithmic predictions. Rather, it is a development that can be observed over the last 40 years. This development – 'risk focusing' in crime control[755] – has not only taken place in substantive criminal law, criminal procedural law and police law, but also has expanded in sanctions law. The focus on risk has permeated every area of crime control. This risk orientation is closely linked to a shift in crime control measures towards the run-up to the actual perpetration of a crime.[756] The feeling of increasing threat in the risk society is accompanied by demands to contain risks using crime control as early as possible in order to secure society as effectively as possible.[757] In the recent past, for example, new government powers in crime control and new criminal laws have often been justified with reference to the particularly urgent dangers associated with Islamist terrorism, and the common good of public security.[758] While the fight against Islamist terrorism is frequently given as the primary reason for new laws, in practice it is not uncommon for new laws to stretch well beyond mere terrorist offences. The moving of crime control interventions further and further away from actual offences thus affects crime control as a whole, not just the extreme area of terrorism. Singelnstein and Stolle have also pointed out that investigative measures in Germany that have been officially introduced to combat particularly serious crime often also apply to 'mild to moderate crime'.[759]

753 See p. 170.
754 Cf. p. 172.
755 Cf. 'Risk legislation' at *Eisenberg/Kölbel* 2017, 276.
756 Cf. *Puschke/ Singelnstein*, Vorwort, in: Singelnstein/Puschke 2018, XI.
757 *Sinn* 2011; Sinn et al. 2011, 20.
758 Cf. already *Jakobs* ZStW 1985, 751, 773 et seq.; *Pintaske*, in: Sinn et al. 2011, 305 with further references.
759 *Singelnstein/Stolle* 2012, 115.

As Germany is certainly a target of Islamist attacks, investigative measures prior to actual offences should not be rejected outright. Terrorism clearly poses an incomparably greater danger than crimes such as the theft of a handbag, and therefore more far-reaching interventions are justified in this case. However, risk orientation and the associated shifting of crime control prior to offences taking place are not justified *indiscriminately*. New legislative measures must be critically examined in each individual case, taking all circumstances into account. Prior intervention should only be used to protect 'important interests [...] that are so sensitive that even actions that only come close to a danger must be prevented by the sharp weapon of criminal law'.[760]

I. Examples of risk-oriented norms

§ 89a (2a) of the German Criminal Code (Strafgesetzbuch – StGB) on the preparation of a serious violent act endangering the state is one example of risk orientation in criminal law. The norm, introduced in 2009, makes it illegal for people to prepare to leave Germany to attend terrorist training camps.[761] Criminal liability – punishable by imprisonment of up to 10 years[762] – applies to a person travelling to a training camp (even before they have arrived) and even if they have yet to cross the German border. What the paragraph is effectively punishing is a risk, that someone who travels abroad might one day perpetrate a particularly serious offence.

§ 129a of the German Criminal Code provides a further example from criminal law: it bans the establishment of a terrorist organization.[763] It was introduced in 1976 and extended in 2003 and is also sanctioned with up to 10 years imprisonment. It, too, punishes a risk, namely that a member of a group might commit particularly serious crimes in the future.

As for criminal procedural law and investigative powers, there, too, has been an expansive trend in recent decades;[764] i.e. the number and intensity of powers of intervention have generally increased.[765] They have also particularly shifted towards a risk orientation. § 100b (2) no. 1a, b of

760 *Pintaske*, in: Sinn et al. 2011, 304.
761 See *Bäcker* 2015, 327; constitutionality confirmed in BGH 3 StR 243/13 sS; critical however, *Zöller* GA 2010, 607 607; *Bäcker* 2015, 377.
762 Cf. *Fischer* StGB, § 89a mn. 45.
763 See *Bäcker* 2015, 323 et seq.
764 See in detail on the Criminal Procedure Law *König* 1993.
765 *Eisenberg/Kölbel* 2017, 276.

the German Criminal Procedural Code, permits a secret, digital search of a person's communication devices if certain facts give rise to the suspicion – i.e. if there is a certain risk – that a person will undertake to leave for a terrorist training camp or become a member of a terrorist organization. This norm allows the police to take preventive action at a much earlier point in time than would be possible without the criminalization of behaviour preceding the occurrence of actual damage.

Further, German sanctions law also has a risk orientation. In contrast to substantive criminal law and criminal procedural law, however, this is nothing novel: sanctions law has had a long-standing need for recidivism prognosis. However, legislative efforts are also being made in sanctions law to further extend its orientation towards risk. An example of this is preventive detention, which was first introduced in 1933 in §§ 66 et seq. of the German Criminal Code. Since 1998, however, there have been continuous extensions inter alia to the maximum time limit for preventive detention,[766] and when it can be ordered by a judge. Most recently, in 2017, §§ 89a and 129a of the German Criminal Code were inserted into § 66 (3) of the German Criminal Code as new offences that may result in preventive detention.[767]

As in criminal procedural law, the number and intensity of powers of intervention in police law has increased in recent decades,[768] and has turned towards averting risks as early as possible. One example of police intervention taken in the run-up to actual damage is the video surveillance permitted by § 15a of the Police Law of the German Federal State of North Rhine-Westphalia PolG NRW. Its purpose is to enable immediate police intervention in places where there is a general risk of future crimes being committed.

This demonstrates that an increasing focus on risks in the run-up to actual damage or danger can be observed in all areas of crime control.

II. Security society

With their concept of the 'security society', Singelnstein and Stolle provide an analytical framework to describe the risk orientation as well as the

766 SexualdelBekG (BGBl. 1998 I, 160), § 67d Para. 2 StGB.
767 53. StÄG (BGBl. I 2017, 1612).
768 *Eisenberg/Kölbel* 2017, 276, *Bäcker* 2015, 192 et seq.

increased focus on economic efficiency in crime control.[769] In addition, the concept shines light on the fact that fear of crime is increasingly becoming a key governing instrument in modern-day societies.[770] It is often by conjuring up images of offenders as outcasts and 'enemies of society'[771] that governments reach consensus on the expansion of crime control measures.[772] In the security society, the pursuit of comprehensive security is the highest value that displaces all other objectives in politics and law.[773] Not only is it accepted in the security society that 'risky individuals' may be excluded from the rule of law, but even every law-abiding citizen is expected to tolerate an invasion of their rights for the greater good of crime control,[774] for example by being expected to tolerate surveillance measures.

Common features of Singelnstein and Stolle's security society and Beck's risk society, described above, emerge to the extent that both are based on the seemingly oppositional pair of risk and security. The need for security as the highest good in a security society can be understood as a response to the fear of increasing risks in the risk society. However, the risk society addresses risks more generally – including in the areas of environmental protection and health – and takes a more descriptive perspective. Singelnstein and Stolle, on the other hand, focus *their* modelling of the security society specifically on crime control. They shed light on how risk narratives can be misused by the state for particular interests. In contrast to Beck,[775] Singelnstein and Stolle see the core difference between present and past societies not in the fact that there are *more* risks today; rather, the risks are the *same* but we *react* differently to them. We are forecasting more risks today than in the past, not primarily because our society has a greater need for security, but because we *can* forecast risks with increasing skill. And because we can predict these risks (or at least we *think* we can), society demands it – which then increases our need for security (the security paradox).[776] Fritzsche also notes in this context that 'the analysis of numerous conceivable horror scenarios makes laypersons aware of them in the first

769 *Singelnstein/Stolle* 2012.
770 *Singelnstein/Stolle* 2012, 143.
771 As opposed to e.g. images of offenders as fellow citizens who have lost their way and need to be supported to return to a lawful life.
772 See *Singelnstein/Stolle* 2012, 115.
773 *Singelnstein/Stolle* 2012, 121 et seq.
774 *Singelnstein/Stolle* 2012, 113, 115.
775 See fn. 690 and accompanying text.
776 *Singelnstein/Stolle* 2012, 25 et seq., 42; *Prittwitz* 1993, 56, *Brunhöber*, in: Zedner 2009, 146; *Banse* 1993, 3 with further references.

place. Because of our inability to grasp small probabilities realistically we do not succeed in erasing these extremely improbable scenarios from our mind again. In this regard, risk analysis seems to have opened a Pandora's box.'[777] Lübbe also assumes that the 'demand for security [...] grows with the level of technical and social security attained'.[778]

Another feature of the security society is the collection of more and more data about more and more people. It becomes increasingly impossible to keep track of which data are stored by which government agency. Singelnstein speaks of a 'criminalization through data collection' in view of the consequences that storage, for example in a police file, can have.[779]

III. The actuarial turn

Another analytical framework for crime control's risk focus is provided by the 'actuarial turn'. It was developed in the US, but mirrors developments found globally, including in Germany. US criminologists Feeley and Simon have been observing what they call 'actuarial justice' in the US criminal justice system, especially in sanctions law, since the 1980s.[780] The term stands for the phenomenon that 'risky persons' are identified on the basis of group risk characteristics and mathematical-statistical calculations and subsequently sorted according to their risk profile for different treatment.[781] The approach of basing the assessment of an individual in crime control on statistical data about a group of people with similar characteristics is by no means self-evident or self-explanatory, but represents a conscious value judgement that accepts a certain degree of generalization in crime control.

An example of the actuarial turn is the use of statistical forecasting instruments mentioned above, such as VRAG, in recidivism decisions in sanctions law.[782] Furthermore, the mentality associated with the actuarial turn, i.e. the anticipated attribution of possible damage, is also spreading

777 *Fritzsche* 1986, 28, 135; *Prittwitz* 1993, 72.

778 *Lübbe* 1989, 22.

779 *Singelnstein* ZStW 2008, 854, 857; cf. on 'social control' through data collection in the USA, *Kohler-Hausmann* 2018.

780 *Feeley/Simon* Criminology 1992, 449, 450 ff; *Simon/Feeley* 1994; cf. *Reichman* Research in Law, Deviance and Social Control 1986, 151; *Cohen* 1985.

781 *Eisenberg/Kölbel* 2017, 457; see also *Simmons* U.C. Davis L. Rev. 2018, 1067, 1097.

782 See above p. 38 et seq.

in other areas such as crime prevention: measures for the situational prevention of crime risks, i.e. the elimination of objective opportunities to commit crimes, including through technical precautions, have long become an integral part of everyday life.[783] This includes, for example, video surveillance of public places where statistical analyses identify high crime rates. Further application examples of mathematical-statistical methods and their algorithm-supported further development can also be found in the detection of crimes already committed, such as in the area of tax crime or corruption.[784] As mentioned above, Germany intends to uncover corruption in the future with the help of artificial intelligence, and artificial intelligence is already being used today to search for certain forms of tax evasion.[785] All this ultimately reveals an increasingly all-encompassing recording of criminal behaviour and the way society deals with it through the mathematical turn. The constant concern about not having made optimal decisions from a risk point of view means that consequences that are ever more distant in the future and ever more uncertain are considered in the calculation of risk.[786]

The calculation of risk in the actuarial turn is no longer about identifying the underlying causes of a person's crime (within a person's inner life or social environment) and then tackling these causes.[787] Instead, it is a matter of 'managing'[788] crime as cost-effectively as possible,[789] virtually from a bird's eye view. The focus is on the phenomenon of crime as a whole instead of the individual motives that a person may have for a crime.[790] It is less a question of the individual's moral responsibility than of reducing risk for society as a whole. This becomes clear when, in the criminal justice system, an individual is no longer assessed on the basis of their personal biography, but solely on the basis of their membership of high-risk groups.[791] An external personality construction occurs through

783 *Kunz* NK 2005, 151, 152; *Peters* 2007, 49.

784 Cf. for the USA with further examples also *Harcourt* 2007, 9 et seq.

785 See fn. 17, 18 and accompanying text.

786 *Kunz* NK 2005, 151, 153.

787 See *Reichman* Research in Law, Deviance and Social Control 1986, 151, 164.

788 *Feeley/Simon* Criminology 1992, 449, 452.

789 *Simon* Law & Soc'y Rev. 1988, 771, 772.

790 *Simon* Law & Soc'y Rev. 1988, 771, 792.

791 Cf. *Wischmeyer* AöR 2018, 1, 29 f; *Van Wel/Royakkers* Ethics and Information Technology 2004, 129 133; cf. in also *Britz* 2008.

the attribution of group characteristics.[792] Accordingly, individuals are held jointly responsible, quasi in preventive 'clan imprisonment', for the misconduct of people with similar traits.

Simon sees a critical side effect of the actuarial turn in the fact that the exercise of penal power with the help of statistics causes less controversy, works less conspicuously and is viewed as objective.[793] The way in which statistical procedures divide people into different 'classes' would actually be perceived as offensive in society and in the legal system. Statistical methods, however, have the 'ideological power' to defuse or completely conceal the moral value judgement that lies in classification.[794] Actuarial justice thus leads to a superficial scientification of criminal policy. It is critical to note that the idea of a strictly rational, mathematical determination of crime risks is, however, not very realistic.[795] It neglects the fact that the definition of risks is ultimately guided by interests. As already described above,[796] it avoids the question of which risks to focus on and ignores the fact that the decision as to when a risk is no longer tolerable is a value judgement.

IV. Summary of status quo

The two interpretative approaches presented above shed light on different, but partly overlapping aspects of risk orientation in crime control. The key components in both frameworks are summarized in the following.

The security society is characterized among other things by:

1. security as a target variable in crime control trumps all other values such as freedom or equality[797]
2. the expansion of crime control measures is justified by narratives of fear and imagery of the criminals as 'enemies of society'[798]
3. demands for special sacrifices from the whole population, e.g. tolerating surveillance, in order to achieve security

---

792 See *Fröhlich/Spiecker* Verfassungsblog of 26.12.2018, accessible at https://perma.cc/9GVX-X564, last accessed 1.1.2022.
793 *Simon* Law & Soc'y Rev. 1988, 771, 792.
794 *Simon* Law & Soc'y Rev. 1988, 771, 794.
795 See *Kunz* NK 2005, 151, 154.
796 See above p. 167 et seq.
797 See fn. 769 above and accompanying text.
798 See fn. 708 above and accompanying text.

4. the possibility of predicting more and more risks increases society's desire for more security (security paradox)[799]

The actuarial turn is characterized among other things by:

1. attributing risk not only to abstract events or places, but also to individuals[800]
2. allocating risk not after a comprehensive individual analysis of a person's biography and circumstances, but by sorting people into risk categories on the basis of group risk characteristics[801]
3. 'managing' without attempting to 'change' deviant behaviour
4. the 'objectivity' of mathematical prognosis methods makes political decisions appear less controversial[802]

The following section describes how these characteristics are not only updated through the use of automated, algorithmic crime prediction, but also how qualitatively they reach a new dimension through a shift to the 'algorithmic turn'.

C. Development: algorithmic crime control and the algorithmic turn

How does person-based predictive policing fit in with the observations just made with regard to the security society and the actuarial turn? First, predictive algorithms may seem like 'islands' of security and certainty among a flood of risks. The promise of mastering modern-day uncertainties, taming them and countering risks at the earliest possible stage is incredibly tempting. Person-based predictive policing thus follows from a development line of risk-oriented crime control that existed before the introduction of algorithms (I). But person-based predictive policing goes further: it introduces new values, ways of thinking and action into crime control that radically change policing and the criminal justice system as a whole. In this sense, the advent of person-based predictive policing constitutes a new 'algorithmic turn' in crime control (II).

799 See fn. 776 above and accompanying text.
800 See fn. 781 above and accompanying text.
801 *Ibid.*
802 See fn. 793 above and accompanying text.

I. Continuation of risk-based crime control

It seems *prima facie* obvious that person-based predictive policing represents a continuation and consolidation of existing risk tendencies. This is true particularly with regard to (1) the focus on the run-up to a crime, (2) the individualized ascription of risk, (3) the promotion of an 'enemy' perspective on offenders and (4) the concealment of political value judgements.

1. Focus on risk well in advance of actual harm

The focus on risk well in advance of actual harm is a phenomenon that existed prior to the arrival of algorithms. However, it is now being solidified by the use of person-based predictive policing through the calculation of probabilities of the future perpetration of crimes and the classification of people into risk categories. Person-based predictive policing acts – as already described above[803] – like a sieve. It 'sieves out' from a mass of people the most dangerous individuals and brings them to the attention of the police. Person-based predictive policing thus intervenes at an early point in the run-up to a crime, a time that was previously inaccessible to traditional police work. Person-based predictive policing theoretically and technically allows risk to be ascribed at a point in time when police officers have no indications of a danger. Algorithms recognize deviations from the norm (the average citizen) by comparing individuals to large amounts of data from past offenders.

2. Individualized risk ascription on the basis of group characteristics

Person-based predictive policing continues the premise of the 'actuarial turn': reducing people to risks and probabilities. In person-based predictive policing, people are either assigned a numerical value to describe the risk of them committing crimes in the future, or are divided into risk categories (high, medium, low).[804] In this approach, general statistical observations about large groups of people are transferred to the individual level. As is typical for the actuarial turn, risk analyses are not based on

803 See above p. 33.
804 See above p. 31.

comprehensive examinations of individual cases, but instead on group characteristics.[805]

3. Enemy perspective

Labelling individuals as having a high probability of committing a crime has the potential to encourage an 'enemy' and 'outcast' perspective (common already to the security society).[806] In particular, person-based predictive policing – such as the Chicago Strategic Subject List[807] – that uses a proportional scale for risk assessment (i.e. it expresses a person's risk by their deviation from the average population) supports the perception of high-risk individuals as 'other' and thus facilitates exclusion. In the Strategic Subject List, a risk score of 500 means that a person has 500 times the risk of committing a crime than the average population.[808] At first glance, this score may seem shockingly high and may prompt police officers to jump to conclusions about the 'abnormal' personality that hides behind such a score. However, people's specific circumstances are ignored when they are reduced to a number. Moreover, in the case of particularly serious and thus *rare* crimes, a 500-fold deviation from the average population may ultimately only correspond to a low single digit probability of committing a crime.[809] The fact that these low percentage probabilities are not explained, and instead are only presented as proportional deviations from the norm, is not without alternatives; rather, it is the result of a conscious value judgement. The consequences of this decision include promoting an image of people classed as at a high risk of committing a crime as 'abnormal'. This ultimately makes it easier to, in good conscience, curtail their protection under the rule of law.

4. Disguising political value judgements

The concealment of political value judgements by framing risk assessments as supposedly objective and alternativeless mathematical methods – em-

805 Cf. Tbl. 2, Tbl. 3 (p. 63, 70) (data input column).
806 See fn. 772 and accompanying text.
807 See above p. 66 et seq.
808 See above p. 66.
809 See above fn. 227 and accompanying text.

phasized by Simon in the 'actuarial turn'[810] – is also inherent in person-based predictive policing. Such disguising is even more true for algorithms than for traditional statistical modes of prediction, as the processes within a predictive policing system are particularly non-transparent for outsiders, as demonstrated above.[811]

The concealment lies in the fact that person-based predictive policing is based on certain assumptions that are political in nature, but which are not disclosed and discussed as such. Political debate is limited to (at best) the question of whether person-based predictive policing, which is presented as neutral and objective, should be used at all. The discussion does not often touch on the many value judgements which are an inherent part of the design of a person-based predictive policing system. Such value judgements include, for example, the question of whether it should be possible to apply statistical findings about groups to individuals. And, if so, whether interventions into their fundamental rights should be permitted; i.e., the question of whether an individual should have to suffer negative consequences because of their belonging to a group of people of which a large number have committed crimes in the past. Other value judgements that are rarely disclosed include acceptable levels of false-positives (the number of individuals wrongly classified as highly dangerous), and the threshold that should be used to classify someone as 'high risk'. The decisions as to whether a risk should be conveyed as a proportion or a percentage also constitutes a value judgement; and this also applies to the selection of training data.[812] Finally, the handling of statistical discrimination is also of a political nature, i.e. the different treatment of, for example, minority groups in person-based predictive policing, as has been shown, for example, in the COMPAS algorithm in the US. These are highly political issues that politicians along the ideological spectrum are likely to answer in very different ways. Public debate on these issues, however, threatens to be stifled by pointing to the seemingly objective calculations used by person-based predictive policing systems. An 'algorithmization' of crime control could thus be detrimental to public debate on crime policy in general.

810 See above fn. 793.
811 See above 124 et seq.
812 See above p. 87 et seq.

5. Summary of risk-based crime control

Closer analysis has confirmed the *prima facie* impression that person-based predictive policing continues existing development lines in crime control. The next step, however, is to examine the extent to which person-based predictive policing also poses new challenges.

II. New challenges associated with the algorithmic turn

The new challenges associated with the algorithmic turn are permeating through crime control at various levels. (1) On the one hand, they are manifested on the level of the social perception of policing, where they can lead to a loss of legitimacy. (2) At the institutional level, criminology is relinquishing its relevance to computer sciences. (3) Further, the outsourcing of responsibility to algorithms threatens to lead crime control into 'self-imposed thoughtlessness' and 'self-imposed nonage'. (4) Finally, law may even be completely subjugated to the internal logic of computer science.

1. Loss of legitimacy due to lack of procedural justice

From a societal perspective, the introduction of person-based predictive policing can affect citizens' perception of the work conducted by the state and the state as a whole. The considerations that need to be taken into account when introducing a new method of crime control should not be limited to increasing efficiency and respecting legal limits. Another important point that has been neglected in the discussion so far[813] is the question of the extent to which new technologies influence citizens' attitudes towards the legitimacy of the police. In the case of person-based predictive policing, it is particularly important to examine whether a lack of 'procedural justice' could lead to a loss of legitimacy.

---

813 See, however, mention at *Wischmeyer* 2020, mn. 61; on loss of trust, *Mittelstadt et al.* Big Data & Society 2016, 1, 7 with further references.

a) Legitimacy and legal compliance

Whether the public considers police actions to be legitimate, i.e. whether the police have the right to call on the public to comply with laws and support crime control through their cooperation,[814] is not only of academic interest, but directly relevant to police practice. The police force is one of the central pillars of the state and citizens' attitudes towards it have an impact on the perception of the rule of the state as a whole.[815] Empirical studies show that perceptions of legitimacy generally correlate positively with legal compliance. Legitimacy thereby acts in a crime-preventive manner.[816] The idea that the legitimacy of an institution has a crucial impact on compliance with standards and voluntary cooperation can already be found in Weber's work:[817] law as a controlling element of society can only fulfil its function if it can count on acceptance and compliance. However, the fact that the majority of society follows laws cannot be explained by the deterrent effect of punishment alone.[818] Rather it is largely based on the fact that state authority is perceived as legitimate.[819] In addition, the police depend not only on compliance with legal norms, but also on the cooperation of the population in the prevention and investigation of criminal offences. This willingness to cooperate also correlates with recognition that the state's authority is legitimate.[820]

b) Basic concept of procedural justice

The circumstances that contribute to the legitimacy of police and judicial decision-making have been examined by empirically grounded social

---

814 See *Tyler* The Annals of the American Academy of Political and Social Science 2004, 84, 86 et seq. definition.

815 *Tyler* 1990; *Tyler/Huo* 2002, 326 ff; *Hough et al.* 2013, 326, 326 et seq.

816 *Tyler* 1990, 8-15.

817 *Weber* 1972, 16.

818 Although the general preventive effect of punishment has been proven in studies, the extent of the effect is small and is not sufficient to explain the high degree of compliance with the law in society, see *Tyler* The Annals of the American Academy of Political and Social Science 2004, 84, 86 with further references.

819 See *Tyler* The Annals of the American Academy of Political and Social Science 2004, 84, 85 et seq. with further references.

820 See *Tyler* The Annals of the American Academy of Political and Social Science 2004, 84, 85 with further references.

psychologists under the headings of procedural justice and procedural fairness. In the 1990s, Tyler, in his seminal book *Why People Obey the Law*, was one of the first to look at people's attitudes to the police from this point of view. He thus paved the way for procedural justice research in criminological debates. His research has subsequently been confirmed inter alia in studies by Groll,[821] Hecker and Starcke[822] as well as Staubli.[823]

The notion of procedural justice is based on the assumption that the reason why people describe an action as legitimate not only depends – as previously assumed – on a beneficial outcome for themselves or on the overall effectiveness of police action (outcome fairness);[824] rather, it is centrally influenced by whether the *procedure* that has led to an outcome is perceived as 'just'. Empirical research on procedural justice has shown that the procedure as such represents a decisive component in the acceptance of a result. It may even be more important for people *how* they are treated in a procedure than *what* outcome they are subject to.[825] *Tyler* showed in empirical studies that the perception of procedural justice in interactions with the police has great influence on people's satisfaction with the outcome.[826] This influence exists regardless of whether an achieved outcome is beneficial or detrimental for a person. Further, the importance of procedural justice is not limited to people who interact directly with the police. The majority of the population rarely has contact with the police. However, studies have shown that people's general notions of procedural treatment of citizens by the police have an impact on the perception of the police as legitimate, regardless of whether a person has had personal contact with the police.[827] In the case of the police, it is therefore not only a question of achieving the best possible result in terms of maximum effectiveness (outcome fairness) in fulfilling its task of averting danger and investigating criminal offences. A core question should also be *how* the police achieve their goals and how this is perceived by the population (procedural fairness). The four core elements of procedural justice are

821 *Groll* 2002, 75.
822 *Hecker/Starcke* Soziale Probleme 2017, 223 223 et seq.
823 *Staubli* Soziale Probleme 2016, 49.
824 *Bussmann* 1996, 98; *Luhmann* 1983.
825 *Lind/Tyler* 1988; see also *Groll* 2002, 75, 87.
826 *Tyler* 1990, 57 et seq.
827 *Tyler* Behavioral Sciences & the Law 2001, 215, 215 ff; *Tyler* The Annals of the American Academy of Political and Social Science 2004, 84, 95 with further references.

participation, neutrality, respectful treatment and trust in the motives of decision-makers.[828]

c) Procedural justice in algorithmic decision-making

While in Germany the population's perception of the legitimacy of the police is high on average,[829] it is markedly lower among immigrants and their direct descendants.[830] A reduction of procedural justice due to the use of algorithms could lead to a further deterioration of perceptions of legitimacy that would affect the general population as well as minority groups.

aa) Participation

A first important factor in procedural justice is participation.[831] This refers to both participation in shaping the rules that are applied to a person in a decision-making process and participation in a decision-making process itself, for example the extent to which a person is given the opportunity to present their view of a dispute and to be heard. The possibility of participation is of great importance in assessing the legitimacy of a procedure, even if people are aware that their own participation cannot alter the outcome of a decision.[832]

In algorithmic risk assessments, however, participation is practically impossible – with regard to the rules that are written into a predictive

---

828 *Tyler* Int. J. Psychol. 2000, 117, 121 et seq.; see also *Tyler/Sevier* Alb. L. Rev. 2013, 1095, 1105; *Tyler* The Annals of the American Academy of Political and Social Science 2004, 84, 94 f; *Blader/Tyler* Personality and Social Psychology Bulletin 2003, 747; *Tyler/Lind* Advances in Experimental Social Psychology 1992, 115, 153 et seq.

829 The confidence of Germans in the police is higher than in other institutions surveyed (political parties, judiciary, military, administration, regional authorities, national government, national parliament, EU, UN), *Europäische Kommission* 2018, T38; cf. similar results for the year 2010 at *Reuband* Soziale Probleme 2012, 5, 5 et seq.; cf. also *Schwind* 2018.

830 *Behr/Oberwittler* Soziale Probleme 2011, 115 with further references.

831 *Tyler et al.* J. Pers. Soc. Psychol. 1985, 72, 79; *Simmons* U.C. Davis L. Rev. 2018, 1067, 1081.

832 *Tyler et al.* J. Pers. Soc. Psychol. 1985, 72, 79; *Simmons* U.C. Davis L. Rev. 2018, 1067, 1081.

policing system, as well as the generation of a specific risk score. An algorithmic system cannot listen to an affected person and adapt its decision according to what it has heard. An algorithmic system cannot make an overall assessment of a situation and consider all of the circumstances and arguments on a case-by-case basis.[833] An algorithm makes its decision solely on the basis of the data points entered into it, without allowing a person to explain the occurrence of those points. Admittedly, an affected person can explain to the police officers who carry out a measure based on predictive policing their own point of view as to why they do not pose a risk. But this communication with the police officer can no longer change the risk assessment of the algorithm itself. It may thus well be that people will view the algorithm as the actual decision-maker and not the police. But such an algorithmic decision-maker is – as explained – unable to engage with an affected individual and thereby unable to facilitate participation.

bb) Neutrality

The next central point of procedural justice is the neutrality of the police. This involves the question of whether decision-makers follow and apply rules impartially and make decisions objectively and based on fact.[834] On the one hand, the advantages of algorithms with regard to this point must be emphasized. Unlike humans, algorithms constantly make the same decisions given the same factual basis, whereas human decisions can be influenced by fluctuating emotions and the particular shape they are in on any particular day.[835] On the other hand, however, there is the danger – as described in detail in Chapter I[836] and Chapter II[837] that human prejudices – which the use of algorithms was actually intended to displace – are unintentionally permanently inscribed into the code of a predictive policing system. An example is the racially uneven error rate of the COMPAS algorithm in the assessment of African Americans described above.[838] In view of this consolidation of human prejudices against certain groups of people

833 See on the lack of overall assessment already pp. 84 et seq.
834 *Tyler* Int. J. Psychol. 2000, 117, 122.
835 See also *Simmons* U.C. Davis L. Rev. 2018, 1067, 1081; *Lee* Big Data & Society 2018, 1, 4; also above fn. 448 and accompanying text.
836 See at 113 et seq.
837 See at 87 et seq.
838 See discussion in fn. 741 and accompanying text.

in predictive policing systems, it is questionable whether algorithms are actually perceived by the population as more neutral than humans, or whether they appear less neutral. A representative survey conducted by the Bertelsmann Stiftung in 2018 confirmed the German population's scepticism about the general neutrality of algorithms. Only 6 per cent of respondents agreed with the statement, 'I think it's better when algorithms judge me instead of people. They make fact-based decisions that are the same for everyone.'[839]

cc) Respectful treatment

Another element of procedural justice is whether a person is treated politely and respectfully during contact with the police, with respect for their dignity, i.e. whether they are recognized as human beings and members of society.[840] At first glance, this point may seem to differ little from traditional policing in the use of predictive policing. Police officers, regardless of whether they have become aware of a person through an algorithm or traditional policing, can decide to take a respectful approach with every individual they encounter.[841] However, as discussed[842] in Chapter II, there is a danger that by integrating an algorithm into policing, a person may be reduced to a collection of numbers and probabilities and treated as a mere object of state security rather than as a human being.[843] In contrast to Chapter II, in which compatibility with the guarantee of human dignity was discussed from a constitutional point of view, the issue here is whether the population *subjectively perceives* objectification as taking place. It is possible that people feel affected in their dignity when they learn that it is not other people but 'machines' that have actually made the decisions that have led to police action against them.[844] A study by Lee on the use of algorithms in the selection of job applicants showed that participants perceived the evaluation of people by algorithms to be 'humi-

---

839 *Fischer/Petersen* 2018, 25.
840 *Tyler* Int. J. Psychol. 2000, 117, 122.
841 *Simmons* U.C. Davis L. Rev. 2018, 1067, 1081.
842 See on the compatibility of person-based predictive policing with the human dignity core of the right to informational self-determination from a constitutional point of view above pp. 153 et seq.
843 *Simmons* U.C. Davis L. Rev. 2018, 1067, 1081.
844 *Simmons* U.C. Davis L. Rev. 2018, 1067, 1081.

liating' and 'dehumanizing'.[845] A 2017 survey of more than 1,000 technology experts, scientists, practitioners and government officials also found that dehumanizing the decision-making process is a major concern over the introduction of algorithmic decision-making systems.[846] In particular, there is concern that people are understood merely as statistical 'input' to an algorithmic process, and not as 'thinking, feeling, changing beings'.[847]

dd) Trust in the motives

Trust in decision-makers' motives and intentions is another key aspect of procedural justice. Trust depends, inter alia, on the ability of a decision-maker to explain their decision well[848] and on whether a statement enables people to predict how a public institution will decide in the future.[849] The extent to which the population trusts decisions that are based on algorithms thus depends on the extent to which considerations of the algorithms can be communicated in a generally comprehensible way.[850] Trust is thus ultimately influenced by the transparency of an algorithm-based decision-making system. In a general study on algorithm-based decision-making systems outside crime control, Lee has shown that algorithms are more trusted than people when they only make decisions within the framework of mechanical activities.[851] However, if they have to make weighing and evaluation decisions about people (as is the case with predictive policing), they are less trusted.[852] Dietvorst et al. have further shown that as a result of errors of an algorithmic system, people lose confidence in the future decisions of the system more quickly than they do in human future decisions after comparable human errors.[853]

---

845 *Lee* Big Data & Society 2018, 1, 12 ('Some thought it was demeaning and dehumanizing to use machines to judge a person').
846 *Rainie et al.* Pew Research Center 2017, 42 f; *Simmons* U.C. Davis L. Rev. 2018, 1067, 1094.
847 *Rainie et al.* Pew Research Center 2017, 42.
848 *Tyler/Lind* Advances in Experimental Social Psychology 1992, 115, 155.
849 *Tyler/Lind* Advances in Experimental Social Psychology 1992, 115, 155; so too *Skogan* Police Quarterly 2005, 298, 314, *Lee* Big Data & Society 2018, 1, 4.
850 *Simmons* U.C. Davis L. Rev. 2018, 1067, 1084.
851 *Lee* Big Data & Society 2018, 1, 9 et seq.
852 *Lee* Big Data & Society 2018, 1, 9 et seq.
853 *Dietvorst et al.* J. Exp. Psychol. Gen. 2015, 114, 114 et seq.

d) Transparency as a response to a lack of procedural justice

Given how predictive algorithms are currently designed and applied, they are likely to reduce the level of procedural justice and thus the legitimacy of the police as a government institution. They offer hardly any space for participation, threaten to be perceived as lacking neutrality, are not an expression of a respectful way of dealing with people and, without explanations of the algorithmic processes, are unlikely to inspire trust. Simmons assumes that the public's attitude towards algorithms will become all the more critical the more algorithmic decision-making systems spread in crime control, the more mistakes they make, and the more these mistakes are addressed in the media.[854] This development is already empirically evident in the first studies conducted in the US, including those by Wang and Lee.[855] Walkman and Martin[856] have also shown that attitudes on legitimacy depend on the type of data that are used in algorithmic decision-making systems: an algorithm that uses data collected specifically for predictive purposes was considered more legitimate than the use of aggregated data from various other sources.[857]

How can a loss of procedural justice and thus a loss of legitimacy be counteracted in this context? In part, negative attitudes on issues of procedural justice are likely to depend on the availability of information, for example about the existence of algorithm-based decision-making systems and the discriminatory effect of algorithm-based procedures. A survey conducted by the Bertelsmann Foundation in 2018 revealed that in Germany many citizens were still unaware that algorithms are used in many areas of life.[858] This fact should not be understood as an incentive to deliberately conceal the existence and processes of algorithmic systems and to inform the population as little as possible. Such an approach is not permitted

---

854 *Simmons* U.C. Davis L. Rev. 2018, 1067, 1081.

855 *Wang* SSRN 2018, 4, 7 ('Respondents strongly disapprove of algorithms as a matter of fairness, a preference of policy, and a source of legitimacy'), see also *Lee* Big Data & Society 2018, 1, 8; pointing in a different direction, however, the study results at *Simmons* U.C. Davis L. Rev. 2018, 1067, 1106.

856 *Waldman/Martin* (Im-)Perfect Enforcement Conference des Yale Information Society Projects v. 6.4.2019 (unpublished manuscript at author) 2019.

857 *Waldman/Martin* (Im-)Perfect Enforcement Conference des Yale Information Society Projects v. 6.4.2019 (unpublished manuscript at author) 2019, 10.

858 *Fischer/Petersen* 2018, 13 et seq., see also *Harcourt* 2007, 3.

by the law.[859] Instead, the requirements of procedural fairness must be met by system adaptation. This means, in particular, that the decisions of an algorithm-based system must be explained and justified to those affected.[860] Explaining algorithmic processes can help people feel respected instead of objectified and to build trust in the police. Instead of simply referring to the fact that an algorithm has calculated a high risk for a person concerned, the details of the algorithmic decision-making process must be provided.[861] Algorithms must be transparent for outsiders. The police must be able to explain the processes of an algorithm to the people affected and in a way that they understand. Thus, it is not only the constitution that may impose transparency obligations on predictive policing,[862] but such an obligation may also arise with regard to the consideration of procedural justice.[863]

While, as mentioned, people are also 'organic black boxes' whose brains cannot fully be understood,[864] Simmons rightly notes[865] that humans have the ability to make assumptions about other people's states of consciousness and draw conclusions about their intentions.[866] This ability, described in psychology and cognitive sciences as the 'theory of mind', means that in the vast majority of cases people can, or believe they can, understand the decisions of police officers.[867] In contrast, there is no 'theory of mind' for algorithms as people cannot intuitively understand them. In order to create the feeling of comprehensibility in this situation, which is important for respect and trust, the algorithm's underlying processes must be explained clearly.

Finally, in a study on the use of predictive recidivism algorithms during sentencing, Wang shows that people prefer transparent algorithms whose inner workings are made accessible to the public. Non-transparent algorithms are rejected more frequently, even when participants are told a transparent algorithm would cost $3 million more than a non-transparent

859 See obligation to notify about the use of algorithm-based decision-making systems, p. 139.
860 See on the duty to state reasons from a legal point of view p. 142 et seq.
861 *Simmons* U.C. Davis L. Rev. 2018, 1067, 1081, 1087 et seq.
862 See above p. 120 et seq.
863 *Simmons* U.C. Davis L. Rev. 2018, 1067, 1081.
864 See already above p. 147.
865 *Simmons* U.C. Davis L. Rev. 2018, 1067, 1085.
866 See *Premack/Woodruff* Behavioral and Brain Sciences 1978.
867 *Simmons* U.C. Davis L. Rev. 2018, 1067, 1085.

one.[868] In a survey conducted in Germany in 2017 on the use of algorithms in the private sector, the majority of respondents also supported the disclosure of algorithm data by manufacturers. If there is no disclosure, respondents are more likely to perceive automated decisions as a threat.[869] This empirical finding also fits in with the demand for transparency developed in the preceding chapters.

e) Summary on legitimacy and procedural justice

Even though average levels of trust in the police is currently high in Germany compared to the US,[870] the loss of police legitimacy in the US is generally regarded by many as a harbinger of a development that will sooner or later take place in other western industrial nations.[871] This loss of legitimacy could be triggered by the use of new police technologies such as predictive policing. The introduction of predictive policing systems without regard for perceived procedural justice threatens to run counter to the objective of predictive policing systems, i.e. creating more security. The effectiveness of policing must not remain the only factor that guides the introduction of person-based predictive policing. Procedural justice and legitimacy as variables directly linked to the willingness to comply with the law must not be neglected in the introduction of person-based predictive policing.[872]

2. Crime control without criminology

The introduction of predictive policing systems does not only have an impact on the population's perception of policing, but also on which scientific disciplines that decision-makers in police and politics perceive as practically relevant to criminal policy. In the future, computer sciences may replace social sciences. Criminology has always had its place in the middle between scholarly research and practice,[873] and although the influ-

868 *Wang* SSRN 2018, 14, 20.
869 *Verbraucherzentrale Bundesverband* 2017, 4.
870 For Germany see fn. 829; for the USA see *Congressional Research Service* 2018, 2.
871 *Reuband* Soziale Probleme 2012, 5, 7.
872 Cf. in general for any kind of police actions, *Behr/Oberwittler* Soziale Probleme 2011, 115.
873 Cf. *Jehle/Beier* 2003, 1 et seq.

ence of criminology on crime policy is limited,[874] it threatens to vanish completely with the advent of algorithmic big data methods. Technological developments have always questioned the self-image of established professions. As early as the 1960s, Forsthoff, for example, wrote about the technologist's critical view of the lawyer: 'Seen through the eyes of the technologist, the lawyer is a functionary who claims to be able to do everything, [...] even though he has learned nothing in a technological sense'.[875] Will computer scientists and police practitioners soon look down on a criminology that has learned nothing in the computer science sense? We can only guess how the development of predictive algorithms will actually affect criminal policy in this area in the long term. However, some important voices in the public debate are already warning against a one-sided shift of focus towards computer science.[876] Since these warnings cannot be completely denied plausibility, the arguments should be taken seriously and accounted for in future developments.

For some years now, the advent of machine learning algorithms has led to proclamations of the 'end of theory' in science.[877] This refers to the increasingly widespread view that computers, algorithms and big data can generate supposedly more revealing, useful and accurate results than scientists who carefully and purposefully develop hypotheses and research strategies in traditional ways.[878] This is complemented by the view that since the arrival of machine learning it is no longer necessary to work with hypotheses and theories.[879] Instead, researchers only need to let themselves be led by the 'machines' to the patterns, trends and relationships in the social, economic, political and crime control fields.[880] Uprichard even speaks of a 'methodological genocide' in the social sciences due to

874 *Kunz/Singelnstein* 2016, 381; *Schüler-Springorum* KritV 1990, 315.

875 *Forsthoff* 1964, 191.

876 *Anderson* Wired of 23.6.2008, accessible at https://perma.cc/CE9Y-3ZYR, last accessed 1.1.2022; *Graham* The Guardian of 9.3.2012, accessible at https://perma.cc/2V2T-2F44, last accessed 1.1.2022;*Mayer-Schönberger/Cukier* 2013, 30, 67, 71.

877 *Anderson* Wired of 23.6.2008, accessible at https://perma.cc/CE9Y-3ZYR, last accessed 1.1.2022; *Mayer-Schönberger/Cukier* 2013, 30, 67, 71; *Chan/Bennett Moses* Theoretical Criminology 2016, 21, 29.

878 See *Graham* The Guardian of 9.3.2012, accessible at https://perma.cc/2V2T-2F44, last accessed 1.1.2022.

879 Cf. above the hypothetical example of a correlation between shoe size and crime, fn. 308.

880 See *Graham* The Guardian of 9.3.2012, accessible at https://perma.cc/2V2T-2F44, last accessed 1.1.2022.

self-learning algorithms.[881] An investigation of causal connections of social facts is replaced by an exclusive orientation towards correlations uncovered by algorithms. Mayer-Schönberger and Cukier also warn that questions of causality in science could lose importance in the future.[882] They argue that more and more people, through big data and machine learning, are resigning themselves to simply understanding *what* has happened, without understanding *why* it has happened. Moreover, this constitutes a revolution in our knowledge practices, which have been established for centuries, and a fundamental change in our understanding of reality.[883] As shown in Chapter I, machine learning algorithms can actually generate statements without the need for social science theory or proof of causalities, and do so solely on the basis of correlations.[884] The problems start when algorithmically generated results are perceived as absolute and generally error-free. What may also happen is that experts from specific social science disciplines could lose their discourse-guiding function with regard to empirical understandings of the world.[885] Generalist data analysts may one day completely replace social science experts.[886] From the perspective of some authors, criminology as a social science is thus threatened with a loss of significance. Theories are a central component of criminology, not only for theoretical criminologists, but also for empirical criminologists, who create new theories through their work and test the usefulness of existing ones.

Should decision-makers in police and politics in Germany actually adopt this perspective, the prophesied 'end of theory' threatens to become reality for criminology as well. But it is important to bear in mind that the 'end of theory' is to be understood less as a fact than as an increasingly widespread view. It does not reflect reality: the arrival of even the most precise new machine learning algorithm has yet to make hypotheses and theories obsolete in the social sciences.[887] As described in previous chapters,[888]

881 *Uprichard* Discover Society. Focus 2013, 3, 4.
882 *Mayer-Schönberger/Cukier* 2013, 30, 67.
883 *Harkin* The Financial Times of 1.3.2013, accessible at https://perma.cc/SS9R-JFDY, last accessed 1.1.2022.
884 See above p. 85 et seq.
885 *Mayer-Schönberger/Cukier* 2013, 30, 67; *Chan/Bennett Moses* Theoretical Criminology 2016, 21, 22.
886 *Mayer-Schönberger/Cukier* 2013, 30, 67; different, however, *Chan/Bennett Moses* Theoretical Criminology 2016, 21, 35.
887 Also critical *Chan/Bennett Moses* Theoretical Criminology 2016, 21
888 See above p. 87 et seq. and p. 113 et seq.

data are by no means always neutral and objective, but can contain social prejudices, value judgements and assumptions.[889] This applies to cut-off points[890] and error rates,[891] and all are written into the algorithm by people. The assertion that data speaks 'for itself' in a completely unmediated way is a fallacy.[892] If we rely solely on big data and its interpretation by data scientists as a mirror of our social, economic and political reality, we run the risk of ignoring important nuances.[893] Even with the advent of big data, social science experts must continue to play an important role in conceptualizing data analysis and providing insights into the causal functioning of correlations. Hypothesis-driven and data-driven approaches are not opposites, but complement each other.[894]

The alarmism around the 'end of theory' cannot be fully endorsed at this point.[895] However, this should not be a reason for stagnation in criminology. In 2007, Zedner posed the question in *Pre-Crime and Post-Criminology* of whether criminology in particular was being side-lined because it could no longer keep up with fundamental innovations in automated crime control.[896] Zedner also argues that if the objects of criminology research, including crime control, change fundamentally, criminology must also change, or risk becoming obsolete.[897]

In order to adequately meet the new technological challenges of the twenty-first century, criminology must therefore develop awareness of algorithms.[898]

889 See *Graham* The Guardian of 9.3.2012, accessible at https://perma.cc/2V2T-2F44, last accessed 1.1.2022.
890 See above p. 45 et seq.
891 See above p. 94 et seq.
892 See the anthology titled 'Raw Data Is an Oxymoron' by Gitelman 2013.
893 See *Graham* The Guardian of 9.3.2012, accessible at https://perma.cc/2V2T-2F44, last accessed 1.1.2022.
894 See *Ozkan* Soc. Sci. J. 2019, 208, 10.
895 See *Chan/Bennett Moses* Theoretical Criminology 2016, 21.
896 *Zedner* Theoretical Criminology 2007, 261, 267 ('Where crimes are regarded as continuous with normal behaviour; where future crimes are anticipated by actuarial calculation and forestalled by pre-emptive endeavour; where past crimes are conceived less as wrongs than losses; and where responsibility for limiting loss lies as much with the individual or the company as the State, then criminology must also adapt or risk being rendered marginal, even obsolete').
897 *Zedner* Theoretical Criminology 2007, 261, 261.
898 See *Smith et al.* Br. J. Criminol. 2017, 259; see also *Powell et al.* 2018.

a) Algorithmic criminology

This requires criminology on the one hand to adopt new algorithmic methods of crime analysis as a *supplement* (not a substitute!) to traditional criminological methods. On the other hand, criminology must learn to understand new technologies such as predictive methods in detail so that it can then accompany and study their application in practice in a computer-scientifically sound, critical yet independent manner.[899] In the English-speaking world, the advances made by Smith et al.[900] and Powell et al.[901] have already given rise to new theoretical approaches to 'algorithmic criminology' and 'digital criminology'. In view of the introduction of person-based predictive policing in Germany, disciplinary expansion is urgently needed in Germany as well. In order to remain relevant as a discipline in the 'algorithmic turn', criminologists need to act today.[902]

It would therefore make sense to open up criminology to the computer sciences, for example through interdisciplinary teaching at university or with a compulsory 'machine learning' module in criminology courses.[903] Criminology has always been multidisciplinary, has points of contact with neighbouring disciplines such as sociology, psychology and law, and accommodates a variety of research methods. Therefore, there is nothing that speaks against opening up criminology to computer science as a neighbouring discipline.

The more knowledge there is about algorithmic processes within criminology, the more resources it has to point out weaknesses in a government system and to draw up alternatives.

b) Summary of crime control without criminology

Algorithm-based big data analysis is undoubtedly useful in addressing many societal problems, including crime. However, it is essential that police and political decision-makers are not misled by big data's false promises

899 Cf. the importance of social science for the development of 'safe' artificial intelligence *Irving/Askell* Distill 2019.

900 *Smith et al.* Br. J. Criminol. 2017, 259.

901 *Powell et al.* 2018.

902 A different point of view, however, in *Chan/Bennett Moses* Theoretical Criminology 2016, 21, 26, who see no new challenges for criminology.

903 See *Uprichard* Discover Society. Focus 2013, 4.

and claims that theories are superfluous.[904] The central task of informing decision-makers and the public about the dangers of the new technology falls to the new sub-discipline 'algorithmic criminology'.

3. Self-imposed algorithmic thoughtlessness

Having discussed the influence of algorithms on the attitudes of the population and on the relevance of criminological knowledge, the following section now turns to the *users* of algorithmic risk scores. This section argues that algorithmic systems that help people make decisions lead users to assume less responsibility for their own actions and threaten to draw them into self-imposed 'algorithmic thoughtlessness'.[905]

In 1963, Hannah Arendt used the term 'thoughtlessness' (German: Gedankenlosigkeit) to describe how ordinary people[906] were able to commit war crimes by switching off their ability to think during the Third Reich, despite the fact that they had no overtly 'evil' intentions. An essential factor for the emergence of this attitude was integration into a bureaucratic apparatus. The Nazi war criminal Eichmann, for example, repeatedly claimed to have merely followed instructions.[907] Arendt saw the great danger here in the inability of people to reflect on the scope of their own actions. Under certain circumstances, this inability could affect almost every average person, which Arendt views as the 'banality' of evil.[908]

Of course, predictive algorithms do not linearly lead to crimes against humanity. And yet the concept of thoughtlessness is useful in an algorithmic context,[909] since it expresses how people in a system rely on the decisions of others, do not question them, and simply follow them. As justification, they refer to higher authority and the need to follow rules in the interest of a functioning system. This situation is quite comparable to the way people deal with the result of algorithmic calculations.[910] The con-

---

904 See *Graham* The Guardian of 9.3.2012, accessible at https://perma.cc/2V2T-2F44, last accessed 1.1.2022.

905 The term was first coined by *McQuillan* 2015.

906 Arendt describes Eichman as an 'average, normal human being' *Arendt* 2007, 99 et seq.

907 *Arendt* 2007, 99 et seq., 231 et seq.

908 *Arendt* 2007, 57 on the criticism of the concept of banality, however, e.g. *Robinson* Science and Society 1966, 368.

909 See also *McQuillan* 2015.

910 *McQuillan* 2015.

cept of thoughtlessness – though not explicitly named as such – can also be found in Arendt's later works. She chooses the rubric of the 'worldless mind' (German: weltloser Verstand), which is reduced to mere observance of rules. For example, in the context of mathematical-statistical procedures she writes, 'As this producing [of phenomena by modern science] takes place in the sense of mathematical formulas and equations, it [science] can now move in a world that corresponds exactly to what a *worldless mind* finds in itself'.[911]

a) The social psychology perspective on 'thoughtlessness'

That Arendt's observations on thoughtlessness are not merely abstract philosophical concepts has been demonstrated by the social psychologist Bandura, among others, in his research on moral disengagement. Under this heading, Bandura describes various psychological mechanisms that enable people to shut off their ability to think critically, and therefore enable them to commit actions that contradict with their values, and to do so without a conflict of conscience. According to Bandura, moral disengagement does not only emerge among perpetrators of the Nazi regime[912] and the My Lai massacre in Vietnam carried out by the US army. It also manifests itself in the famous Milgram experiment conducted at Yale University,[913] in which people, based on the instructions of the laboratory staff, put their counterparts through supposedly increasingly painful electric shocks without questioning the instructions.[914] Finally, moral disengagement has also been observed in the execution of cruel counterterrorism strategies, such as waterboarding and other ill-treatment that the US applied to suspected terrorists in the Abu Ghraib prison in Iraq.[915] However, moral disengagement is not limited to these extreme situations of serious human rights violations. It can also be observed in

911 *Arendt* 1994 [1958], 277 (emphasis by author).

912 *Bandura* 2016, 58 et seq., *Bandura* Personality and Social Psychology Rev. 1999, 193, 196, s. also *Gigerenzer* 2007, 263 (on the mass murder of the reserve police battalion 101 in Poland 'Actually they tried not to think anything').

913 *Milgram* J. Abnorm. Soc. Psychol. 1963, 371

914 *Bandura* 2016, 58 f; *Bandura* Personality and Social Psychology Rev. 1999, 193, 202.

915 *Bandura* 2016, 356 ff; *Bandura* 2004, 121; cf. also *McAlister et al.* J. Soc. Clin. Psychol. 2006, 141

unethical and criminal behaviour in the business world and is associated, among other things, with the world financial crisis.[916]

Bandura identifies two core causes of moral disengagement: first, situations that promote the dehumanization of a counterpart,[917] and second, situations that displace an actor's responsibility.[918] Dehumanization occurs when a counterpart is excluded from the values and norms otherwise applicable to all citizens. When responsibility is displaced, it is shifted to external decision-making bodies (e.g. superiors). If an actor views a source of authority as calling on them to enact a particular form of behaviour, this call goes unquestioned and the actor refrains from seeking indicators that could stand in the way of its execution. People do not view themselves as actors, and instead believe that they have no power to act themselves; therefore, they can *only* carry out instructions.[919] This frees them psychologically from personal responsibility, enables them to cease thinking for themselves and thus to act 'thoughtlessly'.

b) Moral disengagement algorithmic decision support systems

Both of the core triggers for moral disengagement described by Bandura are found in algorithmic systems used to provide support to decision-makers: dehumanization and displacement of responsibility.

aa) Dehumanization – the 'moral buffer'

The dehumanizing effect associated with these systems has been discussed in preceding sections from a constitutional point and the perception of the population. Bandura has demonstrated that 'digital dehumanization', i.e. the reduction of a person to mere data points, is directly related to moral disengagement of the users in the field of computer-assisted drone warfare.[920] Cummings bases his research on Bandura's when he writes that

---

916 *Bandura* 2016, 203 et seq.; see also *Bazerman/Gino* Annu. Rev. Law. Soc. Sci. 2012, 85; *Bazerman/Tenbrunsel* Harv. Bus. Rev. 2011, 58; see also 'Ethical Blindspots' in *Bazerman/Tenbrunsel* 2011.

917 *Bandura* Personality and Social Psychology Rev. 1999, 193, 200; *Bandura* 2016, 84 et seq.

918 *Bandura* 2016, 58 et seq.

919 *Bandura* 2016, 58 et seq.

920 *Bandura* The Psychologist 2017, 39-43; see also *Bandura* 2004, 121.

algorithmic decision support systems act like 'moral buffers'.[921] Computer systems create a special spatial[922] and emotional distance to the object of a decision.[923] When a person is represented by dots and numbers on a screen, they are no longer perceived as a complex feeling, thinking counterpart. The consequences that one's own actions have on such a human 'data point' can more easily be disregarded.[924] Such 'buffer' effects are also conceivable when it comes to systems providing support to police decision-making: the head of a predictive policing project in Germany recently described criminals as a 'bad weather front', which implies that they are devoid of human characteristics.[925]

bb) Displacement of responsibility – from tool to authority figure

Although algorithm-based systems were initially designed as tools subordinate to the user, in practice they can take on a more dominating role. They can take on a role that is similar to that of an authority figure who the user looks up to,[926] such as a superior whose 'orders' are executed without question.[927] Algorithmic systems that provide support to decision-makers are markedly different from other tools used by the police, such as weapons or video surveillance technology, in that they have the potential to completely replace the human decision-making process – even if this is undesirable from a legal point of view. Psychological studies of systems that

---

921 *Cummings* Journal of Technology Studies 2006, 23, 26.

922 Cf. with regard to distance already the Milgram experiment, in which the persons harmed are not visible, *Milgram* J. Abnorm. Soc. Psychol. 1963, 371.

923 *Cummings* Journal of Technology Studies 2006, 23, 26.

924 *Cummings* Journal of Technology Studies 2006, 23, 26.

925 See above fn. 28.

926 Cf. as a popular example for the interaction of man and technology in this sense Hegel's 'Master-slave dialectic', with which he described the priority of the means over their purpose, *Hegel* 1970, 145 et seq.; see on reception today, e.g., *Almerud et al.* Nursing Philosophy 2008, 55, 56; *Berger* 1991, 39 et seq.

927 Cf. also the distribution of moral responsibility in algorithmic systems described by *Floridi*, which leads to a situation where nobody feels responsible, since each participant made only a contribution to a result which appears negligible in itself. *Floridi* Phil. Trans. R. Soc. A 2016, 374: 20160112, *Floridi* Science and Engineering Ethics 2013, 727, 728 ('the macroscopic and growing phenomenon of global moral actions and non-individual responsibilities, resulting from the "invisible hand" of systemic interactions among multiagent systems (comprising several agents, not all necessarily human) at a local level').

provide support to decision-makers in the medical field and aviation[928] have shown that people find it very difficult to go against the results of algorithmic calculations. This even applies when a result is intended as only *one* of several factors that should inform a decision. The phenomenon known as automation bias (already described in Chapter I)[929] leads people to refrain from collecting and evaluating information themselves, and even to deliberately ignore evidence that clearly contradicts the result of an algorithm.[930] People are less confident in their own expertise than in complex, opaque algorithmic processes. This is even truer if, in light of time pressure and rationalization, making decisions *against* 'the machine' involves more time and explanation, than making decisions in line *with* 'the machine'. As a result, algorithmic calculations, which are only intended as an aid to decision-making (a mere tool), determine the decision.[931] The human user outsources their own responsibility to the algorithmic process.

Insisting under such circumstances that 'a human in the loop'[932] would suffice to control faulty algorithms is misleading.[933] In this constellation, the algorithm, with its supposedly certain probabilities, ultimately becomes the decisive authority figure. The human succumbs to 'thoughtlessness', in light of the imposition of having to make a decision. Uncertainty demands normative decisions from humans, a demand we are tempted to free ourselves from by following the certainty that the algorithm seems to offer.[934] The more a process is automated, the easier it is for people to become 'thoughtless' and indifferent to its results. The more crime control is automated, the easier it will be for officials using the system to feel that they are no longer responsible for actions taken on the basis of the system. Ultimately, this, too, is a question of shifting responsibility from the traditional actors of crime control to computer scientists.

---

928 Cf. *Manzey* 2012, 333, 333; cf. also on decision support for aircraft pilots, *Skitka et al.* Int. J. Hum. Comput. Stud. 1999, 991; *Mosier et al.* Int. J. Aviat. Psychol. 1998, 47, 63

929 See above p. 60.

930 E.g. *Skitka et al.* Int. J. Hum. Comput. Stud. 2000, 701; *Skitka et al.* Int. J. Aviat. Psychol. 2000, 85; *Skitka et al.* Int. J. Aviat. Psychol. 2000, 85; *Mosier et al.* Int. J. Aviat. Psychol. 1998, 47; *Skitka et al.* Int. J. Hum. Comput. Stud. 1999, 991;*Parasuraman* Ergonomics 2000, 931.

931 *Cummings* 2006, 1249, 7.

932 Cf. above p. 146.

933 Cf. *Citron* Wash. L. Rev. 2007, 1249, 1277.

934 See Gigerenzer/Engel 2006, 13.

No safeguards have yet been installed against displacement of responsibility in any person-based predictive policing system in Germany. Further, the effectiveness of the little safeguards that have been installed in the US is questionable:[935] the Wisconsin Supreme Court has, for example, stated that each risk score calculated by the COMPAS algorithm[936] has to be accompanied by simple 'warning notices' on, among other things, the lack of transparency and potentially discriminatory effect of the system vis-à-vis minorities.[937] These warnings are unlikely to truly counteract the strong psychological effects of automation bias and moral disengagement.

cc) Conclusion on moral disengagement

In summary, algorithmic systems that provide support to decision-makers inherently promote the thoughtlessness of users, i.e. prevent them from making a comprehensive assessment of all the factors in a situation and fully considering the consequences of their actions. Such thoughtlessness is self-imposed insofar as we, as a society in the algorithmic turn, willingly choose to use predictive policing that promotes our thoughtlessness.

c) Self-imposed nonage – willingly entering into a situation of 'not being able to understand'

Hannah Arendt warned that 'it is in the nature of science to follow every path once taken to the end'.[938] Self-imposed thoughtlessness, however, does not yet stand at the end of the logic of the algorithmic turn, but only at its beginning. If the algorithmic turn in crime control continues, self-imposed thoughtlessness threatens to become self-imposed nonage. In addition to situations that make it easy to refrain from thinking, there are situations that make it *impossible* to think. This may happen because decision-makers 'unlearn' their expertise by relying too often on algorithmic calculations – this phenomenon, 'deskilling', has already been observed in

935 See, critical of the approach of the Wisconsin Supreme Court, e.g. *Freeman* NCJL & Tech. On. 2016, 75, 95 et seq.
936 See on COMPAS above fn. 143.
937 State v. Loomis, 881 N.W.2d 749 (WI 2016) (mn. 66).
938 *Arendt* 1994 [1958], 9.

aviation[939] and medicine.[940] It may also happen by using inherently non-transparent algorithmic systems[941] (e.g. neural networks, but also complex decision forests)[942] in which the details of an algorithm's decision paths can no longer be unravelled *ex post* even by experts.[943] Consciously choosing such methods may equate with the conscious abandonment of the possibility to understand a decision.

aa) Deskilling

The more we rely on machines, the more unnecessary our own mental efforts may seem.[944] The abilities to observe, evaluate, draw conclusions and to weigh up evidence are all under threat.[945] Some authors fear that the use of algorithmic decision-making in crime control will systematically discourage future generations of civil servants to exercise judgement and to think critically.[946]

bb) Non-transparent algorithms

Although non-transparent algorithms such as neural networks may provide highly accurate results, their results cannot always be explained in a manner that people can understand.[947] Such non-transparent algorithms may classify a person as 'highly dangerous' and having a 90 per cent probability of committing a crime. Blind acceptance of such risk scores by human decision-makers may ultimately result in police action being taken

---

939 See *Manzey* 2012, 333, 333.

940 Cf. *Cabitza et al.* Jama 2017, 517; *Hoff* Health Care Management Review 2011, 338.

941 On various types of intransparency pp. 124 et seq.

942 See above fn. 157.

943 See above p. 153 et seq.

944 See on deskilling in detail *Carr* 2014.

945 *Capus* Die Republik of 19.9.2018, accessible at https://perma.cc/LVD2-64KA, last accessed 1.1.2022; experiments show that skill preservation requires the user to actively try to mentally comprehend the automatic process, *Endsley/Kiris* Human Factors 1995, 381; *Lorenz et al.* Aviation, Space, and Environmental Medicine 2002, 886.

946 Cf. exemplary *Capus* Die Republik of 19.9.2018, accessible at https://perma.cc/LVD2-64KA, last accessed 1.1.2022.

947 See above fn. 157.

without any understanding of *why* an algorithm calculated such a high risk score. By using algorithms that lack transparency, we consciously enter a situation of 'not being able to understand'. Algorithms then generate legal and social realities[948] that are no longer directly accessible to human experiences. The more opaque the algorithmic procedures are for humans, the greater the distance from human perception. If we resign ourselves to just knowing *what* will happen without knowing *why*, then the way we seek to understand the world and the knowledge we act upon will change.[949]

cc) 'Supra-human' knowledge mediation

In a future dominated by algorithmic decision-making, knowledge of the world in core legally and socially relevant areas would only be mediated via 'supra-human' artificial intelligence. This would mean abandoning the basic premise of the Enlightenment: understanding the world independently, without the direction of another person, and only by using one's own mind.[950] For 'the maxim of the Enlightenment is to always think for yourself'.[951]

It is the paradox of the Enlightenment, which Horkheimer and Adorno called 'dialectics',[952] that if we consistently pursue the ideals of the Enlightenment right up to the end, then the Enlightenment threatens to turn into its opposite. Weizenbaum has already analysed this tendency of the Enlightenment specifically in the context of computer technology:[953] considering that human reason and logic – the core concept of the Enlightenment – are embodied in algorithms, the use of complex and non-transparent 'rational' algorithms bars people from directly accessing knowledge about the world.

Although machine learning technologies, on the one hand, have the ability to shed light on data that was previously inaccessible to the human mind,[954] they threaten to lead to a detachment from human comprehensibility and understanding.

---

948 Cf. also 'By drawing up risk and danger forecasts it [the police] acquires a power of definition over social reality' *Singelnstein/Stolle* 2012, 199.

949 See *Mayer-Schönberger/Cukier* 2013, 7.

950 Cf. *Kant* Berlinische Monatsschrift 1784, 481 et seq.

951 *Kant* Berlinische Monatsschrift 1786, 304, 330.

952 *Adorno/Horkheimer* 1947.

953 *Weizenbaum* 1976, 258-280.

954 *Wischmeyer* 2020, mn. 52.

By using algorithms that we cannot understand, we voluntarily put ourselves in a situation (self-imposed) in which we can no longer verify our own decisions based on the new technology. One may speak of a reversion of our way of understanding the world into a pre-Enlightenment state.

Broad areas of knowledge are now only accessible to us through the mediation of a supra-human entity (in the past this entity was God mediated by the priesthood, in the future artificial intelligence mediated by data scientists). It should therefore not be surprising that the religious and mystical features of artificial intelligence have been pointed out in many places in the literature.[955]

To put it bluntly, the algorithmic turn is moving toward 'self-imposed nonage';[956] precisely what the Enlightenment of the eighteenth century had freed us from.

d) Conclusion on self-imposed algorithmic thoughtlessness

In short, algorithm-based big data analytics are useful in addressing many social issues, including crime. However, policy-makers must not be tempted by the false promises of the infallibility of big data or allow themselves to fall into the trap of self-imposed thoughtlessness or even self-inflicted nonage.[957]

955 See *O'Neil* 2016, 3, 8 ('Like gods, these mathematical models were opaque, their workings invisible to all but the highest priests in their domain: mathematicians and computer scientists'); *Legnaro/Kretschmann* KrimJ 2015, 94, 107 ('quasi-religious expectation of salvation'); see also the title at *Kurzweil* 2005 'The Singularity is Near', which is based on the saying of John the Baptist 'the kingdom of heaven is near' (Matthew 3: 2); see also the description of AI as 'mythology' by *boyd/Crawford* Information, Communication & Society 2012, 662, 663; cf. *Adorno/Horkheimer* 1947, 37 on the mystical elements of rationalization.

956 See *Kant* 2016 [1784], 7.

957 See *Arendt* 2007, 57.

4. From the logic of the law to the logic of algorithms – 'machine logic'

'If one applies [statistical] laws [...] to the objects of politics and history indiscriminately, then these objects have already been wilfully, quietly obliterated, namely they have been levelled as deviations into the medium in which they appear, but which they are not.'
Hannah Arendt – Vita Activa[958]

After having discussed the loss of legitimacy, the need for algorithmic criminology and the threat of self-imposed thoughtlessness, the following focuses on an aspect of the algorithmic turn that connects all of these points: 'machine logic'.

The logic of the law is at odds with the logic of algorithms.[959] The question is which mode of 'thinking' will prevail during the present algorithmic turn in crime control. 'Machines' make decisions in different ways, fact-finding and prognoses are made on a different basis than humans. Hilgendorf calls this a 'paradigm shift' and 'no less than another way of establishing the truth'.[960]

Will law subordinate technology, harness its powers for its own interests, mould it to its own internal logic, as concepts such as 'privacy by design' or 'transparency by design'[961] may imply? Are the new algorithmic models of knowledge creation and processing a gift for the legal system that will enable it to expand its reach and strengthen the rule of law?

In short, will we be able to embed the values of the law into technology, or will technology embed its values into the law? Will technology subjugate the law to its own internal logic and change our perception and interpretation of even the most fundamental legal guarantees and institutions?

The latter is not as far-fetched as it may seem. The basic prerequisites that have led to the current form and function of our legal system are changing. Even firmly established pillars of the legal system such as the

958 *Arendt* 1994 [1958], 43. [*German*: 'Wendet man also die [statistischen] Gesetze [...] unbesehen auf die Gegenstände der Politik und der Geschichte an, so hat man diese Gegenstände bereits unter der Hand eliminiert, sie nämlich als Abweichungen in dasjenige Medium eingeebnet, in dem sie zwar erscheinen, das sie aber gerade nicht sind'; translation by author.]

959 Cf. also *Hilgendorf* 2019, 229, 249 (discussing a departure from the logic of the law through the use of AI in criminal justice contexts).

960 *Hilgendorf* 2019, 229, 250.

961 *Yeung* Information, Communication & Society 2017, 118; *Hildebrandt* Legisprudence 2011, 223 *Balboni/Macenaite* Computer Law & Security Review 2013, 330.

principle of the rule of law can prove less stable than expected in the face of technological change.[962] Our legal system has always been decisively shaped by technologies and it cannot be thought of independently of them. Our current legal system is particularly shaped by three technologies of knowledge production and retention: language, writing and printing.[963] Reducing and replacing the significance of the processing of information through speaking and writing with new technologies of knowledge production that differ substantially from their predecessors can have an effect on the basic structures of the legal system. The production and storage of knowledge in algorithmic form, which is no longer *directly* accessible to humans, can be regarded as a technological revolution with culture-changing significance.[964]

The view of the fundamental pillars of our legal system as monolithic and immutable is thus highly doubtful,[965] and cannot be blindly relied upon. Some authors fear that the fundamental pillars of the legal system could be in danger if algorithmic rationalities and understandings of the world are applied to the law and crime control. This would lead algorithmic rationalities, 'machine logic', so to speak, to form the basis of governmental and regulatory decisions. In turn, this would lead to a fundamental shift in values and, in the long run, even self-harm of the legal system.[966]

---

962 *Hildebrandt* 2015, 47 et seqq; *Hildebrandt* Mod. L. Rev. 2016, 1, 3-4. Her approach is an extension of earlier theories of media analysis by e.g. *Marshall McLuhan* to the field of law. See her reference to him in *Hildebrandt* 2015, 49-50; *McLuhan* assumes that changes in the dominant forms of communication (i.e. the modes of knowledge production) lead to fundamental changes in human thinking; see *McLuhan* 1962; *McLuhan* 1994 [orig. 1964]; see also *Ong* 2012 [orig. 1982].

963 *Hildebrandt* Mod. L. Rev. 2016, 1, 3; cf. also *Legendre* 2001, 17 ('Man can only access the world through the mediation of the medium of language and thus through representation').

964 *Mayer-Schönberger/Cukier* 2013, 30, 67.

965 *Hildebrandt* Mod. L. Rev. 2016, 1, 2, 4 ('We cannot take for granted that law will interact with an artificially intelligent information and communications technology infrastructure (ICTI) in the same way as it has interacted with written and printed text'; 'We cannot take for granted that the current mode of existence of law and the Rule of Law are sustainable once the ICTI of data-driven agency takes over').

966 Cf. *Kerr*, in: Hildebrandt/de Vries 2013, 105, 112 ('a broad uptake of predictive and preemptive approaches across the social order might reach a tipping point wherein our systems of social control could no longer properly be called a 'legal system'); cf. opposition of 'government by the law' and 'algorithmic government' by *Rouvroy*, in: Hildebrandt/de Vries 2013, 143, 153 et seqq.; more

According to the Homeric tale of Ulysses, the Trojans joyfully moved a wooden horse they thought was a gift left at their gates into their fortified city. Once inside, however, Greek warriors disembarked from the horse and destroyed Troy from the inside out.[967] The object, which at first seemed like a gift, turned out to be disastrous in retrospect. By adapting to established cultural techniques (the exchange of gifts) and through a welcomed symbolism (the peaceful withdrawal of the Greeks), the Greeks induced the Trojans to participate in their own destruction. Pointedly, some modern-day authors[968] could be given the name *Laocoon*,[969] because they fear that now, as new technologies such as algorithmic crime predictions stand at the gates of jurisprudence, they, too, could turn out to be an unwholesome gift and take over the law from within. Popular authors,[970] but also legal scholars[971] and philosophers,[972] critically note that algorithm-based decision-making systems transform areas from the inside out once they have become established. This transformation consists in a subordination to the 'logic and rationalities of the machine', or, as Arendt formulated it for statistical procedures, in the 'levelling' of algorithm-external areas of life *into* machine logic, thereby extinguishing the areas' idiosyncrasies and modes of thinking.

The term 'machine logic' in this context refers to a totality of interwoven mutually reinforcing phenomena accompanying the current algorithmic turn:

---

cautious, *Zalnieriute et al.* Mod. L. Rev. 2019, 425, 455 ('The rule of law is not a static concept. It evolves in response to changing societal values and the operation of government. As technology reshapes society, and government interacts with the community, it can be expected in turn that our understanding of the rule of law will shift. Values such as transparency and accountability, predictability and consistency and equality before the law may remain central to conceptions of the rule of law, but their interpretation and application may change.').

967 See. Hom. Od. 4, 271–289; 8, 492–520; 11, 523–532.

968 Cf. *Kerr*, in: Hildebrandt/de Vries 2013, 105, 112; cf. generally critical of algorithmic processes *O'Neil* 2016; for use in crime control *ibid.* 26 et seqq., 71 et seqq.; cf. for the importance technologies as a prerequisite for the (further) development of a legal system, *Hildebrandt* 2015, 47 et seqq.

969 Laocoon warns the Trojans of the horse, using his spear to stab the horse in order to examine it for threats from within, Verg. Aen. II, 40–53.

970 Cf. *O'Neil* 2016.

971 Cf. *Zalnieriute et al.* Mod. L. Rev. 2019, 425, 455; Kerr, in: Hildebrandt/de Vries 2013, 105, 112

972 Cf. *Hildebrandt* 2015, 47 et seqq.; *Rouvroy*, in: Hildebrandt/de Vries 2013, 143, 153 et seqq.

- The focus on correlations instead of causalities[973] and an impending resignation to decision-making systems that – like e.g. neural networks – operate beyond the humanly comprehensible[974]
- The limitation of the legal system's field of vision to the mathematically quantifiable[975]
- A view of 'social physics' – represented e.g. by Pentland[976] and 'data behaviourism' as described by Rouvroy[977] – according to which all human behaviour can be calculated as if it were a scientific phenomenon; a view in conflict with the presumption of free will, underlying the legal system[978]
- The reduction of human beings to data processes,[979] in the words of the computer theorist Negroponte, to 'information bits',[980] and the neglect, if not negation of their characteristics as sentient, thinking beings[981]
- The lack of disclosure of the normativity of algorithm-based decisions in the legal system[982]
- The impending inability of humans to make decisions that contradict the predictions of complex algorithmic system (automation bias)[983]
- The loss of human expertise and the growing dependence on machine rationality that is already apparent in other areas of automation (deskilling).[984] Future generations of civil servants are in danger of losing their ability to form opinions without algorithms[985]

---

973 See above p. 85 et seq.; 193 et seq.

974 See above p. 127 et seq.; see also *Kroll et al.* U. Pa. L. Rev. 2017, 633, 638 ; *Knight* MIT Technol. Rev. 2017.

975 See above for missing overall consideration by algorithms p. 84 et seq.

976 *Pentland* 2014.

977 *Rouvroy*, in: Hildebrandt/de Vries 2013, 143 et seqq.

978 See *Prinz* 2008, 593; *Dreher* 1987, 28 et seqq.; cf. also BGHSt 2, 194 (200) ('The inner reason for the reproach of guilt lies in the fact that man is designed for free, responsible, moral self-determination [...]').

979 Cf. also *Puschke* 2017, 256.

980 *Negroponte* 1995.

981 See above on 'dehumanization' from a socio-psychological point of view, pp. 200 et seq.

982 See above for the numerous hidden value judgements in an algorithm 87 et seq.

983 See above p. 60 et seq.

984 See on 'deskilling' in detail, *Carr* 2014

985 *Capus* Die Republik of 19.9.2018, accessible at https://perma.cc/LVD2-64KA, last accessed 1.1.2022.

- The adoption of efficiency as a leitmotif in all forms of crime control and a subsequent relaxation of legal guarantees such as the principle of equal treatment in Article 3 of the German Constitution[986]

Each of these phenomena brings its own challenges, and the list could be extended further. However, it is precisely the interplay of all these phenomena, so the concern is in legal scholarship, that the law as leading variable of crime control could be displaced or fundamentally changed from within.

So far, there is little empirical evidence to suggest that such a change is actually taking place. The technology is still in its infancy, at least in Germany. Due to the multitude of possible applications and different technical designs of predictive algorithms, no general statement can be made about the overall impact of algorithmic crime control. The question of whether it will actually turn out to be an ominous gift for the legal system cannot yet be answered with certainty. Nevertheless, the existing concerns should not be ignored. Rather, it is essential that legal scholars are vigilant and examine the use of algorithms to ensure that these concerns do not become reality.

D. *Conclusion on the algorithmic turn*

Person-based predictive policing not only continues existing trends of risk orientation in crime control; it involves fundamental innovation on the legal, social and psychological levels. Overall, these changes amount to such a significant divergence from previous modes of crime control that they constitute far more than a continuation: they amount to a 'turn' in crime control.

Although person-based predictive policing is not illegal, a number of constitutional limits must be respected.[987]

If we accept that certain challenges posed by the algorithmic turn to crime control must be counteracted, a return to the Enlightenment's claim that all human action should be based on reflection offers a starting point.

This includes not just a focus on Horkheimer's and Adorno's criticism of instrumental reason, but also demands our focus on the fundamental guiding principle of the Enlightenment: '*sapere aude* – dare to use your

---

986 Cf. on statistically justified discrimination p. 92.

987 See above pp. 97 et seq.

own intellect'.[988] People must be able to maintain their ability to in theory understand central decision-making processes in society and the legal system *themselves.* Applied to day-to-day policing, this means the seemingly trivial: individual police officers should understand the facts on which their own decisions are based, and they should not confuse algorithmic normative results with facts. This also means that it is important to undertake a thorough reflection on the broad societal impacts of algorithmic systems.

Forty years ago, Horst Herold, the former president of the German Police Force and the 'father' of dragnet investigations in Germany, stated that whoever rejects the modern methods of the computer in crime control is suppressing knowledge and acting anti-Enlightenment.[989] Even if we admit that big data and machine learning open up numerous new ways with which to gain knowledge, Herold's blanket statement is problematic. It is important to differentiate between information, knowledge, and taking rational decisions and action, and these need to be evaluated on their own terms. In fact, it is entirely *within* the spirit of the Enlightenment to scrutinize the application of complex new technologies in crime control and, if their lack of transparency prevents scrutiny, to prohibit their use in crime control altogether. Introducing new technologies into crime control is not an end in itself. Crime control should not uncritically adopt the technology industry's marketing slogans of salvation. Only deliberate legal and criminological scrutiny of the new technologies can point the way forward. The following chapter explores the legal and organizational infrastructure that is needed to make such scrutiny possible.

988 *Kant* 2016 [1784], 7.
989 *Cobler* TransAtlantik 1980, 29, 38; critical *Kreissl* KJ 1981, 128.

Chapter IV. Minimum requirements for algorithmic crime prediction

This chapter is based on the results of the investigation so far. It outlines minimum requirements for algorithmic crime prediction and the future development and use of person-based predictive policing.[990] These requirements are primarily aimed at the programmers of person-based predictive policing systems, but also at decision-makers in the police and politics, at newly established government control bodies and at judges who review police measures based on predictive policing scores. The minimum requirements address the times during algorithm design when value judgements should not be made by programmers alone but should be put up for democratic debate. They point out sources of impending unconstitutionality and demand the use of technical innovation to counteract unconstitutionality within algorithm design. The requirements form the basis for future binding and uniform standards for person-based predictive policing, which a government control body must develop in detail. Even before the implementation of such standards, these requirements are aimed at assisting all parties involved in critically assessing the significance of any predictive policing score. The minimum requirements can be divided into three categories: 'development modalities', 'deployment modalities' and 'control modalities'.

A. Development modalities

It is crucial that minimum requirements do not only regulate the deployment stage of predictive policing, but are already steer the development phase.[991] The core decisions that underly a predictive policing system are

---

990 In contrast to the minimum requirements on recidivism prognosis published in 2006 by *Boetticher et al.* NStZ 2006, 537 which were drafted by a whole group of experts from different disciplines and occupational fields, the recommendations here are a first attempt by a single author to compile core points; they are intended to give impetus for further thought and expansion of the requirements in the future together with an interdisciplinary team of experts.

991 See also *Fröhlich/Spiecker* Verfassungsblog of 26.12.2018, accessible at https://perma.cc/9GVX-X564, last accessed 1.1.2022.

made during the development phase. Once a predictive policing system has been set up without respect for minimum requirements, it can only be retrofitted to a limited extent and at great expense. Once a predictive policing tool has been developed at great expense of time and money – with or without respecting minimum criteria – decision-makers in crime control are under pressure to use it.[992] A system that fails to follow minimum developmental requirements should, however, not be deployed.

I. Transparency

All decisions made during the developmental phase of a person-based predictive policing system should be logged in a way that people can understand. Cooperation with a private company in the development of a person-based predictive policing system should only take place if the company forgoes trade secret protection and therefore permits inspection of the algorithm's development phase.[993]

The obligation to log information includes the selection of the training data, the definition of the target variables (which offences are to be predicted within which period) and of the input variables and decisions in the calibration phase of the learning process. The origin of all data sources used in a training dataset and the considerations that led to the selection of a particular input variable (e.g. previous criminological research) must be recorded. To indicate the perpetration of an offence, any person-based predictive policing system should not merely refer to police *arrest* data but preferably base its calculation on harder to come by but more reliable court *conviction* data.[994] Furthermore, the weighting of the individual input variables within a prediction model should be recorded,[995] as should the position at which the cut-off point is set, i.e. the minimum threshold used to classify people as 'high risk'.[996] The way in which the error rate is calibrated, i.e. how many 'harmless' people are classified as dangerous in order to correctly identify one actually dangerous person also needs to be stated. The same applies to the calibration of the relationship between

992 *Weßlau* 1989, 241 et seq.
993 See on trade secrets above p. 149.
994 On selecting the target variable above p. 40.
995 . *Sachverständigenrat für Verbraucherfragen* 2018, 42.
996 See on the cut-off point p. 45; cf. *Eaglin* Emory L.J. 2017, 59, 118.

false-positive and false-negative errors during the design phase (the asymmetric cost ratio).

Two categories of quality measures are available to assess the predictive power of a person-based predictive policing system: measures, such as Area Under the Curve (AUC), which concern the discriminatory power of a system, and methods for measuring the positive predictive value of a model, i.e. the question of how many of the people identified by the algorithm as high risk actually go on to commit a crime. The predictive power of a person-based predictive policing system should be reported using *both* quality measures.

The use of particularly non-transparent machine learning processes such as neural networks, the exact processes of which are not comprehensible even to experts, should not be used in the fundamental rights-sensitive area of individualized crime prediction.[997] Rather, any system must be designed in such a way that it is possible to *ex post* identify the input variables that were decisive for a score and to determine each input variable's weighting in individual cases.

II. Impartiality

The impartiality of the algorithm must be ensured by reviewing the dataset for discrimination as early as the development phase. During and after completion of the person-based predictive policing model, the system should also be reviewed using various mathematical equality measures: Overall Accuracy Equality, Statistical Parity, Conditional Procedure Accuracy Equality, Conditional Use Accuracy Equality and Treatment Equality.[998] The results of the examination should be logged. If an inequality according to one of the above measures is found (which is to be expected, since not all equality measures can be fulfilled at the same time)[999] and if

997 See above p. 153 et seq.

998 See overview at *Gesellschaft für Informatik* 2018b, 39; *Berk et al.* Sociological Methods & Research 2018, 1, 13 et seq.; three different definitions in *Corbett-Davies et al.* ACM SIGKDD 2017, 797, 798; four different definitions in *Huq* Duke L.J. 2019, 1043, 56 et seq.; see also *Zweig/Krafft* 2018, 204, 213 ff; *Sachverständigenrat für Verbraucherfragen* 2018, 50 f; *Hacker* Common Market L. Rev. 2018, 1143, 1143 et seq.

999 See *Zweig/Krafft* 2018, 204, 216 et seq.; *Huq* Duke L.J. 2019, 1043, 63 ff; *Berk et al.* Sociological Methods & Research 2018, 1, 5; *Kleinberg et al.* ITCS, 43:1, 5

such inequality is not eliminated, a reason must be given for this, so that the decision can be subsequently reviewed.

Computer scientific methods of 'non-discrimination by design' must be used to eliminate discrimination.[1000]

B. *Deployment modalities*

I. Statutory basis

At the level of deployment modalities, a person-based predictive policing system should only be set up and used after a legal basis for the deployment has been established by parliamentary law. The system should only be deployed to provide *support*, not as a complete substitute for a police officer's decision. Person-based predictive policing should not be used to develop risk scores for suspicion-generating purposes on a city-wide or nation-wide scale; risk scores should only be calculated on request in individual cases and only if there is a specific danger to a particularly important legally protected good.[1001] The creation of a risk score must be communicated to the person concerned as soon as the situation permits, at the latest, after any police action has been taken.

II. Risk communication

When communicating the likelihood of a future crime to police officers, various aspects need to be considered. The probability of committing a criminal offence is to be communicated numerically with explicit mention of the target variables, i.e. for example '10 % probability of committing terrorist motivated homicides within the next 6 months'. Statements of probability that solely use terms such as 'high, medium and low risk' without disclosing the percentages behind them (as is the case with the RADAR-iTE programme,[1002] a precursor of person-based predictive policing) should be avoided. This also applies to the use of measures such

et seq.; cf. on procedures to investigate the different effects of different fairness measures on different groups *Chouldechova/G'Sell* arXiv 2017.

1000 See 'Non-Discrimination by Design' fn. 346,472 and accompanying text.

1001 See above p. 106 et seq.

1002 See above p. 71 et seq.

as 'a person has an x times higher probability of committing a crime than the average population', as with the Chicago Strategic Subject List.[1003] In addition to the probability of a criminal offence being committed, the system's error rates should also be reported, because police officers who are aware of the error rate can search particularly thoroughly for possible counter-indications. Further, as far as is known, the base rate of predicted crimes should be provided, i.e. the frequency of a certain crime within the general population. The base rate is important for the proper assessment of any prediction;[1004] without it, misjudgements may occur.[1005] Finally, the input variables that had the greatest influence on the result should be reported for each individual case.[1006]

C. Control modalities

The development and deployment of person-based predictive policing systems should be paused until appropriate control infrastructures have been established for both stages. Any approach to controlling algorithms should be based on the transparency triangle consisting of public registration obligations, the subjective rights of those affected and the establishment of a government control body (Fig. 6).

1003 See above p. 66.
1004 *Kröber et al.* 2006, 84; see also *Nedopil* 2017, 347 et seq.
1005 *Gigerenzer* 2000, 251 ff; *Ginosar/Trope* J. Exp. Soc. Psychol. 1980, 228, 228 ff; *Kahneman/Tversky* Psychol. Rev. 1973, 237, 237 et seq.
1006 See DyRiAS, fn. 267 and accompanying text.

Fig. 6. Triangle of algorithmic transparency for person-based predictive policing[1007]

The decisions recorded in the development phase of the algorithm should be deposited with a registration body in a publicly accessible manner before the first use of the algorithm.[1008] When risk scores are calculated, the individuals affected must be informed about the input variables used for their individual score result. They should also be given the opportunity to challenge a score in court and any police measures based on that score. Finally, an interdisciplinary government control body is required to set standards and systematically monitor predictive policing systems before and during their deployment. The benefits of the participation of pluralistic expert bodies in the context of the design of technical systems are already known from elsewhere in administrative law, such as the German Biosafety Commission.[1009] A mere blanket statement by a control body that a predictive policing system meets 'current standards of science and technology' would be too vague and therefore inappropriate in the context of person-based predictive policing.[1010] Instead, a government control bo-

1007 Printed already on p. 159.
1008 See above fn. 557.
1009 *Meyer* JZ 2017, 429, 438
1010 *Meyer* JZ 2017, 429, 438.

dy must define which methodological foundations, quality criteria and evaluation standards are appropriate for predictive policing.[1011]

Person-based predictive policing systems should only be developed and used *after* the establishment of uniform standards. It is only possible to sanction defective predictive policing systems once precise quality standards have been drawn up.[1012] Manufacturers of person-based predictive policing can only optimize their model training if optimization criteria have been uniformly defined. When setting standards and defining optimization goals, the government control body will have to make a number of value judgements. These decisions should be made as transparently as possible in order to ensure that they are open for public debate. This includes the issues of:

- prediction accuracies (AUC and Positive Predictive Value) that a person-based predictive policing system must meet
- acceptable error rates (false-positive and false-negative)
- the mathematical equality measure on which a person-based predictive policing system should be founded

D. Checklist

The minimum requirements for algorithm-based crime prediction described above can be summarized in the checklist on the following page.

1011 *Meyer* JZ 2017, 429, 438.
1012 *Wischmeyer* AöR 2018, 1, 25.

Minimum requirements for algorithmic crime predictions

☐ Development modalities

☐ **Transparency**

☐ Logging of
- ☐ Selection of training database
- ☐ Defining of target variables
  - o Type of predicted offence
  - o Time period of prediction
  - o Based NOT merely on arrest data, but on conviction data
- ☐ Defining input variables
  - o Risk-increasing variables
  - o Risk-reducing variables
- ☐ Weighting of input variables
- ☐ Cut-off point
- ☐ Error rate
- ☐ Asymmetric cost ratio
- ☐ Predictive accuracy
  - o Area Under the Curve
  - o Positive Predictive Value

☐ No deployment of algorithms with system inherent intransparency (e.g. neural networks).

☐ In individual cases, input variables that are decisive for a score can be identified retrospectively.

In the case of cooperation with private company

☐ The private company may not invoke trade secret protection against an inspection of the algorithm's design process.

☐ **Impartiality**

☐ Search for discrimination in training dataset

☐ Search for discrimination in algorithm model

Overall equality
- ☐ Overall Accuracy Equality
- ☐ Statistical Parity

Error rate equality
- ☐ Conditional Procedure Accuracy Equality
- ☐ Conditional Use Accuracy Equality
- ☐ Treatment Equality

☐ Giving reason for non-elimination of recorded inequalities

☐ Use of non-discrimination by design methods

☐ Deployment modalities

☐ Statutory basis in the form of parliamentary legislation
- ☐ Decision-supporting, NOT decision-substituting
- ☐ Use only in case of concrete danger
- ☐ Only to protect legal interest of particularly high value
- ☐ No widespread suspicion-generating use (e.g. all residents of a city)
- ☐ Obligation to notify people for whom a score is calculated

☐ Risk communication
- ☐ Percentage probability, NOT just abstract risk categories
- ☐ Naming of target variable
  - o Predicted offences
  - o Forecast period
- ☐ Error rate
- ☐ Base rate
- ☐ List of the most important input variables for the risk score

☐ Control modalities

☐ Development and deployment of person-based predictive policing only after control structures have been established
- ☐ Registration requirements
- ☐ Subjective rights
- ☐ Government control body

☐ Development and deployment of person-based predictive policing only after the development of uniform standards, e.g. on
- ☐ Predictive accuracy
- ☐ Error rate
- ☐ Equality measures

Chapter V. Closing remarks: Tyrannicide and a new beginning

It may well be that future generations, or at least their well-off elites, will look back on our critical analyses of algorithmic crime control with amusement; perhaps with the same amusement which we feel today when we read about *Plato's* warning against the 'technology' of writing[1013] or *Trithemius'* warning about the negative effects of the printing press.[1014] Both warnings are concerned with a loss of control and negative impacts on society as a whole, which, in turn, are associated with the systematic mass transfer of knowledge production and storage from individuals to external media (written/printed words).

A less advantaged segment of future societies, however, consisting of citizens who have not been able to benefit from digital progress and who suffer from the consequences of negative algorithmic assumptions about themselves,[1015] might look back more reproachfully on this century's choices and ask why no safeguards for the rule of law and protection of fundamental rights were included in the new technology. In imagining the scenario of such a future assessment of our present-day actions and in the speculations about the good or bad end of the algorithmic turn, our introductory theme of tyrannicide and of real or only imagined possibilities re-emerges:[1016] is the algorithmic turn an 'old beldam from Argos' that preventively protects society from countless 'Pyrrhoi'? Or is the algorithmic turn a 'Caesar' from which society will retrospectively wish a 'Brutus' had freed them?

This work cannot predict what answer will be given, or what part of this scenario is more likely to shape the future. Instead, it merely invites the reader to consider whether, in a digital age that has now also reached crime control, the traditional tools of the rule of law are sufficient to pre-

1013 *Platon*, 341b–e; 344c–d; *Platon*, 275A.

1014 *Trithemius* 1973.

1015 *See* as an example of 'risk inequalities', the fact that members of minority groups may have a higher likelihood of being falsely identified as carrying high risk [false-positives], the COMPAS algorithm in which African-American defendants were twice as likely as white defendants to be wrongly labelled as future criminals, *Angwin et al.* ProPublica 2016.

1016 See above p. 1.

serve the *status quo* of existing fundamental rights protection, or whether the use of new technologies and their promises must be questioned from the ground up.

The narrative framework of being able to prevent crimes before they happen is tempting. But it should not blind us to the real limitations of predictive algorithms and the risks of this form of 'uncertainty absorption'[1017] for society and the rule of law.

In view of the legitimate legal objective of increasing security through predictive algorithms, a balance must be sought and found with compensatory provisions for the protection of freedom. In a society aimed at security and prevention, the realization of fundamental rights must be promoted actively and offensively;[1018] this is all the more true as encroachments on fundamental rights are increasingly moving into an opaque digital space.

This book is a warning against considering each and every citizen as nothing more than a potential crime risk in the algorithmic turn,[1019] and pleads against a view of humans as 'recidivism automatons'.[1020]

It concludes with a reference to what is threatening to be lost in a future calculated from data of the past: the new beginning, a basic condition of human existence. Arendt described it in her philosophy of 'natality' as follows:[1021]

> 'The new always happens against the overwhelming odds of statistical laws and their probability, which for all practical, everyday purposes amounts to certainty; the new therefore always appears in the guise of a miracle. The fact that man is capable of action means that the unexpected can be expected from him, that he is able to perform what is infinitely improbable.'

1017 See *Meyer* JZ 2017, 429, 429.
1018 Cf. *Hassemer* Vorgänge, Zeitschrift für Bürgerrechte und Gesellschaftspolitik 2002, 10 10 et seq.
1019 See *Creemers/Guagnin* KrimJ 2014, 134, 147.
1020 See *Kröber*, 173.
1021 *Arendt* 1998 [1958], 178.

Chapter VI. Theses

Theses on the foundations of person-based predictive policing:

1. § 4 FlugDaG provides the first explicit statutory basis for person-based predictive policing in Germany in the form of flight data pattern recognition.[1022]
2. The constitutionality of § 4 FlugDaG is problematic, among other aspects in view of its widespread suspicion-generating character, the absence of a specific risk threshold and the lack of an appropriate control infrastructure.[1023]
3. Programs such as Palantir Gotham in Hesse and RADAR-iTE represent preliminary stages of person-based predictive policing in Germany.[1024]
4. Due to 'automation bias', i.e. the limited willingness of humans to question and deviate from the results of computer programs, the decision-making corridor of police officers is de facto pre-set by predictive policing recommendations.[1025]

Theses on legal limits of person-based predictive policing:

5. It follows from the right to informational self-determination that person-based predictive policing may only be used if there is a specific danger and only to protect high-ranking legal interests.[1026]
6. As human dignity is at the core of the right to informational self-determination and the principle of the rule of law, the use of system-inherent non-transparent algorithms for crime control should be banned, i.e. the use of algorithms whose internal connections can no longer be understood in detail even by experts, for example, artificial intelligence in the form of neural networks.[1027]
7. Contrary to widespread belief, person-based predictive policing is not inherently more neutral and objective than decisions made by police officers. Rather, it reproduces existing social prejudices, for example,

1022 See above p. 80 et seq.
1023 See above p. 107 et seq.
1024 See above p. 69 et seq.
1025 See above p. 60.
1026 See above p. 106 et seq.
1027 See above p. 158.

towards minorities, if these prejudices are not recognized and eliminated in the data underlying the algorithm.[1028]

8. The risks associated with person-based predictive policing for the right to informational self-determination, for the ban on discrimination and for the rule of law must be countered by a transparency triangle of public registration, the subjective rights of people affected, and government control structures.[1029]

Theses on the algorithmic turn in crime control:

9. The use of predictive algorithms is not merely a continuation of previous trends of risk focus in crime control.[1030] Rather, the outsourcing of decisions and responsibility to algorithms represents a new level of crime control whose various effects can be summarized under the headline of the 'algorithmic turn'.[1031]
10. Due to the lack of procedural justice associated with predictive algorithms with regard to participation, neutrality, respectful treatment and trust in the motives of decision-makers, there is a danger that predictive policing will reduce the legitimacy of the police in the eyes of the population.[1032]
11. Criminology's relevance in crime control threatens to be diminished compared to the computer sciences. In connection with this, questions of causality threaten to take a back seat to mere correlations. In order to be able to accompany these technical developments in a computer-scientifically sound, critical and independent manner, criminology must understand the processes of machine learning and develop a new sub-discipline of 'algorithmic criminology'.[1033]
12. The use of predictive algorithms promotes 'self-imposed thoughtlessness' in crime control, i.e. a situation in which a person ignores their own thinking and completely relies on the decisions of others without question or measuring them against their own values.[1034]

1028 See above p. 87 et seq., 113 et seq.
1029 See above p. 158, 217.
1030 See above p. 181 et seq.181
1031 See above p. 184 et seq.
1032 See above p. 184 et seq.
1033 See above p. 193 et seq.
1034 See above p. 198 et seq.

Bibliography

Adorno, Theodor W. / Horkheimer, Max, *Dialektik der Aufklärung*, Amsterdam: de Munter, 1947.

Aghababaei, Somayyeh / Makrehchi, Masoud, 'Mining Social Media Content for Crime Prediction', *IEEE/WIC/ACM International Conference on Web Intelligence*, 2016, 526–531.

Ahlstrom, Vicki / Longo, Kelly, 'Human Factors Design Standard for Acquisition of Commercial-off-the-Shelf Subsystems, Non-Developmental Items, and Developmental Systems', Atlantic City: FAA Technical Center, 2003. Available at: http://www.tc.faa.gov/its/worldpac/techrpt/ct03-5.pdf [https://perma.cc/4LCC-9WR9] (accessed 1.1.2022).

Aitken, Rob, "'All data is credit data': Constituting the Unbanked", *Competition & Change*, 21 (4/2017): 274–300.

Alberdi, Eugenio / Povyakalo, Andrey / Strigini, Lorenzo / Ayton, Peter, 'Effects of Incorrect Computer-Aided Detection (CAD) Output on Human Decision-Making in Mammography', *Academic Radiology*, 11 (8/2004): 909–918.

Albrecht, Günter, 'Probleme der Prognose von Gewalt durch psychisch Kranke', *Journal für Konflikt-und Gewaltforschung*, 5 (1/2003): 97–126.

Albrecht, Peter-Alexis /Lamnek, Siegfried, *Jugendkriminalität im Zerrbild der Statistik: eine Anlayse von Daten und Entwicklungen*, Munich: Juventa, 1979.

Almerud, Sofia /Alapack, Richard J. /Fridlund, Bengt /Ekebergh, Margaretha, 'Beleaguered by Technology: Care in Technologically Intense Environments', *Nursing Philosophy*, 9 (1/2008): 55–61.

Alpaydin, Ethem, M*achine Learning: The New AI*, Cambridge, MA/London: MIT, 2016.

Ananny, Mike, 'Toward an Ethics of Algorithms: Convening, Observation, Probability, and Timeliness', *Science, Technology & Human Values,* 41 (1/2016): 93–117.

Ananny, Mike / Crawford, Kate, 'Seeing without knowing: Limitations of the transparency ideal and its application to algorithmic accountability', *New Media & Society*, 20 (3/2018): 973–989.

Anderson, Chris, 'The End of Theory: The Data Deluge Makes the Scientific Method Obsolete', *The Wired*, 23 June 2008. Available online: www.wired.com/2008/06/pb-theory [https://perma.cc/CE9Y-3ZYR] (last accessed 1.1.2022).

Andrews, Donald Arthur / Bonta, James, *The Psychology of Criminal Conduct*, 6. ed., Cincinnati: Routledge, 2017.

Angwin, Julia / Larson, Jeff / Mattu, Surya / Kirchner, Lauren, 'Machine Bias: There's Software Used Across the Country to Predict Future Criminals. And it's Biased Against Blacks', *ProPublica*, 23 May 2016. Available online: https://www.propublica.org/article/machine-bias-risk-assessments-in-criminal-sentencing [https://perma.cc/LAE9-A656], (accessed 1.1.2022).

Arbeitsgruppe Digitaler Neustart, 'Zwischenbericht der Arbeitsgruppe "Digitaler Neustart" zur Frühjahrskonferenz der Justizministerinnen und Justizminister am 6. und 7. Juni 2018 in Eisenach', 2018. Available online: http://docplayer.org/80392233-Zwischenbericht-der-arbeitsgruppe-digitaler-neustart.html [https://perma.cc/M88A-G9QX], (accessed 1.1.2022).

Arendt, Hannah, *Crises of the Republic: Lying in Politics, Civil Disobedience on Violence, Thoughts on Politics, and Revolution*, New York: Mariner Books, 1972.

Arendt, Hannah, *Vita Activa or Vom tätigen Leben*, Munich: Piper, 1994 [1958].

Arendt, Hannah, The *Human Condition*, 2. ed., Chicago/London: University of Chicago, 1998 [1958].

Arendt, Hannah, *Eichmann in Jerusalem: ein Bericht von der Banalität des Bösen*, 2. ed., Munich: Piper, 2007 [1964]).

Art. 29 Data Protection Working Party, 'Guidelines on Automated individual decision-making and Profiling for the purposes of Regulation 2016/679', 2018. Available online: https://ec.europa.eu/newsroom/article29/item-detail.cfm?item_id=612053 [https://perma.cc/6AL5-TAHS], (accessed 1.1.2022).

Arzt, Clemens, 'Das neue Gesetz zur Fluggastdatenspeicherung – Einladung zur anlasslosen Rasterfahndung durch das BKA', *DÖV*, 24 (2017): 1023–1030.

Arzt, Clemens, 'Stellungnahme zum FlugDaG', *A-Drs.* 18(4)689 F, 2017.

Bäcker, Matthias, Kriminalpräventionsrecht: eine rechtsetzungsorientierte Studie zum Polizeirecht, zum Strafrecht und zum Strafverfahrensrecht, Tübingen: Mohr Siebeck, 2015.

Bacon, Francis, 'Meditationes', in: Spedding, James / Ellis, Robert / Douglas, Heath (eds), *The Works of Francis Bacon Vol. XIV*, Boston: Michigan Scholar Press: 1863, 59–96.

Baer, Susanne, "'Ende der Privatautonomieoder' grundrechtlich fundierte Rechtsetzung? Die deutsche Debatte um das Antidiskriminierungsrecht", *ZRP*, 2002, 7: 290–294.

Bahner, Jennifer Elin, *Übersteigertes Vertrauen in automation: Der Einfluss von Fehlererfahrungen auf complacency und automation bias*, Diss. Technisches Universität Berlin, 2008.

Baier, Dirk / Pfeiffer, Christian / Simonson, Julia / Rabold, Susann, 'Jugendliche in Deutschland als Opfer und Täter von Gewalt: Erster Forschungsbericht zum gemeinsamen Forschungsprojekt des Bundesministeriums des Innern und des KFN', Hannover Kriminologisches Forschungsinstitut Niedersachsen e.V, 2009.

Balasuriya, Lakshika / Wijeratne, Sanjaya / Doran, Derek / Sheth, Amit, 'Finding street gang members on twitter', IEEE/ACM International Conference on Advances in Social Networks Analysis and Mining 2016, 685–692.

Balboni, Paolo / Macenaite, Milda, 'Privacy by design and anonymisation techniques in action: Case study of Ma3tch technology', *Computer Law & Security Review*, 29 (2013): 330–340.

Balogh, Dominik A., 'Near Repeat-Prediction mit PRECOBS bei der Stadtpolizei Zürich', *Kriminalistik*, 5 (2016): 335–341.

Bandura, Albert, 'Moral disengagement in the perpetration of inhumanities', *Personality and Social Psychology Rev.*, 3 (3/1999): 193–209.

Bandura, Albert, 'The role of selective moral disengagement in terrorism and counterterrorism', in: Moghaddam, Fathali M. / Marsella, Anthony J. (eds), *Understanding terrorism: Psychosocial roots, consequences, and interventions*, Washington DC: American Psychological Association, 2004: 121–150.

Bandura, Albert, *Moral Disengagement: How People Do Harm and Live with Themselves*, New York: Worth, 2016.

Bandura, Albert, 'Disengaging Morality from Robotic War', *The Psychologist*, 30 (2017), 38–43.

Banse, Gerhard, *Risiko – Technik – Technisches Handeln (eine Bestandsaufnahme)*, Karlsruhe: Kernforschungszentrum Karlsruhe, 1993.

Barocas, Solon / Selbst, Andrew D., 'Big Data's Disparate Impact', *Calif. L. Rev.*, (104–3/2016): 671–732.

Barr, Michael, 'An Update on Toyota and Unintended Acceleration', *Embedded Gurus*, 2013. Available online: https://embeddedgurus.com/barr-code/2013/10/an-update-on-toyota-and-unintended-acceleration/ [https://perma.cc/GMX4-979H], (accessed 1 January 2022).

Barton, Stephan, 'Benötigen wir psychologische Sachverständige für die Glaubhaftigkeitsbeurteilung?', in: Barton, Stephan / Dubelaar, Marieke / Kölbel, Ralf / Lind, Michael (eds), *'Vom hochgemuten, voreiligen Griff nach der Wahrheit – Fehlurteile im Strafprozess'*, Baden-Baden: Nomos, 2018: 199–224.

Basel-Stadt, 'Regierungsrat des Kantons, Interpellation Nr. 131 Tonja Zürcher betreffend "Radikalismus und Nutzung Software RA-PROF – Radicalisation Profiling"', *JSD/P165546*: 2016.

Bateson, Gregory, *Steps to an Ecology of Mind: Collected Essays in Anthropology, Psychiatry, Evolution, and Epistemology*, Chandler: San Franscico, 1972.

Bazerman, Max H. / Gino, Francesca, 'Behavioral Ethics: Toward a Deeper Understanding of Moral Judgment and Dishonesty', *Annu. Rev. Law. Soc. Sci.*, 8 (2012): 85–104.

Bazerman, Max H. / Tenbrunsel, Ann E., *Blind Spots: Why we fail to do what's right and what to do about it*, Princeton: Princeton University Press, 2011.

Bazerman, Max H. / Tenbrunsel, Ann E., 'Ethical Breakdowns', *Harv. Bus. Rev.*, 4 (2011): 58–65.

Beck, Charlie / McCue, Colleen, 'Predictive Policing – What can we learn from Wal-Mart and Amazon about Fighting Crime in a Recession?', *The Police Chief*, 76 (11/2009): 18–24.

Beck, Ulrich, Risikoges*ellschaft: Auf dem Weg in eine andere Moderne*, Frankfurt a. M.: Suhrkamp, 1986.

Beck, Ulrich, *Gegengifte: die organisierte Unverantwortlichkeit*, Munich: Suhrkamp, 1988.

Behr, Rafael / Oberwittler, Dietrich, 'Polizei und Polizieren in multiethnischen Gesellschaften: Einleitung', *Soziale Probleme*, 23 (2011): 114–118.

Berger, Rainer, *Politik und Technik: Der Beitrag der Gesellschaftstheorien zur Technikbewertung*, Opladen: Westdeutscher Verlag, 1991.

Berk, Richard, *Machine Learning Risk Assessments in Criminal Justice Settings*, Cham: Springer, 2019.

Berk, Richard / Heidari, Hoda / Jabbari, Shahin / Kearns, Michael / Roth, Aaron, 'Fairness in Criminal Justice Risk Assessments: The State of the Art', *Sociological Methods & Research*, 50 (1/2018): 1–42.

Beuth, Patrick, 'Die Polizei, dein Freund und Hellseher', *Zeit Online*, 11 October 2017. Available online: https://www.zeit.de/digital/datenschutz/2017-10/pre-crime-film-predictive-policing [https://perma.cc/T4GL-6U5A], (accessed 1.1.2022).

Beuth, Patrick, 'Maas schlägt digitales Antidiskriminierungsgesetz vor', *Zeit Online*, 3 July 2017. Available online: https://www.zeit.de/digital/internet/2017-07/heiko-maas-algorithmen-regulierung-antidiskriminierungsgesetz [https://perma.cc/Y64R-77TK], (accessed 1.1.2022).

Beyerbach, Hannes, *Die geheime Unternehmensinformation: grundrechtlich geschützte Betriebs- und Geschäftsgeheimnisse als Schranke einfachrechtlicher Informationsansprüche*, Tübingen: Mohr Siebeck, 2012.

Big Brother Watch, 'Press Release: Police use Experian Marketing Data for AI Custody Decisions', 2018. Available at https://bigbrotherwatch.org.uk/all-media/police-use-experian-marketing-data-for-ai-custody-decisions/ [https://perma.cc/CXD4-ASYN], (accessed 1.1.2022).

Blader, Steven L. / Tyler, Tom R., 'A four-component model of procedural justice: Defining the meaning of a "fair" process', *Personality and Social Psychology Bulletin*, 29 (6/2003): 747–758.

Bock, Michael, 'Die Methode der idealtypisch-vergleichenden Einzelfallanalyse und ihre Bedeutung für die Kriminalprognose', in: Dölling, Dieter (ed), *Die Täter-Individualprognose. Beiträge zu Stand, Problemen und Perspektiven der kriminologischen Prognoseforschung*, Heidelberg: Kriminalistik-Verl., 1995: 1–28.

Böckler, Nils / Allwinn, Mirko / Hoffmann, Jens / Zick, Andreas, 'Früherkennung von islamistisch motivierter Radikalisierung. Vorstellung und empirische Validierung eines verhaltensbasierten Instrumentes zum Fallscreening', *Kriminalistik*, 8–9 (2017): 491–497.

Boer, Douglas P, *Manual for the Sexual Violence Risk-20: Professional guidelines for assessing risk of sexual violence*, Burnaby: British Columbia Institute Against Family Violence, 1997.

Boetticher, Axel / Kröber, Hans-Ludwig / Müller-Isberner, Rüdiger / Böhm, Klaus M. / Müller-Metz, Reinhard / Wolf, Thomas, 'Mindestanforderungen für Prognosegutachten', *NStZ 2006*, (13/4): 537–544.

Borchers, Detlef, 'Predictive Analytics bei der Polizei: Tätergruppen als Schlechtwetterfront entlang der Autobahn', *Heise Online*, 2 February. 2016. Available online: https://www.heise.de/newsticker/meldung/Predictive-Analytics-bei-der-Polizei-Taetergruppen-als-Schlechtwetterfront-entlang-der-Autobahn-3119294.html [https://perma.cc/PB9J-T7VG], (accessed 1 January 2022).

Botha, Henk, 'Human dignity in comparative perspective', *Stellenbosch L. Rev.*, 20 (2/2009): 171–220.

Bowers, Kate J. / Johnson, Shane D. / Pease, Ken, 'Prospective Hot-Spotting – The Future of Crime Mapping?', *Brit. J. Crim.*, 44 (5/2004): 641–658.

Bowker, Geoffrey C., *Memory Practices in the Sciences*, Cambridge, MA: MIT, 2005.

Boyd, Danah / Crawford, Kate, 'Critical Questions for Big Data', *Information, Communication & Society*, 15 (5/2012): 662–679.

Bozdag, Engin, 'Bias in Algorithmic Filtering and Personalization', *Ethics and Information Technology*, 15 (2013): 209–227.

Brendecke, Arndt, *Imperium und Empirie: Funktionen des Wissens in der spanischen Kolonialherrschaft*, Köln/Weimar: Böhlau, 2009.

Brennan-Marquez, Kiel, 'The Constitutional Limits of Private Surveillance', *U. Kan. L. Rev.*, 66 (3/2018): 485–521.

Britz, Gabriele, *Freie Entfaltung durch Selbstdarstellung: eine Rekonstruktion des allgemeinen Persönlichkeitsrechts aus Art. 2 I GG*, Tübingen: Mohr Siebeck, 2007.

Britz, Gabriele, *Einzelfallgerechtigkeit versus Generalisierung: verfassungsrechtliche Grenzen statistischer Diskriminierung*, Tübingen: Mohr Siebeck, 2008.

Bröhmer, Jürgen, *Transparenz als Verfassungsprinzip: Grundgesetz und Europäische Union*, Tübingen: Mohr Siebeck, 2004.

Brühl, Jannis, 'Gotham am Main', *Süddeutsche Zeitung*,18 October 2018. Available online: https://sz.de/1.4175521 [https://perma.cc/6QDL-GD5X], (accessed 1 January 2022).

Brühl, Jannis / Steinke, Ronen, 'Algorithmen gegen Verbrecher: Morgen ein Mörder', *Süddeutsche Zeitung*, 4 March 2019. Available online: https://sz.de/1.4349068 [https://perma.cc/6J55-VGCX], (accessed 1 January 2022).

Bundeskriminalamt, 'Neues Instrument zur Risikobewertung von potentiellen Gewaltstraftätern', 2 February 2017. Available online: https://www.bka.de/DE/Presse/Listenseite_Pressemitteilungen/2017/Presse2017/170202_Radar.html [https://perma.cc/Z89V-CF75], (accessed 1 January 2022).

Bundesministerium des Innern, 'Häufig Nachgefragt: Fluggastdatengesetz (PNR)', 2018. Available online: https://www.bmi.bund.de/SharedDocs/faqs/DE/themen/sicherheit/pnr/pnr-liste.html [https://perma.cc/V8HS-NAT4], (accessed 1 January 2022).

Burgess, Ernest W., 'Factors determining success or failure on parole', in: Bruce, A. A. / Burgess, Ernest W. / Landesco, J. / Harno, A.J. (eds), *The Workings of the Indeterminate Sentence Law and the Parole System in Illinois*, 221–234, Springfield: Northwestern University Press, 1928.

Burrell, Jenna, 'How the Machine "Thinks" – Understanding Opacity in Machine Learning Algorithms', *Big Data & Society*, 3(1/2016): 1–12.

Bussmann, Kai-D., 'Kritische Kriminologie und Systemtheorie', in: Kreissl, Reinhard (ed), *Kritische Kriminologie in der Diskuss*ion, Wiesbaden VS Verlag für Sozialwissenschaften, 1996: 73–122.

Cabitza, Federico / Rasoini, Raffaele / Gensini, Gian Franco, 'Unintended consequences of machine learning in medicine', *Jama*, 318(6/2016): 517–518.

Capers, I. Bennett, 'Race, Policing, and Technology', *N.C. L. Rev.*, 95 (4/2017): 1241–1292.

Capus, Nadja, 'Die Tyrannei des Wahrscheinlichen in der Justiz', *Die Republik*, 19 September 2018. Available online: https://www.republik.ch/2018/09/19/die-tyrannei-des-wahrscheinlichen-in-der-justiz [https://perma.cc/LVD2-64KA], (accessed 1 January 2022).

Carr, Nicholas, *The Glass Cage: Automation and Us*, New York: Norton, 2014.

Carter, Shan / Armstrong, Zan / Schubert, Ludwig / Johnson, Ian / Olah, Chris, 'Exploring Neural Networks with Activation Atlases', *Distill*, 2019. Available online: https://distill.pub/2019/activation-atlas/ [https://perma.cc/Z2LV-8VQN], (accessed 1 January 2022).

Center for the Governance of Change, 'European Tech Insights 2019'. Available online: https://www.ie.edu/cgc/news-events/events/european-tech-insights-2019/ [https://perma.cc/E8XR-YFTT], (accessed 1 January 2022).

Chan, Janet / Bennett Moses, Lyria, 'Is Big Data Challenging Criminology?', *Theoretical Criminology*, 20(1/2016): 21–39.

Chander, Anupam, 'The Racist Algorithm?', *Mich. L. Rev.*, 115(6/2017): 1023–1045.

Chicago Police Department, 'News Release: CPD Welcomes the Opportunity to Comment on Recently Published RAND Review', 17 August 2016. Available online: http://4abpn833c0nr1zvwp7447f2b.wpengine.netdna-cdn.com/wp-content/uploads/2016/08/RAND_Response-1.pdf [https://perma.cc/7A9H-97U8] (accessed 1 January 2022).

Chouldechova, Alexandra / G'Sell, Max, 'Fairer and More Accurate, But For Whom?', *arXiv 2017*. Available online: https://arxiv.org/abs/1707.00046 [https://perma.cc/D65U-V7JW], (accessed 1 January 2022).

Citron, Danielle Keats, 'Technological Due Process', *Wash. L. Rev.*, 85 (2007): 1249–1313.

Citron, Danielle Keats / Pasquale, Frank A., 'The Scored Society: Due Process for Automated Predictions', *Wash. L. Rev.*, 1 (2014): 1–33.

Cobler, Sebastian, 'Herold gegen alle', *TransAtlantik*, 11 (1980): 29–40.

Cofone, Ignacio, 'Antidiscriminatory Information Rules', *SMU L. Rev.*, 2019: 139–176.

Cohen, Stanley, *Visions of Social Control: Crime, Punishment and Classification*, Cambridge: Polity Press, 1985.

Confessore, Nicholas / Rosenberg, 'Matthew, Spy Contractor's Idea Helped Cambridge Analytica Harvest Facebook Data', *The New York Times*, 27 February 2018. Available online: https://nyti.ms/2GhF55r [https://perma.cc/4E2X-2CKD], (accessed 1 January 2022).

Congressional Research Service, 'Public Trust and Law Enforcement – A Discussion for Policymakers', 2018. Available online: https://fas.org/sgp/crs/misc/R43904.pdf [https://perma.cc/YP9M-7CGP], (accessed 1 January 2022).

Corbett-Davies, Sam / Pierson, Emma / Feller, Avi / Goel, Sharad / Huq, Aziz, 'Algorithmic Decision Making and the Cost of Fairness', *ACM SIGKDD* 2017, 797–806.

Creemers, Niklas / Guagnin, Daniel, 'Datenbanken in der Polizeipraxis: Zur computergestützten Konstruktion von Verdacht', *KrimJ*, 3 (24/2014): 134–148.

Cummings, Mary. L., 'The social and ethical impact of decision support interface design', in: Karwowski, Waldemar (ed), *International Encyclopedia of Ergonomics and Human Factors*, 2. ed. New York: CRC Press, 2006: 1249–1253.

Cummings, Mary L., 'Automation and Accountability in Decision Support System Interface Design', *Journal of Technology Studies*, 31 (1/2006): 23–31.

Danziger, Shai / Levav, Jonathan / Avnaim-Pesso, Liora, 'Extraneous factors in judicial decisions', *PNAS*, 108 (17/2011): 6889–6892.

Darnstädt, Thomas, 'Ein personenbezogener Gefahrbegriff–Analyse der Bedingungen des Bundesverfassungsgerichts an Vorfeld-Ermächtigungen im BKA-Gesetz', *DVBL*, 132 (2/2017): 88–96.

Darnstädt, Thomas / Horning, Frank / Müller, Martin U. / Rosenbach, Marcel / Schmundt, Hilmar, 'Freiheit@unendlich.welt', *Der Spiegel*, 9 August 2009. Available online: https://www.spiegel.de/politik/freiheitanunendlich-welt-a-116a4dc0-0002-0001-0000-000066360414 (accessed 1 January 2022).

DARPA, 'Broad Agency Announcement: Explainable Artificial Intelligence (XAI)', 2016. Available online: https://www.darpa.mil/attachments/DARPA-BAA-16-53.pdf [https://perma.cc/FL9C-W2RJ] (accessed 1 January 2022).

Datenethikkommission, 'Empfehlungen der Datenethikkommission für die Strategie Künstliche Intelligenz der Bundesregierung', 2018. Available online: https://www.bmjv.de/SharedDocs/Downloads/DE/Ministerium/ForschungUndWissenschaft/DEK_Empfehlungen.pdf;jsessionid=C7003E376DBB74AD0D32E6A93A45B3B0.1_cid289?__blob=publicationFile&v=2 [https://perma.cc/TS9Q-H7LR] (accessed 1 January 2022).

Datenschutzbeauftragte des Bundes und der Länder, *Big Data zur Gefahrenabwehr und Strafverfolung: Risiken und Nebenwirkungen beachten*, 89. Konferenz der Datenschutzbeauftragten des Bundes und der Länder, 2015. Available online: https:// www.datenschutzkonferenz-online.de%2Fmedia%2Fen%2F20150318_en_BigData.pdf&usg=AOvVaw1jiJ07f3H58GwlQtpCJ_6G (accessed 1.1.2022).

Datta, Anupam / Sen, Shayak / Zick, Yair, 'Algorithmic transparency via quantitative input influence: Theory and experiments with learning systems', 2016 IEEE symposium on security and privacy (SP): 598–617.

Davey, Monica, 'Chicago Police Try to Predict Who May Shoot or Be Shot', *The New York Times*, 23 May 2016. Available online: http://nyti.ms/1s4fQfh [https://perma.cc/MCL2-EZXN], (accessed 1 January 2022).

de Keijser, Jan W. / Roberts, Julian V. / Ryberg, Jesper (ed), *Predictive Sentencing: Normative and Empirical Perspectives*, Oxford: Hart Publishing, 2019.

Dean, Jeff / Patterson, David / Young, Cliff, 'A new golden age in computer architecture: Empowering the machine-learning revolution', *IEEE Micro*, 2018: 21–29.

Denninger, Erhard, 'Das Recht auf informationelle Selbstbestimmung und Innere Sicherheit: Folgerungen aus dem Volkszählungsgesetzurteil des Bundesverfassungsgerichts', *KJ*, 18 (3/1985): 215–244.

Diakopoulos, Nicholas, 'Algorithmic Accountability: On the Investigation of Black Boxes, *Tow Center for Digital Journalism*, 2014. Available online: https://doi.org/10.7916/D8ZK5TW2 (accessed 1 January 2022).

Dick, Philip K., 'Minority Report', in: Dick, Philip K. (ed), *Selected Stories of Philip K. Dick*, New York: Houghton Mifflin Harcourt, 2013 [1956]: 223–260.

Dietvorst, Berkeley J / Simmons, Joseph P / Massey, Cade, 'Algorithm aversion: People erroneously avoid algorithms after seeing them err', *J. Exp. Psychol. Gen.*, 144 (1(2015): 114–126.

Dollinger, Bernd, 'Sicherheit als politische Narration: Risiko-Kommunikation und die Herstellung von Un-/Sicherheit', in: Dollinger, Bernd / Schmidt-Semisch, Henning (eds), *Sicherer Alltag?: Politiken und Mechanismen der Sicherheitskonstruktion im Alltag*, Wiesbaden: Springer, 2016: 57–80.

Doshi-Velez, Finale / Kim, Been, 'Towards a Rigorous Science of Interpretable Machine Learning', *arXiv*, 2017. Available online: https://arxiv.org/abs/1702.08608 [https://perma.cc/893G-SBCE], (accessed 1 January 2022).

Doshi-Velez, Finale / Kortz, Mason / Budish, Ryan / Bavitz, Chris / Gershman, Sam / O'Brien, David / Schieber, Stuart / Waldo, James / Weinberger, David / Wood, Alexandra, 'Accountability of AI Under the Law: The Role of Explanation', *arXiv*, 2017. Available online: https://arxiv.org/pdf/1711.01134.pdf [https://perma.cc/QTP5-F854], (accessed 1 January 2022).

Douglas, Kevin S. / Hart, Stephen D. / Webster, Christopher D. / Belfrage, Henrik / Guy, Laura S. / Wilson, Catherine M., 'Historical-clinical-risk management-20, version 3 (HCR-20V3): development and overview', *Int. J. Forensic Ment Health*, 13 (2/2014): 93–108.

Douglas, Kevin S. / Webster, Christopher D., 'The HCR-20 violence risk assessment scheme: Concurrent validity in a sample of incarcerated offenders', *Criminal justice and behaviour*, 26 (1/1999): 3–19.

dpa, 'Journalisten wurde zu Unrecht Akkreditierung entzogen', *Zeit Online*, 30 August 2017. Available online: https://www.zeit.de/gesellschaft/zeitgeschehen/2017-08/datenschutz-datenspeicherung-bka-heiko-maas-rechtswidrig-aufklaerung [https://perma.cc/6Z45-CSRZ], (accessed 1 January 2022).

Dräger, Jörg, 'Ein Tüv für Algorithmen', *Handelsblatt*, 21 August 2017. Available online: https://www.handelsblatt.com/meinung/gastbeitraege/gastkommentar-zum-digitalen-wandel-ein-tuev-fuer-algorithmen/20212180.html?ticket=ST-912292-A6FvzJRe0bEXgzXLLXgu-ap2 [https://perma.cc/6M6X-GXTT], (accessed 1 January 2022).

Dreher, Eduard, *Die Willensfreiheit: ein zentrales Problem mit vielen Seiten*, Munich: C.H. Beck, 1987.

Dressel, Julia J / Farid, Hany, 'The Accuracy, Fairness, and Limits of Predicting Recidivism', *Science Advances*, 4 (1/2018): 1–5.

Drewer, Petra, Die *kognitive Metapher als Werkzeug des Denkens. Zur* Rolle *der Analogie bei der Gewinnung und Vermittlung wissenschaftlicher Erkenntnisse*, Tübingen: Gunter Narr, 2003.

Duhigg, Charles, 'How Companies Learn Your Secrets', *The New York Times*, 19 February 2012. Available online: https://nyti.ms/2jEboTD [https://perma.cc/UU 4W-YVPH], (accessed 1 January 2022).

Dumke, Mick / Main, Frank, 'A Look Inside the Watch List Chicago Police Fought to Keep Secret', 2017. Available online: https://chicago.suntimes.com/2017/5/ 18/18386116/a-look-inside-the-watch-list-chicago-police-fought-to-keep-secret [https://perma.cc/9DG9-TZAF], (accessed 1 January 2022).

Duwell, Marcus, 'Human Dignity: Concept, Discussions, Philosophical Perspectives: Interdisciplinary Perspectives', in: Düwell, Marcus / Braarvig, Jens / Brownsword, Roger / Mieth, Dietmar (eds), *Cambridge Handbook on Human Dignity*, Cambridge: Cambridge University Press, 2014: 23–50.

DyRiAS, 'Broschüre: Screener Islamismus', Darmstadt, 2018. Available online: https://www.dyrias.com/images/Screener_Islamismus/DyRiAS_Broschuere_ Screener_Radikal.pdf [https://perma.cc/Y8X2-8UC5], (accessed 1 January 2022).

Eaglin, Jessica M., 'Constructing Recidivism Risk', *Emory L.J.*, 67 (1/2017): 59–122.

Eckstein, Ken, Ermittlungen zu Lasten Dritter, Tübingen: Mohr Siebeck, 2013.

Egbert, Simon, 'On Security Discourses and Techno-Fixes – The Political Framing and Implementation of Predictive Policing in Germany', *European Journal for Security Studies*, 3 (2018): 95–114.

Egbert, Simon / Krasmann, Susanne, 'Predictive Policing. Eine ethnographische Studie neuer Technologien zur Vorhersage von Straftaten und ihre Folgen für die polizeiliche Praxis. Projektabschlussbericht', Hamburg 2019. Available online: https://www.wiso.uni-hamburg.de/fachbereich-sowi/professuren/hentsch el/forschung/predictive-policing/egbert-krasmann-2019-predictive-policing-proje ktabschlussbericht.pdf [https://perma.cc/96H9-2Q2E], (accessed 1 January 2022).

Eichenhofer, Johannes, 'Privatheit und Transparenz in der Demokratie', *Forschungsjournal Soziale Bewegungen*, 30 (2/2017): 133–142.

Eifert, Martin, 'Das Allgemeine Persönlichkeitsrecht des Art. 2 I GG', *JURA*, 37 (11/2015): 1181–1191.

Eisenberg, Ulrich / Kölbel, Ralf, *Kriminologie – Ein Lehrbuch*, 7. ed., Tübingen: Mohr Siebeck, 2017.

Elish, M. C. / boyd, danah, 'Situating methods in the magic of Big Data and AI', *Communication Monographs*, 85 (1/2017): 1–24.

Elmering, Hermann, *Die kriminologische Frühprognose: Überprüfung der Glueck'schen fünfpunktigen sozialen Prognosetafel an Hand von hundert mit Jugendstrafe bestraften Jugendlichen*, Hamburg: Kriminalistik Verlag, 1969.

Endrass, Jérôme, 'Die Stigmatisierung junger Muslime wäre kontraproduktiv', *Frankfurter Allgemeine Zeitung*, 19 July 2017. Available online: http://plus.faz.net/natur-und-wissenschaft/2017-07-19/die-stigmatisierung-junger-muslime-waere-kontraproduktiv/33009.html [https://perma.cc/6XY2-H6H8], (accessed 1 January 2022).

Endrass, Jérôme / Rossegger, Astrid, 'Herausforderungen im Bedrohungsmanagement und das Octagon als neuer Ansatz', *format magazine – Zeitschrift für Polizeiausbildung und Polizeiforschung*, 7 (2017): 36–41.

Endsley, Mica R. / Kiris, Esin O., 'The out-of-the-loop performance problem and level of control in automation', *Human Factors*, 37 (2/1995): 381–394.

Europäische Kommission, *Generaldirektion Kommunikation, Standard Eurobarometer 90, Die öffentliche Meinung in der Europäischen Union*, Brussels: European Commission, 2018.

Evers, Adalbert, "Risiko und Individualismus. Was in Ulrich Becks 'Risikogesellschaft' unbegriffen bleibt", *Kommune*, 6 (1989), 33–49.

Ewald, François, *Der Vorsorgestaat*, trans. W. Bayer and H. Kocyba, 2. ed., Frankfurt: Suhrkamp, 1993.

Farrell, Graham / Sousa, William, 'Repeat Victimization and Hot Spots – The Overlap and its Implications for Crime Control and Problem-Oriented-Policing', in: Farrell, Graham / Pease, Ken (ed), *Crime Prevention Studies*, volume 12 (2001): 221–240.

Fazel, Seena / Singh, Jay P. / Doll, Helen / Grann, Martin, 'Use of risk assessment instruments to predict violence and antisocial behaviour in 73 samples involving 24 827 people: systematic review and meta-analysis', *BMJ*, 345 (2012): e4692.

Feeley, Malcolm / Simon, Jonathan, 'The New Penology: Notes on the Emerging Strategy of Corrections and Its Implications', *Criminology*, 30 (4/1992): 449–474.

Feldman, Michael / Friedler, Sorelle A. / Moeller, John / Scheidegger, Carlos / Venkatasubramanian, Suresh, 'Certifying and removing disparate impact', *ACM SIGKDD*, 2015: 259–268.

Ferguson, Andrew G., 'Big Data and Predictive Reasonable Suspicion', *U. Pa. L. Rev.*, 163 (2/2015): 327–310.

Ferguson, Andrew G., The *Rise of Big Data Policing – Surveillance, Race, and the Future of Law Enforcement*, New York: NYU Press, 2017.

Fischer, Sarah / Petersen, Thomas, Was *Deutschland über Algorithmen weiß und denkt. Ergebnisse einer repräsentativen Bevölkerungsumfrage im Auftrag der Bertelsmann Stiftung*, Gütersloh: BertelsmannStiftung, 2018.

Fischer, Thomas, *Beck'scher Kurz-Kommentar StGB*, 65. ed., Munich: C.H. Beck, 2018 (Fischer StGB).

Flade, Florian, 'So funktioniert das Radar für radikale Islamisten', *Die Welt*, 12 June 2017. Available online: https://www.welt.de/politik/deutschland/plus165451390/So-funktioniert-das-Radar-fuer-radikale-Islamisten.html [https://perma.cc/2MLX-A6ST], (accessed 1 January 2022).

Floridi, Luciano, 'Distributed morality in an information society', *Science and Engineering Ethics*, 19 (3/2013): 727–743.

Floridi, Luciano (ed), *The Onlife Manifesto – Being Human in a Hyperconnected Era*, Heidelberg: Springer, 2015.

Floridi, Luciano, 'Faultless responsibility: on the nature and allocation of moral responsibility for distributed moral actions', *Phil. Trans. R. Soc. A*, 374 (2083/2016).

Fong, Ruth C. / Vedaldi, Andrea, 'Interpretable Explanations of Black Boxes by Meaningful Perturbation', *Proceedings of the IEEE International Conference on Computer Vision* 2017: 3429–3437.

Forsthoff, Ernst, *Rechtsstaat im Wandel: verfassungsrechtliche Abhandlungen 1950–1964*, Stuttgart: Kohlhammer, 1964.

Foucault, Michel, 'Macht und Wissen', in: Foucault, Michel (ed), *Dits et Ecrits. Schriften*, Frankfurt a. M.: Suhrkamp, 2003: 515–534.

Freeman, Katherine, 'Algorithmic Injustice: How the Wisconsin Supreme Court Failed to Protect Due Process Rights in State V. Loomis', *NCJL & Tech. On.*, 18 (15/2016): 75–180.

Frei, Andreas, 'Die Risikoeinschätzung von schwerwiegender häuslicher Gewalt anhand des computerisierten Prognoseinstrumentes DyRiAS', unpublished manuscript.

Freitas, Alex A., 'Comprehensible classification models: a position paper', *ACM SIGKDD explorations newsletter*, 15 (1/2014): 1–10.

Freund, Georg, *Normative Probleme der 'Tatsachenfeststellung': eine Untersuchung zum tolerierten Risiko einer Fehlverurteilung im Bereich subjektiver Deliktsmerkmale*, Heidelberg: C.F. Müller, 1987.

Frister, Helmut, 'Die Unschuldsvermutung', in: Herzog, Felix / Schlothauer, Reinhold / Wohlers, Wolfgang (eds), *Rechtsstaatlicher Strafprozess und Bürgerrechte. Gedächtnisschrift für Edda Wesslau, Schriften zum* Strafrecht, 297 (2016): 149–163.

Fritzsche, Andreas F., *Wie sicher leben wir?*, Köln: TÜV Rheinland, 1986.

Fröhlich, Wiebke / Spiecker, Indra, 'Können Algorithmen diskriminieren?', *Verfassungsblog*, 26 December 2018. Available online: https://verfassungsblog.de/koennen-algorithmen-diskriminieren/ [https://perma.cc/9GVX-X564], (accessed 1 January 2022).

Fuchs, Christian (2002), *Krise und Kritik in der Informationsgesellschaft*, Norderstedt: BoD, 2002.

Gandomi, Amir / Haider, Murtaza, 'Beyond the hype: Big data concepts, methods, and analytics', *IJIM*, 35 (2/2015): 137–144.

Garzcarek, Ursula / Steuer, Detlef, 'Approaching Ethical Guidelines for Data Scientists', *arXiv*, 2019. Available online: https://arxiv.org/abs/1901.04824 [https://perma.cc/RZ5S-P24W], (accessed 1 January 2022).

Geißler, Rainer, "'Ausländerkriminalität' – Vorurteile, Mißverständnisse, Fakten", *Zeitschrift für Migration und soziale Arbeit*, 1 (2000): 20–27.

Gershgorn, Dave, 'Software used to predict crime can now be scoured for bias', *Quarz*, 22 March 2017. Available online: https://qz.com/938635/a-predictive-policing-startup-released-all-its-code-so-it-can-be-scoured-for-bias/ [https://perma.cc/QJ6P-WB8N], (accessed 1 January 2022).

Gerstner, Dominik, *Predictive Policing als Instrument zur Prävention von Wohnungseinbruchdiebstahl – Evaluationsergebnisse zum Baden-Württembergischen Pilotprojekt P4*, Freiburg: edition iuscrim, 2017.

Gerth, Juliane, *Risk-Assessment bei Gewalt- und Sexualdelinquenz – Standardisierte Risk-Assessment Instrumente auf dem Prüfstand*, Diss. Universität Konstanz, 2015.

Gerth, Juliane / Rossegger, Astrid / Singh, Jay P. / Endrass, Jérôme, 'Assessing the Risk of Severe Intimate Partner Violence: Validating the DyRiAS in Switzerland', *Archives of Forensic Psychology*, 1 (2015): 1–15.

Gesellschaft für Informatik, 'Gesetzentwurf für ein Gesetz zur Neuausrichtung des Verfassungsschutzes in Hessen', 2018a. Available online: https://gi.de/themen/beitrag/gesetzentwurf-fuer-ein-gesetz-zur-neuausrichtung-des-verfassungsschutzes-in-hessen/ [https://perma.cc/H88C-GQRC], (accessed 1 January 2022).

Gesellschaft für Informatik, 'Technische und rechtliche Betrachtungen algorithmischer Entscheidungsverfahren', Berlin, 2018b. Available online: http://www.svr-verbraucherfragen.de/wp-content/uploads/GI_Studie_Algorithmenregulierung.pdf [https://perma.cc/MZC5-C9L7], (accessed 1 January 2022).

Giddens, Anthony, *The Consequences of Modernity*, Stanford: Stanford University Press, 1990.

Gigerenzer, Gerd, 'How to make cognitive illusions disappear: Beyond "heuristics and biases"', *Eur. Rev. Soc. Psychol.*, 2 (1/1991): 83–115.

Gigerenzer, Gerd, *The Empire of Chance: How Probability Changed Science and Everyday Life*, Cambridge: Cambridge University Press, 1997.

Gigerenzer, Gerd, *Adaptive Thinking: Rationality in the Real World*, Oxford: Oxford University Press, 2000.

Gigerenzer, Gerd, *Bauchentscheidungen: Die Intelligenz des Unbewussten und die Macht der Intuition*, Gütersloh: C. Bertelsmann Verlag, 2007.

Gigerenzer, Gerd, *Risiko: Wie man die richtigen Entscheidungen trifft*, Gütersloh: C. Bertelsmann Verlag, 2013.

Gigerenzer, Gerd, *Risk savvy: How to make good decisions*, London: Penguin Books, 2015.

Gigerenzer, Gerd / Engel, Christoph (ed), *Heuristics and the Law*, Cambridge, MA: MIT Press, 2006.

Gigerenzer, Gerd / Rebitschek, Felix G. / Wagner, Gert G., 'Eine vermessene Gesellschaft braucht Transparenz', *Wirtschaftsdienst*, 98 (2018): 860–868.

Ginosar, Zvi / Trope, Yaacov, 'The effects of base rates and individuating information on judgments about another person', *J. Exp. Soc. Psychol.*, 16 (3/1980): 228–242.

Gitelman, Lisa (ed), *'Raw Data' Is an Oxymoron*, Cambridge, MA: MIT Press, 2013.

Gless, Sabine, 'Predictive Policing und operative Verbechensbekämpfung', in: Herzog, Felix / Schlothauer, Reinhold / Wolfgang, Wohlers (eds), *Rechtsstaatlicher Strafprofzess und Bürgerrechte – Gedächtnisschrift für Edda Weßlau*, Berlin: Duncker & Humblot 2016: 165–180.

Glover, Anthony J. J. / Churcher, Frances P. / Gray, Andrew L. / Mills, Jeremy F. / Nicholson, Diane E., 'A cross-validation of the Violence Risk Appraisal Guide – Revised (VRAG-R) within a correctional sample', *Law and Human Behavior*, 41 (6/2017): 507–518.

Gluba, Alexander, 'Predictive Policing – eine Bestandsaufnahme', *Kriminalistik*, 68 (6/2014): 347–352.

Glueck, Eleanor / Glueck, Sheldon, 'Identification of potential delinquents at 2–3 years of age', *Int. J. Soc. Psychiatr.*, 12 (1/1966): 5–16.

Glueck, Sheldon / Glueck, Eleanor, 'Potential juvenile delinquents can be identified: What next', *Brit. J. Criminol.*, 4 (3/1963): 215–226.

Goddard, Kate / Roudsari, Abdul / Wyatt, Jeremy C, 'Automation bias: a systematic review of frequency, effect mediators, and mitigators', *J. Am. Med. Inform. Assn.*, 19 (1/2011): 121–127.

Goldhammer, Klaus / Wiegand, André, *Ökonomischer Wert von Verbraucherdaten für Adress- und Datenhändler – Studie im Auftrag des Bundesministeriums der Justiz und für Verbraucherschutz*, Berlin: Bundesministerium der Justiz und für Verbraucherschutz, 2017.

Goodman, Bryce / Flaxman, Seth, 'European Union Regulations on Algorithmic Decision-Making and a "Right to Explanation"', *AI Magazine*, 38 (3/2017): 50–57.

Göppinger, Hans, *Kriminologie*, Munich: C.H. Beck, 2008.

Graham, Mark, 'Big Data and the End of Theory?', *The Guardian*, 9 March 2012. Available online: http://www.theguardian.com/news/datablog/2012/mar/09/big-data-theory [https://perma.cc/2V2T-2F44], (accessed 1 January 2022).

Green, Ben, 'Data Science as Political Action: Grounding Data Science in a Politics of Justice', *arXiv*, 2018. Available online: https://arxiv.org/pdf/1811.03435.pdf [https://perma.cc/G7HG-UG4Y], (accessed 1 January 2022).

Grgic-Hlaca, Nina / Zafar, Muhammad Bilal / Gummadi, Krishna P. / Weller, Adrian, 'The Case for Process Fairness in Learning: Feature Selection for Fair Decision Making', *NIPS Symposium on Machine Learning and the Law 2016*.

Groff, Elizabeth R. / LaVigne, Nancy G., 'Forecasting the Future of Predictive Crime Mapping', *Crime Prevention Studies*, 13 (2002): 29–57.

Groll, Kurt H. G., '"Die Bevölkerung vertraut der Polizei!" – Empirische Befunde zur Entwicklung des Vertrauens in Westdeutschland und Problematisierung der Aussagekraft der Vertrauensfrage', in: Bornewasser, Manfred (ed), *Empirische Polizeiforschung III*, Herbolzheim: Centaurus-Verl., 2002: 75–88.

Grossenbacher, Timo, 'Polizei-Software verdächtigt zwei von drei Personen falsch', *SRF*, 5 April 2018. Available online: https://www.srf.ch/news/schweiz/predictive-policing-polizei-software-verdaechtigt-zwei-von-drei-personen-falsch [https://perma.cc/7ZY8-6HCS], (accessed 1 January 2022).

Grymer, Herbert, 'Anmerkungen zum Begriff des Risikos in den Gesellschaftswissenschaften', in: Compes, Peter C. (ed), *Risiko – subjektiv und objektiv*, Wuppertal: Wirtschaftsverlag für neue Wissenschaften, 1989: 133–171.

Guidotti, Riccardo / Monreale, Anna / Ruggieri, Salvatore / Turini, Franco / Giannotti, Fosca / Pedreschi, Dino, 'A survey of methods for explaining black box models', *ACM Computing Surveys (CSUR)*, volume 51 (5/2018), article 93, 1–42.

Gundlach, Thomas / Menzel, Thomas, *Fehlerquellen der Polizeilichen Kriminalstatistik und ihre Auswirkungen am Beispiel Hamburg*, Schriftenreihe Polizei-Führungskademie, 1992: 60–83.

Gusy, Christoph, '§ 23 Informationsbeziehungen zwischen Staat und Bürger', in: Hoffmann-Riem, Wolfgang / Schmidt-Aßmann, Eberhard / Voßkuhle, Andreas (eds), *Grundlagen des Verwaltungsrechts*, 2. ed., Munich: C.H. Beck, 2012.

Gusy, Christoph / Eichenhofer, Johannes, 'Menschenwürde und Privatheitsschutz', in: Lorenzmeier, Stefan / Folz, Hans-Peter (eds), *Recht und Realität – Festschrift für Christoph Vedder*, Baden-Baden: Nomos 2017: 132–157.

Hacker, Philipp (2018), 'Teaching fairness to artificial intelligence: Existing and novel strategies against algorithmic discrimination under EU law', *Common Market L. Rev.*, 55 (4/2018): 1143–1185.

Häfele, Wolf / Renn, Ortwin / Erdmann, Georg, Risiko, 'Unsicherheit und Undeutlichkeit', in: Häfele, Wolf (ed), *Energiesysteme im Übergang unter den Bedingungen der Zuku*nft, Landsberg a. L.: mi-Poller, 1990: 373–423.

Hannah-Moffat, Kelly, 'The Uncertainties of Risk Assessment: Partiality, Transparency, and Just Decisions', *Fed. Sent'g Rep.*, 27 (2014): 244–247.

Harcourt, Bernard E., *Against Prediction: Sentencing, Policing, and Punishing in an Actuarial Age*, Chicago/London: Chicago University Press, 2007.

Harcourt, Bernard E., 'Risk as a proxy for race: The dangers of risk assessment', *Fed. Sent'g Rep.*, 27 (2014): 237–243.

Hardt, Moritz, 'Approaching Fairness in Machine Learning, *Moody Rd*, 2016. Available online: http://blog.mrtz.org/2016/09/06/approaching-fairness.html [https://perma.cc/EU2R-NEU4], (accessed 1 January 2022).

Hardt, Moritz / Price, Eric / Srebro, Nathan, 'Equality of Opportunity in Supervised Learning', *NIPS* 29 (2016).

Harford, Tim, 'Big data: A big mistake?', *Significance*, 11 (5/2014): 14–19.

Harkin, James, '"Big Data", "Who Owns the Future?" and "To Save Everything, Click Here"', *The Financial Times*, 1 March 2013. Available online: https://www.ft.com/content/afc1c178-8045-11e2-96ba-00144feabdc0 [https://perma.cc/SS9R-JFDY], (accessed 1 January 2022).

Hart, Hornell, 'Predicting Parole Cuccess', *J. Am. Inst. Crim. L. & Criminology*, 14 (3/1923): 405–413.

Hassemer, Winfried, 'Kennzeichen und Krisen des modernen Strafrechts', *ZRP*, 25 (10/1992): 378–383.

Hassemer, Winfried, 'Zum Spannungsverhältnis von Freiheit und Sicherheit. Drei Thesen', *Vorgänge, Zeitschrift für Bürgerrechte und Gesellschaftspolitik*, 159 (41/2202): 10–15.

Hastie, Charles / Group, Clutch, 'Compliance Playing Catch-Up with Regulators in Data Analytics Race', *Legaltech* News, 19 April 2017. Available online: http://at.law.com/g974zy [https://perma.cc/2NEG-S98Z], (accessed 1 January 2022).

Hauber, Judith / Jarchow, Esther / Rabitz-Suhr, Simone, *Prädiktionspotenzial schwere Einbruchskriminalität, Ergebnisse einer wissenschaftlichen Befassung mit Predictive Policing*, Hamburg: Landeskriminalamt Hamburg, 2020.

Haugeland, John, *Artificial Intelligence: the very idea*, Cambridge, MA: MIT Press, 1989.

Hecker, Meike / Starcke, Jan, 'Sozialer Zusammenhalt und Polizeivertrauen', *Soziale Probleme*, 28 (2/2017): 223–239.

Hegel, Georg Wilhelm Friedrich, *Phänomenologie des Geistes (Werke in zwanzig Bänden)*, Frankfurt a. M.: Suhrkamp, 1970.

Heilmann, Klaus / Urquhart, John, *Keine Angst vor der Angst: Risiko: Element unseres Lebens und Motor des Fortschritts*, Munich: Kindler, 1983.

Heinz, Wolfgang, '"Alle 5 Sekunden geschieht eine Straftat" "Wer hier wohnt, lebt auf Nummer sicher". Von Schwierigkeiten und Fehlern der Berichterstattung über Kriminalität', in: Dörmann, Uwe (ed), *Zahlen sprechen nicht für sich. Aufsätze zu Kriminalstatistik, Dunkelfeld und Sicherheitsgefühl aus drei Jahrzehnten*, Neuwied: Luchterhand, 2004: 359–412.

Hessischer Landtag, 'Zwischenbericht des Untersuchungsausschusses' 19/3 (2019). Available online: http://starweb.hessen.de/cache/DRS/19/4/06864.pdf [https://perma.cc/G698-DDLZ], (accessed 1 January 2022).

Hildebrandt, Mireille, 'Legal Protection by Design. Objections and Refutations.', *Legisprudence*, 5 (2/2011): 223- 248.

Hildebrandt, Mireille, 'Who Needs Stories if You Can Get the Data? ISPs in the Era of Big Number Crunching', *Philos. Technol.*, 24 (2011): 371–390.

Hildebrandt, Mireille, *Smart Technologies and the End(s) of Law*, Cheltenham/Northampton, MA: Edward Elgar, 2015.

Hildebrandt, Mireille, 'Law as Information in the Era of Data-Driven Agency', *Mod. L. Rev.*, 79 (1/2016): 1–30.

Hildebrandt, Mireille, 'Law as Computation in the Era of Artificial Legal Intelligence – Speaking Law to the Power of Statistics', *UTLJ*, 68 (1/2018): 12–35.

Hildebrandt, Mireille, 'Preregistration of machine learning research design. Against P-hacking', in: Bayamlıoğlu, Emre / Baraliuc, Irina / Janssens, Liisa / Hildebrandt, Mireille (eds), *Being Profiled: Cogitas Ergo Sum*, Amsterdam: Amsterdam University Press, 2018: 102–105.

Hildebrandt, Mireille / de Vries, Katja (ed), *Privacy, Due Process and the Computational Turn: The Philosophy of Law Meets the Philosophy of Technology*, Abingdon: Routledge, 2013.

Hilgendorf, Eric, '"Die Schuld ist immer zweifellos?" – Offene Fragen bei Tatsachenfeststellung und Beweis mit Hilfe "intelligenter" Maschinen', in: Fischer, Thomas (ed), *Beweis*, Baden-Baden: Nomos, 2019: 229–252.

Hoff, Timothy, 'Deskilling and adaptation among primary care physicians using two work innovations', *Health Care Management Review*, 36 (4/2011): 338–348.

Höffler, Katrin, 'Risikokriminologie', *Monatsschrift für Kriminologie und Strafrechtsreform*, 95 (4/2012): 252–268.

Höffler, Katrin / Sommerer, Lucia M. / Gatzmaga, Felix, 'Radikalisierung im digitalen Zeitalter entschlüsseln–Prognosen ermöglichen?', *NK* 29 (2017): 424–439.

Hoffmann, Anika / Illgner, Christian / Leuschner, Fredericke / Rettenberger, Martin, *Extremismus und Justizvollzug: Literaturauswertung und empirische Erhebungen*, Wiesbaden: Kriminologische Zentralstelle e.V, 2017.

Hoffmann, Jens, 'Drohungen, Gewalt und Stalking am Arbeitsplatz', *SafetyPlus*, 2014, Vol. 40: 40–42.

Hoffmann, Jens / Glaz-Ocik, Justine, 'DyRiAS-Intimpartner: Konstruktion eines online gestützten Analyse-Instruments zur Risikoeinschätzung von tödlicher Gewalt gegen aktuelle oder frühere Intimpartnerinnen', *Polizei & Wissenschaft*, 2 (2012): 45–57.

Hoffmann, Jens / Roshdi, Karoline / Allwinn, Mirko, 'DyRiAS-Schule: Entwicklung und Validierung eines online gestützten Analyse-Instruments zur Risikoeinschätzung von schwerer zielgerichteter Gewalt an Schulen', *Polizei & Wissenschaft*, 2 (2013): 49–59.

Hoffmann-Riem, Wolfgang, 'Rechtliche Rahmenbedingungen für und regulative Herausforderungen durch Big Data', in: Hoffmann-Riem, Wolfgang (ed), *Big Data-Regulative Herausforderungen*, Baden-Baden: Nomos 2018, 12–76.

Hoffmann-Riem, Wolfgang / Schmidt-Aßmann, Eberhard / Vosskuhle, Andreas (eds), *Grundlagen des Verwaltungsrechts*, vol. 2, 2. ed. Munich: C.H. Beck, 2012.

Hofmann, Hasso, 'Die versprochene Menschenwürde', *AöR*, 118 (3/1993): 353–377.

Hornung, Gerrit, 'Erosion traditioneller Prinzipien des Datenschutzrechts durch Big Data', in: Hoffmann-Riem, Wolfgang (ed), *Big Data-Regulative Herausforderungen*, Baden-Baden: Nomos, 2018: 79–98.

Hough, Mike / Jackson, Jonathan / Bradford, Ben, 'Legitimacy, trust and compliance: An empirical test of procedural justice theory using the European Social Survey', in: Tankebe, Justice / Liebling, Alison (eds), *Legitimacy and Criminal Justice: an International Exploration*, Oxford: Oxford University Press, 2013: 326–352.

Hüfner, Jörg, *Wie sicher ist sicher genug? Zur Definition, Abschätzung und Bewertung von Risiken*, Karlsruhe: Deukalion, 1989.

Huq, Aziz Z., 'Racial Equity in Algorithmic Criminal Justice, *Duke L.J.*, 68 (2019): 1043–1134.

Irving, Geoffrey / Askell, Amanda, 'AI Safety Needs Social Scientists', *Distill*, 2019: e14.

Isensee, Josef / Kirchhof, Paul (ed), *Handbuch des Staatsrechts*, vol. VIII, 3. ed., Heidelberg: Müller, 2010 (Handbuch Staatsrecht: Handbuch Staatsrecht).

Jäkel, Olaf, *Wie Metaphern Wissen schaffen: die kognitive Metapherntheorie und ihre Anwendung in Modell-Analysen der Diskursbereiche Geistestätigkeit, Wirtschaft, Wissenschaft und Religion*, Hamburg: Dr Kovac Verlag, 2003.

Jakobs, Günther, 'Kriminalisierung im Vorfeld einer Rechtsgutsverletzung', *ZStW*, 97 (5/1985): 751–785.

Jansen, Frank / Fiedler, Maria, 'Interview: "Die Gefährderzahl hat sich verfünffacht"', Bundeskriminalamt, 19 December 2018. Available online: https://www.bka.de/DE/Presse/Interviews/2018/181219_InterviewMuenchTagesspiegel.html [https://perma.cc/6HPV-4HYU], (accessed 1 January 2022).

Jehle, Jörg-Martin / Beier, Klaus M., *Kriminologie zwischen Grundlagenwissenschaften und Praxis*, Mönchengladbach: Forum Verlag Godesberg, 2003.

Joh, Elizabeth E., 'Beyond Surveillance: Data Control and Body Cameras', *Surveillance & Society*, 14 (1/2016): 1–5.

Johnson, David S., 'Repeat Burglary Victimisation: A Tale of Two Theories', *J. Exp. Criminol.*, 4 (2008): 215–240.

Johnson, Shane D. / Birks, Daniel J. / McLaughlin, Lindsay / Bowers, Kate J. / Pease, Ken, *Prospective crime mapping in operational context*, 19 (07/2007), London: Home Office.

Jolls, Christine / Sunstein, Cass R., 'The Law of Implicit Bias', Calif. L. Rev., 94 (2006): 969–996.

Jones, Michael D. / McBeth, Mark K. / Shanahan, Elizabeth A., 'Introducing the Narrative Policy Framework', in: Jones, Michael D. / McBeth, Mark K. / Shanahan, Elizabeth A. (eds), *The Science of Stories*, New York: Palgrave Macmillan, 2014, 1–25.

Jöns, Johanna, 'Daten als Handelsware', Hamburg, 2016. Available online: https://www.divsi.de/wp-content/uploads/2016/03/Daten-als-Handelsware.pdf [https://perma.cc/2T9K-KFPM], (accessed 1 January 2022).

Jordan, Benedikt / Gresser, Ursula, 'Wie unabhängig sind Gutachter', *Der Sachverständige*, 4 (2014): 71–84.

Jouvenal, Justin, 'The new way police are surveilling you: Calculating your threat "score"', *The Washington Post*, 10 January 2016. Available online: https://www.washingtonpost.com/local/public-safety/the-new-way-police-are-surveilling-you-calculating-your-threat-score/2016/01/10/e42bccac-8e15-11e5-baf4-bdf37355da0c_story.html [https://perma.cc/P4FG-6WH8], (accessed 1 January 2022).

Joyce, James, *Ulysses*, London: Penguin, 2000.

Kahneman, Daniel, *Thinking, Fast and Slow*, London: Penguin, 2011.

Kahneman, Daniel / Tversky, Amos, 'Subjective probability: A judgment of representativeness', *Cognitive Psychology*, 3 (3/1972): 430–454.

Kahneman, Daniel / Tversky, Amos, 'On the Psychology of Prediction', Psychol. Rev., 80 (4/1973): 237–251.

Kaiser, Günther, *Kriminologie: ein Lehrbuch*, 3. ed., Heidelberg: Verlagsgruppe Hüthig-Jehle-Rehm, 1996.

Kaminski, Margot E. / Witnov, Shane, 'The Conforming Effect: First Amendment Implications of Surveillance, Beyond Chilling Speech', *U. Rich. L. Rev.*, 49 (2014): 465–518.

Kamishima, Toshihiro / Akaho, Shotaro / Asoh, Hideki / Sakuma, Jun, 'Fairness-Aware Classifier with Prejudice Remover Regularizer', *Joint European Conference on Machine Learning and Knowledge Discovery in Databases 2012*, 35–50.

Kant, Immanuel. 'Beantwortung der Frage: Was ist Aufklärung?', *Berlinische Monatsschrift*, 1784: 481–494.

Kant, Immanuel, 'Was heißt: sich im Denken orientieren?', *Berlinische Monatsschrift*, 1786: 304–330.

Kant, Immanuel, *Beantwortung der Frage: was ist Aufklärung?*, Berlin: CreateSpace, 2016 [1784].

Kaspar, Johannes, 'Sentencing Guidelines statt freies tatrichterliches Ermessen – Brauchen wir ein neues Strafzumessungsrecht? – Gutachten zum 72. Deutschen Juristentag', Munich: C.H. Beck, 2018.

Kasperkevic, Jana, 'Google says sorry for racist auto-tag in photo app', *The Guardian*, 1 July 2015. Available online: https://www.theguardian.com/technology/2015/jul/01/google-sorry-racist-auto-tag-photo-app [https://perma.cc/P2KT-8GEV], (accessed 1 January 2022).

Kaufmann, Franz-Xaver, *Sicherheit als soziologisches und sozialpolitisches Problem. Untersuchungen zu einer Wertidee hochdifferenzierter Gesellschaften*, Münster: LIT Verlag, 2012.

KI Bundesverband, *KI Gütesiegel*, Berlin, 2019. Available online: https://ki-verband.de/ki-guetesiegel-ai-made-in-germany (accessed 1 January 2022).

Kießling, Andrea, 'Gefahraufklärungsbefugnisse in der Polizeirechtsdogmatik – Überlegungen anlässlich des Urteils des Bundesverfassungsgerichts zum BKAG', *Verwaltungsarchiv*, 2017: 282–302.

Kindhäuser, Urs / Neumann, Ulfrid / Paeffgen, Hans-Ullrich (ed), *Strafgesetzbuch*, vol. 1, 5. ed., Baden-Baden: Nomos, 2017 (NK-StGB: NK-StGB).

King, Sonja / Bender, Doris / Lösel, Friedrich, 'Instrumente zur Risikobeurteilung extremistisch motivierter Straftäter: Eine Synopse', *Kriminologische Welt in Bewegung*, 2018: 191–203.

Kischel, Uwe (2003), *Die Begründung: zur Erläuterung staatlicher Entscheidungen gegenüber dem Bürger*, Tübingen: Mohr Siebeck, 2003.

Kitchin, Rob, *The Data Revolution: Big Data, Open Data, Data Infrastructures and their Consequences*, Thousand Oaks: Sage, 2014.

Kleinberg, Jon / Mullainathan, Sendhil / Raghavan, Manish, 'Inherent Trade-Offs in the Fair Determination of Risk Scores', *ITCS 2017*, 43:1–43:23.

Klingele, Cecilia, 'The Promises and Perils of Evidence-Based Corrections', *Notre Dame L. Rev.*, 91 (2/2016): 537–584.

Knauer, Christoph / Kudlich, Hans / Schneider, Hartmut (eds), *Münchener Kommentar zur Strafprozessordnung*, vol. 2, 3, Munich: C.H. Beck, 2016 (MüKo-StPO: MüKo-StPO).

Knierim, Antonie, 'Kumulation von Datensammlungen auf Vorrat', *Zeitschrift für Datenschutz*, 1 (2011): 7–23.

Knight, Ben, 'Wie gefährlich sind Gefährder?', *Deutsche Welle*, 19 December 2017. Available online: https://p.dw.com/p/2peFf [https://perma.cc/3QQC-7MDC], (accessed 1 January 2022).

Knight, Will, 'The Dark Secret at the Heart of AI', *MIT Technol. Rev*, 2017. Available online: https://www.technologyreview.com/s/604087/the-dark-secret-at-the-heart-of-ai/ [https://perma.cc/3RL5-DURR], (accessed 1 January 2022).

Knobloch, Tobias, *Vor die Lage kommen: Predictive Policing in Deutschland*, Berlin: BertelsmannStiftung, 2018.

Kohler-Hausmann, Issa, *Misdemeanorland: Criminal Courts and Social Control in an Age of Broken Windows Policing*, Princeton/Oxford: Princeton University Press, 2018.

Kölbel, Ralf / Selter, Susanne, 'Hostile Intent – The Terrorists Achilles Heel – Observations on Pre-Crime Surveillance by Means of Thought Recognition', *Eur. J. Crime Crim. L. & Crim. Just.*, 18 (3/2010): 237–259.

Köllisch, Tilman, *Vom Dunkelfeld ins Hellfeld: Anzeigeverhalten und Polizeikontakte bei Jugenddelinquenz*, Freiburg, 2004.

Konferenz der Informationsfreiheitsbeauftragten, 'Positionspapier: Transparenz der Verwaltung beim Einsatz von Algorithmen für gelebten Grundrechtsschutz unabdingbar', 2018. Available online: https://www.datenschutzzentrum.de/uploads/informationsfreiheit/2018_Positionspapier-Transparenz-von-Algorithmen.pdf [https://perma.cc/U9N5-K68A], (accessed 1 January 2022).

König, Olaf, *Die Entwicklung der strafprozessualen Zwangsmassnahmen im Ermittlungsverfahren seit 1877: Tendenzen zur Verpolizeilichung des Ermittlungsverfahrens durch präventiv ausgerichtete Zwangsbefugnisse*, Frankfurt a. M.: Peter Lang, 1993.

Kosinski, Michal / Stillwell, David / Graepel, Thore, 'Private traits and attributes are predictable from digital records of human behaviour', *PNAS*, 110 (10/2013): 5802–5805.

Kostka, Genia, 'China's social credit systems and public opinion: Explaining high levels of approval', *New Media & Society*, 21 (7/2019): 1565–1593.

Krafft, Tobias D. / Zweig, Katharina A., 'Wie Gesellschaft algorithmischen Entscheidungen auf den Zahn fühlen kann', in: Mohabbat Kar, Resa / Thapa, Basanta E. P. / Parycek, Peter (eds), *(Un)berechenbar? Algorithmen und Automatisierung in Staat und Gesellschaft*, Berlin: Fraunhofer-Institut für Offene Kommunikationssysteme FOKUS, 2018: 471–492.

Kranzberg, Melvin, 'Technology and History: "Kranzberg's Laws"', *Technology and Culture*, 27 (3/1986): 544–560.

Krebs, Walter, *Kontrolle in staatlichen Entscheidungsprozessen: ein Beitrag zur rechtlichen Analyse von gerichtlichen, parlamentarischen und Rechnungshof-Kontrollen*, Heidelberg: C.F. Müller, 1984.

Kreissl, Reinhard, 'Die präventive Polizei – Auf dem Weg zur gläsernen Gesellschaft?', *KJ*, 14 (2/1981): 128–140.

Krempel, Stefan, 'Berlin will mit Künstlicher Intelligenz Korruption bekämpfen', *Heise Online*, 20 August 2018. Available online: https://www.heise.de/newsticker/meldung/Berlin-will-mit-Kuenstlicher-Intelligenz-Korruption-bekaempfen-4141873.html [https://perma.cc/CRK2-4KUL], (accessed 1 January 2022).

Kreye, Andrian, 'Neue Weltsprache, *Süddeutsche Zeitung*', 22 July 2014. Available online: https://www.sueddeutsche.de/digital/bedeutung-von-algorithmen-neue-weltsprache-1.2051528 [https://perma.cc/8FMT-B2Q8], (accessed 1 January 2022).

Krieger, Linda Hamilton, 'The content of our categories: A cognitive bias approach to discrimination and equal employment opportunity', *Stan. L. Rev.*, 37 (6/1995): 1161–1248.

Kröber, Hans-Ludwig, 'Kriminalprognose an hirndeterminierten Rückfallautomaten? – Über die Freiheit des Verbrechers', in: Fink, Helmut / Rosenzweig, Rainer (eds), *Verantwortung als Illusion*, Münster: Mentis, 2012: 173–187.

Kröber, Hans-Ludwig / Dölling, Dieter / Leygraf, Norbert / Sass, Henning, *Handbuch der Forensischen Psychiatrie: Band 3 Psychiatrische Kriminaltherapie und Kriminaltherapie*, Heidelberg: Springer, 2006.

Krohn, Wolfgang / Weyer, Johannes, 'Gesellschaft als Labor: die Erzeugung sozialer Risiken durch experimentelle Forschung', *Soziale Welt*, 40 (3/1989): 349–373.

Krohn, Wolfgang / Weyer, Johannes, 'Die Gesellschaft als Labor', in: Japp, Klaus-Peter / Halfmann, Jost (eds), *Riskante Entscheidungen und Katastrophenpotentiale*, Wiesbaden: Springer, 1990: 89–122.

Kroll, Joshua A. / Huey, Joanna / Barocas, Solon / Felten, Edward W. / Reidenberg, Joel R. / Robinson, David G. / Yu, Harlan, 'Accountable Algorithms', *U. Pa. L. Rev.*, 165 (3/2017): 633–705.

Kröner, Carolin, *Rückfallprognosen in der forensischen Psychiatrie*, Diss. LMU Munich, 2005.

Krüger, Wolfgang, 'Risiken als Gegenstand der Sicherheitswissenschaft', in: Compes, Peter C. (ed), *Technische Risiken in der Industriegesellschaft. Erfassung, Bewertung, Kontrolle*, Wuppertal: GFS-Sommer-Symposion, 1986: 299–315.

Kugelmann, Dieter, *Die informatorische Rechtsstellung des Bürgers: Grundlagen und verwaltungsrechtliche Grundstrukturen individueller Rechte auf Zugang zu Informationen der Verwaltung*, Tübingen: Mohr Siebeck, 2001.

Kuhlmann, Albert, 'Risikogestaltung in einer von Technik geprägten Welt', in: Hohlneicher, Georg / Raschke, Ehrhard (ed), *Leben ohne Risiko*, Köln: TÜV Rheinland, 1989: 15–35.

Kuhn, Thomas S., *The structure of scientific revolutions*, 2. ed., Chicago: University of Chicago Press, 1970.

Kunz, Karl-Ludwig, 'Grundzüge der heutigen Kriminalpolitik', *NK*, 17 (4/2005): 151–156.

Kunz, Karl-Ludwig, *Die wissenschaftliche Zugänglichkeit von Kriminalität*, Wiesbaden: VS Research, 2008.

Kunz, Karl-Ludwig, *Kriminologie: eine Grundlegung*, 6. ed., Bern: UTB, 2011.

Kunz, Karl-Ludwig / Singelnstein, Tobias, *Kriminologie: eine Grundlegung*, 7. ed., Bern: UTB, 2016.

Kurzweil, Ray, *The Singularity is Near: When Humans Transcend Biology*, New York: Viking, 2005.

Lackner, Karl / Kühl, Kristian (ed), *Strafgesetzbuch*, 29. ed., Munich: C.H. Beck, 2018.

Lakoff, George / Johnson, Mark, *Metaphors We Live By*, Chicago: University of Chicago Press, 2003.

Lakoff, George / Wehling, Elisabeth, *'Auf leisen Sohlen ins Gehirn'. Politische Sprache und ihre heimliche Macht*, 4. ed., Heidelberg: Carl-Auer Verlag, 2016.

Laney, Doug, '3D Data Management: Controlling Data Volume, Velocity and Variety', *META Group Research Note*, 2001. Available online: https://perma.cc/YQ5B-3HCJ [https://perma.cc/YQ5B-3HCJ], (accessed 1 January 2022).

Larson, Jeff / Mattu, Surya / Kirchner, Lauren / Angwin, Julia, 'How We Analyzed the COMPAS Recidivism Algorithm', *ProPublica*, 2016. Available online: https://www.propublica.org/article/how-we-analyzed-the-compas-recidivism-algorithm [https://perma.cc/7WKZ-NCU9], (accessed 1 January 2022).

Lee, Min Kyung, 'Understanding perception of algorithmic decisions: Fairness, trust, and emotion in response to algorithmic management', *Big Data & Society*, 5 (1/2018): 1–16.

Legendre, Pierre (2001), *De la société comme texte: linéaments d'une anthropologie dogmatique*, Paris: Fayard, 2001.

Legnaro, Aldo / Kretschmann, Andrea, 'Das Polizieren der Zukunft', *KrimJ*, 2 (2015): 94–111.

Lehr, David / Ohm, Paul, 'Playing with the Data: What Legal Scholars Should Learn About Machine Learning', *UCDL Rev.*, 51 (2017): 653–717.

Lem, Stanisław, *Summa Technologiae*, transl. Joanna Zylinksa, Minneapolis: University of Minnesota, 2013.

Lessig, Lawrence, 'Code Is Law: On Liberty in Cyberspace', *Harvard Magazine*, 1 January 2000. Available online: http://harvardmagazine.com/2000/01/code-is-law-html [https://perma.cc/59RX-P6VK], (accessed 1 January 2022).

Lessig, Lawrence, *Code: And Other Laws of Cyberspace*, 2. ed., New York: Basic Books, 2006.

Levy, Steven, 'Inside Deep Dreams', *Wired*, 11 December 2015. Available online: https://www.wired.com/2015/12/inside-deep-dreams-how-google-made-its-computers-go-crazy/ [https://perma.cc/HTY5-Y299], (accessed 1 January 2022).

Lewin, Jonathan H. / Wernick, Miles, 'Chicago Police Department Data Analytics and Predictive Policing', *IACP Conference 2015*.

Lewis, David, *Counterfactuals*, Boston: Springer 1973.

Liebl, Karlhans, *Kriminalitätsbelastung und Viktimisierungen im Zeitlauf*, Baden-Baden: Nomos, 2010.

Limbach, Jutta, *Ist die kollektive Sicherheit der Feind der individuellen Freiheit?*, Köln: Heymanns, 2002.

Lind, E. Allan / Tyler, Tom R. (1988), *The Social Psychology of Procedural Justice*, New York: Springer, 1988.

Lindner, Josef Franz, 'Der Verfassungsrechtssatz von der Unschuldsvermutung', *AöR*, 2008: 235–260.

Lisken, Hans / Denninger, Erhard (ed), *Handbuch des Polizeirechts*, 6. ed., Munich: C.H. Beck, 2018 (Handbuch Polizeirecht: Handbuch Polizeirecht).

Lloyd, Monica / Dean, Christopher, 'The Development of Structured Guidelines for Assessing Risk in Extremist Offenders', *Journal of Threat Assessment and Management*, 2 (1/2015): 40–52.

Löffelmann, Markus, 'Schriftliche Stellungnahme zum Gesetzentwurf der Fraktionen der CDU und BÜNDNIS 90/DIE GRÜNEN für ein Gesetz zur Neuausrichtung des Verfassungsschutzes in Hessen – Ausschussvorlage INA 19/63 – Part 1-', *Hessischer Landtag*, 2018.

Lorenz, Bernd / Di Nocera, Francesco / Röttger, Stefan / Parasuraman, Raja, Automated fault-management in a simulated spaceflight micro-world, *Aviation, Space, and Environmental Medicine*, 73 (9/2002): 886–897.

Löwe, Ewald / Rosenberg, Werner (eds) *Die Strafprozeßordnung und das Gerichtsverfassungsgesetz, Großkommentar*, vol. 3, 11, 26. ed. Berlin, 2012/2014 (Löwe/Rosenberg-StPO: Löwe/Rosenberg-StPO).

Lowry, Stella / Macpherson, Gordon, 'A Blot on the Profession', *BMJ*, 296 (6623/1988): 657–658.

Lübbe, Hermann, 'Risiko und Lebensbewältigung', in: Hosemann, Gerhard (ed), *Risiko in der Industriegesellschaft. Analysen, Vorsorge und Akzeptanz*, Erlangen: Universitätsbund Erlangen-Nürnberg., 1989: 15–41.

Lücke, Jörg, *Begründungszwang und Verfassung: zur Begründungspflicht der Gerichte, Behörden und Parlamente*, Tübingen: Mohr, 1987.

Luhmann, Niklas, *Recht und Automation in der öffentlichen Verwaltung*, Berlin: Duncker und Humblot, 1966.

Luhmann, Niklas, *Legitimation durch Verfahren*, Frankfurt a. M.: Suhrkamp, 1983.

Luhmann, Niklas, *Soziologie des Risikos*, Berlin: W. de Gruyter, 1991.

Lukas, Tim, 'Kriminalisierung als Diskriminierung', *Sozial Extra*, 35 (2011): 43–47.

Lum, Kristian / Isaac, William, 'To predict and serve?', *Significance*, 13(5/2016): 14–19.

Maas, Heiko, 'Zusammenleben in der digitalen Gesellschaft – Teilhabe ermöglichen, Sicherheit gewährleisten, Freiheit bewahren'. Pressemitteilung, 2018. Available online: https://www.bmjv.de/SharedDocs/Reden/DE/2017/07032017_digitales_Leben.html [https://perma.cc/ZTR6-4E4K], (accessed 1 January 2022).

Macnish, Kevin, 'Unblinking Eyes: the Ethics of Automating Surveillance', *Ethics and Information Technology*, 14 (2012): 151–167.

Manzey, Dietrich, 'Systemgestaltung und Automatisierung', in: Badke-Schaub, Petra / Hofinger, Gesine / Lauche, Kristina (ed), *Human Factors – Psychologie sicheren Handelns in Risikobranchen*, 2. ed., Berlin/Heidelberg: Springer, 2012: 333–352.

Marshall, Arrian / Davies, Alex, 'Uber's self-driving car saw the Woman it killed', *Wired*, 24 May 2018. Available online: https://www.wired.com/story/uber-self-driving-crash-arizona-ntsb-report/ [https://perma.cc/F2T9-Q2DY], (accessed 1 January 2022).

Marthews, Alex / Tucker, Catherine, 'Government surveillance and internet search behaviour', *SSRN*, 2017. Available online: https://papers.ssrn.com/sol3/papers.cfm?abstract_id=2412564 [https://perma.cc/6QTW-S7CP], (accessed 1 January 2022).

Martini, Mario, 'Big Data als Herausforderung für den Persönlichkeitsschutz und das Datenschutzrecht', *DVBL*, 2014: 1481–1489.

Martini, Mario, 'Wie neugierig darf der Staat im Cyberspace sein? Social Media Monitoring öffentlicher Stellen–Chancen und Grenzen', *Verwaltungsarchiv*, 2016: 307–358.

Martini, Mario, 'Transformation der Verwaltung durch Digitalisierung', *DÖV*, 11 (2017): 443–455.

Martini, Mario / Nink, David, 'Wenn Maschinen entscheiden ... – vollautomatisierte Verwaltungsverfahren und der Persönlichkeitsschutz', *NVwZ – Extra*, 10 (2017): 1–14.

Martini, Mario / Nink, David / Wenzel, Michael, 'Bodycams zwischen Bodyguard und Big Brother-zu den rechtlichen Grenzen filmischer Erfassung von Sicherheitseinsätzen durch Miniaturkameras und Smartphones', *NVwZ – Extra*, 12 (2016): 1–18.

Matthias, Andreas, 'The Responsibility Gap: Ascribing Responsibility for the Actions of Learning Automata', *Ethics and Information Technology*, 6 (2003): 175–183.

Maunz, Theodor / Dürig, Günter (eds), *Grundgesetz, Kommentar, Loseblattsammlung*. Munich: C.H. Beck, Werkstand: 87. EL. 2019 (Maunz/Dürig, GG: Maunz/Dürig, GG).

Mayer-Schönberger, Victor / Cukier, Kenneth, *Big Data – A Revolution that will transform how we live, work and think*, New York: John Murray, 2013.

Mayson, Sandra G., 'Dangerous Defendants', *Yale L.J.*, 127 (3/2018): 490–568.

McAlister, Alfred L. / Bandura, Albert / Owen, Steven V., 'Mechanisms of Moral Disengagement in Support of Military Force: The Impact of Sept. 11', J. *Soc. Clin. Psychol.*, 25 (2/2006): 141–165.

McCrank, John, '"Siri, catch market cheats": Wall Street watchdogs turn to A.I.', *Reuters*, 25 October 2016. Available online: https://ca.reuters.com/article/idCAKCN12P0FJ [https://perma.cc/VA8R-XL7N], (accessed 1 January 2022).

McLuhan, Marshall, *The Gutenberg Galaxy: The Making of Typographic Man*, Toronto: University of Toronto Press, 1962.

McLuhan, Marshall, *Understanding Media: The Extensions of Man*, 1964, Cambridge, MA: MIT Press, 1994.

McQuillan, Dan, 'Hannah Arendt and Algorithmic Thoughtlessness', 2015. Available online: http://danmcquillan.io/arendtandalgorithms.html [https://perma.cc/U7Q6-XCXA], (accessed 1 January 2022).

Meloy, J. Reid / Roshdi, Karoline / Glaz-Ocik, Justine / Hoffmann, Jens, 'Investigating the individual terrorist in Europe', *Journal of Threat Assessment and Management*, 2 (3–4/2015): 140–152.

Meyer, Stephan, 'Kriminalwissenschaftliche Prognoseinstrumente im Tatbestand polizeilicher Vorfeldbefugnisse', *JZ*, 72 (9/2017): 429–439.

Milgram, Stanley, 'Behavioral Study of Obedience', *J. Abnorm. Soc. Psychol.*, 67 (4/1963): 371–378.

Ministerium für Inneres und Kommunales des Landes Nordrhein-Westfalen, 'Antwort der Landesregierung auf die Kleine Anfrage des Abgeordneten Marc Lürbke (FDP)', *LT-Drs.* 16/6453: 2014.

Mittelstadt, Brent Daniel / Allo, Patrick / Taddeo, Mariarosaria / Wachter, Sandra / Floridi, Luciano, 'The Ethics of Algorithms: Mapping the Debate', *Big Data & Society*, 3(2/2016): 1–21.

Mnookin, Jennifer L. / West, Nancy, 'Theaters of Proof: Visual Evidence and the Law in Call Northside 777', *Yale JL & Human.* 13 (2/2001): 329–390.

Mohler, George O. / Short, Martin B. / Brantingham, P. J. / Schoenberg, F. P. / Tita, G. E., 'Self-Exciting Point Process Modeling of Crime', *J. Am. Stat. Assoc.*, 106 (493/2011): 100–108.

Montavon, Grégoire / Samek, Wojciech / Müller, Klaus-Robert, 'Methods for interpreting and understanding deep neural networks', *Digital Signal Processing*, 73 (2018): 1–15.

Mosier, Kathleen L. / Skitka, Linda J. / Burdick, Mark D. / Heers, Susan Tj., 'Automation Bias, Accountability, and Verification Behaviors', *Proceedings of the Human Factors and Ergonomics Society Annual Meeting*, 40 (4/1996): 204–208.

Mosier, Kathleen L. / Skitka, Linda J. / Heers, Susan / Burdick, Mark, 'Automation Bias: Decision Making and Performance in High-Tech Cockpits', *Int. J. Aviat. Psychol.*, 8 (1/1998): 47–63.

Münkler, Herfried / Bohlender, Matthias / Meurer, Sabine (ed), *Sicherheit und Risiko: über den Umgang mit Gefahr im 21. Jahrhundert*, Bielefeld: Transcript Verlag, 2010.

Nave, Gideon / Minxha, Juri / Greene, David M. / Kosinski, Michal / Stillwell, David / Rentfrow, Jason, 'Musical Preferences Predict Personality: Evidence from Active Listening and Facebook Likes', *Psychological Science*, (29/7): 2018: 1145–1158.

Nedopil, Norbert (1986), 'Kriterien der Kriminalprognose bei psychiatrischen Gutachten', *Forensia*, 1986: 167–183.

Nedopil, Norbert, *Forensische Psychiatrie*, 5. ed., Stuttgart/New York: Thieme, 2017.

Nedopil, Norbert / Gross, Gregor, *Prognosen in der Forensischen Psychiatrie: ein Handbuch für die Praxis*, Berlin: Lengerich, 2005.

Negroponte, Nicholas, *Being Digital*, London: Hodder & Stoughton, 1995.

Nissenbaum, Helen, 'Accountability in a Computerized Society', *Science and Engineering Ethics*, 2 (1996): 25–42.

O'Neil, Cathy, *Weapons of Math Destruction – How Big Data Increases Inequalities and Threatens Democracy*, New York: Crown, 2016.

Olah, Chris / Mordvintsev, Alexander / Schubert, Ludwig, 'Feature Visualization', *Distill*, 2017. Available online: https://distill.pub/2017/feature-visualization [https://perma.cc/A5B4-4L3Y], (accessed 1 January 2022).

Olah, Chris / Satyanarayan, Arvind / Johnson, Ian / Carter, Shan / Schubert, Ludwig / Ye, Katherine / Mordvintsev, Alexander, 'The Building Blocks of Interpretability', *Distill*, 2018. Available online: https://distill.pub/2018/building-blocks/ [https://perma.cc/94PQ-X4NP], (accessed 1 January 2022).

Ong, Walter J., *Orality and literacy*, Oxon: Routledge. 2012 [1982].

Ortigosa, Alvaro / Carro, Rosa M. / Quiroga, José Ignacio, 'Predicting User Personality by Mining Social Interactions in Facebook', *J. Comput. Syst. Sci.*, 80 (1/2014): 57–71.

Oswald, Marion / Grace, Jamie / Urwin, Sheena / Barnes, Geoffrey, 'Algorithmic risk assessment policing models: Lessons from the Durham HART model and "Experimental" proportionality', *Information & Communications Technology Law*, 27 (2/2018): 223–250.

Ozkan, Turgut, 'Criminology in the age of data explosion: New directions', *Soc. Sci. J.*, 56 (2/2019): 208–219.

Palacio, Sebastian / Folz, Joachim / Hees, Jörn / Raue, Federico / Borth, Damian / Dengel, Andreas, 'What do Deep Networks Like to See?', *Proceedings of the IEEE Conference on Computer Vision and Pattern Recognition 2018*: 3108–3117.

Palmetshofer, Walter / Semsrott, Arne / Alberts, Anna, *Der Wert persönlicher Daten: Ist Datenhandel der bessere Datenschutz? Studien und Gutachten im Auftrag des Sachverständigenrats für Verbraucherfragen*, Berlin: Bundesministerium der Justiz und für Verbraucherschutz, 2016.

Pandolfini, Bruce, *Kasparov and Deep Blue: The historic chess match between man and machine*, New York: Fireside, 1997.

Papachristos, Andrew V., 'Murder by Structure: Dominance Relations and the Social Structure of Gang Homicide', *Am. J. Sociol.*, 15 (1/2009): 74–128.

Papachristos, Andrew V. / Braga, Anthony A. / Hureau, David M., 'Six-Degrees of Violent Victimization: Social Networks and the Risk of Gunshot Injury', *Researchgate*, 2011. Available online: https://www.researchgate.net/profile/Andrew_Papachristos/publication/227399776_Social_Networks_and_the_Risk_of_Gunshot_Injury/links/563d12af08ae8d65c0117d49.pdf [https://perma.cc/E9ML-2J5Q], (accessed 1 January 2022).

Papachristos, Andrew V. / Braga, Anthony A. / Hureau, David M., 'Social Networks and the Risk of Gunshot Injury', *J. Urban Health*, 89 (6/2012): 992–1003.

Parasuraman, Raja, 'Designing automation for human use: empirical studies and quantitative models', *Ergonomics*, 43 (7/2000): 931–951.

Parasuraman, Raja / Riley, Victor, 'Humans and automation: Use, misuse, disuse, abuse, Human factors', 3 9(2/1997): 230–253.

Pasquale, Frank A., *The Black Box Society – The Secret Algorithms That Control Money and Information*, Cambridge: Harvard University Press, 2015.

Paulus, Christoph, *Das Amok-Puzzle: Psychologische Erklärungsansätze und Täterprofile*, Marburg: Tectum Wissenschaftsverlag, 2016.

Pedreschi, Dino / Giannotti, Fosca / Guidotti, Riccardo / Monreale, Anna / Pappalardo, Luca / Ruggieri, Salvatore / Turini, Franco, 'Open the Black Box Data-Driven Explanation of Black Box Decision Systems', *arXiv*, 2018. Available online: https://arxiv.org/abs/1806.09936 [https://perma.cc/4VJR-UZBW], (accessed 1 January 2022).

Penney, Jonathon W., 'Chilling Effects: Online Surveillance and Wikipedia Use', *Berkeley Tech. LJ*, 7 (5700/2016): 117–182.

Pentland, Alex, *Social Physics: How Good Ideas Spread – the Lessons from a New Science*, New York: Penguin, 2014.

Perry, Walter L. / McInnis, Brian / Price, Carter C. / Smith, Susan C. / Hollywood, John S., *Predictive Policing – The Role of Crime Forecasting in Law Enforcement Operations*, Santa Monica: Rand, 2013.

Peters, Hans-Peter, 'Durch Risikokommunikation zur Technikakzeptanz? Die Konstruktion von Risiko "wirklichkeitendurch" Experten, Gegenexperten und Öffentlichkeit', in: Krüger, Jens / Ruß-Mohl, Stephan (ed), *Risikokommunikation: Technikakzeptanz, Medien und Kommunikationsrisiken*, Berlin: Sigma, 1991: 11–16.

Peters, Helge, 'Schlechte Aussichten. Über goldene und triste Zeiten der Kriminalsoziologie', in: Liebl, Karlshans (ed), *Kriminologie im 21. Jahrhundert*, Wiesbaden: VS Verl. für Sozialwiss., 2007: 43–55.

Petersilia, Joan / Reitz, Kevin R. (ed), *The Oxford Handbook of Sentencing and Corrections*, Oxford: Oxford University Press, 2012.

Pieroth, Bodo, 'Die planende Verwaltung zwischen Geheimhaltung und Öffentlichkeit', *JuS*, 21 (1981): 625–635.

Podesta, John / Pritzker, Penny / Moniz, Ernest / Holdren, J. / Zients, J., *Big Data: Seizing Opportunities, Preserving Values*, Washington DC, 2014.

Pollähne, Helmut, *Kriminalprognostik: Untersuchungen im Spannungsfeld zwischen Sicherheitsrecht und Rechtssicherheit*, Berlin, 2011.

Pomberger, Gustav / Dobler, Heinz, *Algorithmen und Datenstrukturen: eine systematische Einführung in die Programmierung*, Munich, 2008.

Posadas, Brianna, 'How strategic is Chicago's "Strategic Subjects List"?', *Medium*, 22 June 2017. Available online: https://medium.com/equal-future/how-strategic-is-chicagos-strategic-subjects-list-upturn-investigates-9e5b4b235a7c [https://perma.cc/2A9A-8LMG], (accessed 1 January 2022).

Powell, Anastasia / Stratton, Gregory / Cameron, Robin, *Digital Criminology: Crime and Justice in Digital Society*, Abingdon: Routledge, 2018.

Premack, David / Woodruff, Guy, 'Does the chimpanzee have a theory of mind?', *Behavioral and Brain Sciences*, 1 (4/1978): 515–526.

Prentky, Robert / Righthand, Sue, *Juvenile sex offender assessment protocol-II (J-SOAP-II) manual*, Washington DC: Office of Juvenile Justice and Delinquency Prevention's Juvenile Justice, 2003.

Pressman, D. Elaine, *Risk Assessment Decisions for Violent Political Extremism*, Ottawa: Public Safety Canada, 2009.

Pressman, Elaine D. / Duits, Nils / Rinne, Thomas / Flockton, John, *VERA-2R Violent Extremism Risk Assessment Version 2 Revised: a Structured Professional Judgement Approach*, Utrecht, 2016.

Pretrial Justice Institute, 'Where Pretrial Improvements are Happening', 2017. Available online: https://portal.ct.gov/-/media/Malloy-Archive/Reimagining-Justice/Reimagining-Justice---Where-Pretrial-Improvements-are-Happening.pdf?la=en [https://perma.cc/9ZJU-7A8B], (accessed 1 January 2022).

Price, W. Nicholson, II., 'Describing Black-Box Medicine', *BUJ Sci. & Tech. L.*, 4 (2015): 347–356.

Prinz, Marius, *Der Schutz von Betriebs-und Geschäftsgeheimnissen im Informationsfreiheitsrecht*, Diss. Universität Münster, 2015.

Prinz, Wolfgang, 'Der Wille als Artefakt', in: Rehberg, Karl-Siegbert (ed), *Die Natur der Gesellschaft*, Frankfurt a. M.: Campus-Verlag, 2008: 642–655.

Prittwitz, Cornelius, *Strafrecht und Risiko*, Frankfurt a. M.: V. Klostermann, 1993.

Puschke, Jens, *Legitimation, Grenzen und Dogmatik von Vorbereitungstatbeständen*, Tübingen: Mohr Siebeck, 2017.

Pütter, Norbert, Prävention – Spielarten und Abgründe einer populären Überzeugung, *Bürgerrechte & Polizei / Cilip*, 86 (2007): 3–15.

Quercia, Daniele / Kosinski, Michal / Stillwell, David / Crowcroft, Jon, *Our twitter profiles, our selves: Predicting personality with twitter, PASSAT and SocialCom*, 2011: 180–185.

Quinsey, Vernon L. / Harris, Grant T. / Rice, Marnie E. / Cormier, Catherine A., *The Law and Public Policy. Violent Offenders: Appraising and Managing Risk*, 2. ed., Washington DC: American Psychological Association, 2006.

Rachlinski, Jeffrey J. / Wistrich, Andrew J., 'Judging the Judiciary by the Numbers: Empirical Research on Judges', *Annu. Rev. Law. Soc. Sci.*, 13 (1/2017): 203–229.

Rademacher, Timo, 'Predictive Policing im deutschen Polizeirecht', *AöR*, 3 (2017): 366–416.

Rademacher, Timo, 'Artificial Intelligence and Law Enforcement', in: Wischmeyer, Thomas / Rademacher, Timo (ed), *Regulating Artificial Intelligence*, Cham: Singer, 2020: 103–121.

Rainie, Lee / Anderson, Janna / Page, D., 'Code-Dependent: Pros and Cons of the Algorithm Age', Pew Research Center 2017. Available online: http://www.pewinternet.org/2017/02/08/code-dependent/ (accessed 1 January 2022).

Rapoport, Anatol, 'Risiko und Sicherheit in der heutigen Gesellschaft: Die subjektiven Aspekte des Risikobegriffs', *Leviathan*, 16(1/1988): 123–136.

Rath, Christian, 'Gefährder: Was ist ein 'hohes Risiko'?', *Vorwärts*, 17 August 2018. Available online: https://www.vorwaerts.de/artikel/gefaehrder-hohes-risiko [https://perma.cc/AT2B-TEQE], (accessed 1 January 2022).

Rehder, Ulrich / Suhling, Stefan, *Rückfallrisiko bei Sexualstraftätern: RRS; Verfahren zur Bestimmung von Rückfallgefahr und Behandlungsnotwendigkeit*, Lingen: Kriminalpädagogischer Verlag, 2006.

Reichman, Nancy, 'Managing crime risks: Toward an insurance based model of social control', *Research in Law, Deviance and Social Control*, (8/15),1986: 151–172.

Renn, Ortwin, 'Risikowahrnehmung und Risikobewertung: soziale Perzeption und gesellschaftliche Konflikte', in: Chakraborty, Sabyasachi / Yadigaroglu, George (eds), *Ganzheitliche Risikobetrachtungen. Technische, ethische und soziale Aspekte*, Köln: TÜV Rheinland, 1991: 06:1–06:62.

Rettenberger, Martin / Gregório Hertz, Priscilla / Eher, Reinhard, *Die deutsche Version des Violence Risk Appraisal Guide-Revised (VRAG-R)*, Wiesbaden: Kriminologische Zentralstelle, 2017.

Rettenberger, Martin / Matthes, Anna / Schilling, Frank / Eher, Reinhard, 'Die Validität dynamisch-veränderbarer Risikofaktoren bei der Vorhersage einschlägiger Rückfälle pädosexueller Straftäter', *Forensische Psychiatrie, Psychologie, Kriminologie*, 5 (1/2011): 45–53.

Rettenberger, Martin / von Franqué, Fritjof, *Handbuch kriminalprognostischer Verfahren*, Göttingen: Hogrefe Verlag, 2013.

Reuband, Karl-Heinz, 'Vertrauen in die Polizei und staatliche Institutionen: Konstanz und Wandel in den Einstellungen der Bevölkerung 1984–2011', *Soziale Probleme*, 23 (2012): 5–39.

Reuter, Markus, 'Datenskandal bei der Polizei: Offenbar zehntausende Unschuldige gespeichert, *Netzpolitik*, 30 August 2017. Available online: https://netzpolitik.org/2017/datenskandal-bei-der-polizei-offenbar-zehntausende-ungerechtfertigt-gespeichert/ [https://perma.cc/GR2W-MKLG], (accessed 1 January 2022).

Ribeiro, Marco Tulio / Singh, Sameer / Guestrin, Carlos, 'Why Should I Trust You?: Explaining the Predictions of Any Classifier', *ACM SIGKDD*, 2016:1135–1144.

Rice, Marnie E. / Harris, Grant T. / Lang, Carol, 'Validation of and revision to the VRAG and SORAG: The Violence Risk Appraisal Guide – Revised (VRAG-R)', *Psychological Assessment*, 25 (3/2013): 951–965.

Rich, Michael L., 'Machine Learning, Automated Suspicion Algorithms, and the Fourth Amendment', *U. Pa. L. Rev.*, 164 (871/2016): 871–930.

Richardson, Rashida / Schultz, Jason / Crawford, Kate, 'Dirty Data, Bad Predictions: How Civil Rights Violations Impact Police Data, Predictive Policing Systems, and Justice', *N.Y.U. L. Rev.*, 2019: 192–232.

Robinson, Jacob, 'And the Crooked Shall Be Made Straight: The Eichmann Trial, the Jewish Catastrophe and Hannah Arendt's Narrative', *Science and Society*, 1966: 368–371.

Roland, Barthes, *Writing Degree Zero*, New York: Hill and Wang, 1968.

Roth, Andrea, 'Machine Testimony', *Yale L.J.*, 126 (7/2017): 1972–2053.

Roth, Andrea, 'Trial by Machine', *Geo. L.J.*, 104 (2017): 1245–1305.

Rubin, Joel, 'Stopping Crime Before it Starts', *LA Times*, 21 August 2010. Available online: http://articles.latimes.com/2010/aug/21/local/la-me-predictcrime-20100427-1 [https://perma.cc/SXX7-9VYF], (accessed 1 January 2022).

Ruch, Andreas, *Dunkelfeld und Anzeigeverhalten bei Delikten gegen die sexuelle Selbstbestimmung. Eine empirische Untersuchung im Zusammenhang mit den §§ 177, 179 StGB*, Holzkirchen: Felix, 2011.

Ruch, Andreas / Feltes, Thomas, 'Gewalttäterdateien: Rechtliche Probleme und kriminologische Risiken', *NK*, 28 (1/2016): 62–77.

Russell, Stuart / Dewey, Daniel / Tegmark, Max, 'Research Priorities for Robust and Beneficial Artificial Intelligence', *AI Magazine*, 36 (4/2015): 105–114.

Rusteberg, Benjamin, 'Die Entscheidung des Bundesverfassungsgerichts zum Bundeskriminalamtsgesetz – Eine Zwischenbilanz des allgemeinen Sicherheitsrechts', *KritV*, 100 (1/2017): 24–35.

Sachs, Michael, *Verfassungsrecht II – Grundrechte*, 3. ed., Berlin: Springer, 2017.

Sachs, Michael (ed), *Grundgesetz, Kommentar*, 8. ed., Munich: C.H. Beck, 2018 (Sachs, GG: Sachs, GG).

Sachverständigenrat für Verbraucherfragen, *Verbrauchergerechtes Scoring*, Berlin: Sachverständigenrat für Verbraucherfragen, 2018.

Sadowski, Friederike / Rossegger, Astrid / Pressman, Elaine / Rinne, Thomas / Duits, Nils / Endrass, Jérôme, 'Das Violent Extremism Risk Assessment Version 2 Revised (VERA-2R): eine Skala zur Beurteilung des Risikos extremistischer Gewalt', *Kriminalistik*, 5 (2017): 335–342.

Sandvig, Christian / Hamilton, Kevin / Karahalios, Karrie / Lan, Cedric (2014), 'Auditing Algorithms – Research Methods for Detecting Discrimination on Internet Platforms, Data and Discrimination: Converting Critical Concerns into Productive Inquiry', *ACM preconference 2014*.

Satzger, Helmut / Widmaier, Gunter / Schluckebier, Wilhelm (ed), *Strafprozessordnung*, 3. ed., Eschborn, 2018 (SSW-StPO: SSW-StPO).

Saunders, Jessica / Hunt, Priscillia / Hollywood, John S. 'Predictions put into practice: a quasi-experimental evaluation of Chicago's predictive policing pilot', *J. Exp. Criminol.*, 12 (3/2016): 347–371.

Schenke, Wolf-Rüdiger / Graulich, Kurt / Ruthig, Josef (eds), *Sicherheitsrecht des Bundes*, 2. ed. Munich: C.H. Beck, 2019 (Schenke/Graulich/Ruthig: Schenke/Graulich/Ruthig).

Scherer, Matthew U., 'Regulating artificial intelligence systems: Risks, challenges, competencies, and strategies', *Harv. JL & Tech.*, 29 (2/2015): 353–400.

Scherzberg, Arno, *Die Öffentlichkeit der Verwaltung*, Baden-Baden: Nomos, 2000.

Scherzberg, Arno, 'Öffentlichkeitskontrolle', in: Hoffmann-Riem, Wolfgang / Schmidt-Aßmann, Eberhard / Voßkuhle, Andreas (ed), *Grundlagen des Verwaltungsrechts*, 2. ed. Munich, Beck, 2013: 665–742.

Schmidt-Bleibtreu, Bruno / Hofmann, Hans / Henneke, Hans-Günter (ed), *Grundgesetz Kommentar*, 14. ed. Köln:, 2017 (Schmidt-Bleibtreu/Hofmann/Henneke, GG: Schmidt-Bleibtreu/Hofmann/Henneke, GG).

Schnabel, Christoph, 'Rechtswidrige Praktiken als Betriebs-und Geschäftsgeheimnisse?', *Computer und Recht*, 5 (2016): 342–348.

Schneider, Frank / Frister, Helmut / Olzen, Dirk, *Begutachtung psychischer Störungen*, Berlin/Heidelberg: Springer, 2015.

Schneider, Hartmut (ed), *Münchener Kommentar zur Strafprozessordnung*, Vol. 2, §§ 151–332 StPO, Munich, 2016.

Schoch, Friedrich, *Informationsfreiheitsgesetz Kommentar*, 2. ed., Munich: Beck, 2016 (*Schoch*, IFG).

Scholze-Stubenrecht, Werner, *Duden – Deutsches Universalwörterbuch*, Berlin: Dudenverlag, 2015.

Schöndorf-Haubold, Bettina, 'Das Recht auf Achtung des Privatlebens – Problemstellungen im Digitalbereich, eine rechtsvergleichende Perspektive: Deutschland' in: Wissenschaftlicher Dienst des Europäischen Parlaments (ed), *Das Recht auf Achtung des Privatlebens*, Brussels: European Parliament, 2018.

Schüler-Springorum, Horst, 'Kriminologie als Herausforderung der Kriminalpolitik', *KritV*, 73 (3–4/1990): 313–326.

Schurz, Gerhard, *Wahrscheinlichkeit*, Berlin: de Gruyter, 2015.

Schütz, Philip, 'Zum Leben zu wenig, zum Sterben zu viel? Die finanzielle und personelle Ausstattung deutscher Datenschutzbehörden im Vergleich', in: Roßnagel, Alexander / Friedewald, Michael / Hansen, Marit (ed), *Die Fortentwicklung des Datenschutzes. Zwischen Systemgestaltung und Selbstregulierung*, Wiesbaden: Springer, 2018: 251–268.

Schwabenbauer, Thomas, *Heimliche Grundrechtseingriffe*, Heidelberg: Mohr Siebeck, 2013.

Schwind, Hans-Dieter, *Kriminologie: eine praxisorientierte Einführung mit Beispielen*, Heidelberg: Kriminalistik Verlag, 2010.

Schwind, Jan-Volker, *Sicherheit und Sicherheitsgefühl in der Stadt: Bochum 2015/2016 ('Bochum IV')*, Holzkirchen: Felix, 2018.

Seibel, Karsten, 'Gegen Kreditech ist die Schufa ein Schuljunge', *Die Welt*, 17 March 2015. Available online: https://www.welt.de/finanzen/verbraucher/article139671014/Gegen-Kreditech-ist-die-Schufa-ein-Schuljunge.html [https://perma.cc/N9XU-98DC], (accessed 1 January 2022).

Selbst, Andrew D. (2017), 'Disparate Impact in Big Data Policing', *Ga. L. Rev.*, 52 (1): 109–195.

Sheehan, Tim, 'Fresno Council Halts Purchase of Data Software Wanted by Police', *Fresno Bee*, 31 March 2016. Available online: http://www.fresnobee.com/news/local/article69337677.html [https://perma.cc/KP2P-YZBM], (accessed 1 January 2022).

Sheridan, Thomas B., 'Speculations on Future Relations Between Humans and Automation', in: Parasuraman, Raja / Mouloua, Mustapha (ed), *Automation and Human Performance: Theory and Applicatio*ns, New York: Lawrence Erlbaum Associates, 1996: 449–460.

Sherman, Lawrence W., 'Policing communities: what works?', *Crime and Justice*, 1986: 343–386.

Simmons, Ric, 'Big Data, Machine Judges, and the Legitimacy of the Criminal Justice System', *U.C. Davis L. Rev.*, 52 (2/2018): 1067–1118.

Simon, Jonathan, 'The Ideological Effects of Actuarial Practices', *Law & Soc'y Rev.*, 22 (1988): 771–800.

Simon, Jonathan / Feeley, Malcolm, 'Actuarial Justice: The Emerging New Criminal Law', in: Nelken, David (ed), *The Futures of Criminology*, Thousand Oaks: Sage, 1994.

Simon, Judith, *Knowing Together: a Social Epistemology for Socio-Technical Epistemic Systems*, Diss. Universität Wien, 2010.

Singelnstein, Tobias, 'Strafprozessuale Verwendungsregelungen zwischen Zweckbindungsgrundsatz und Verwertungsverboten', *ZStW*, 120 (4/2008): 854–893.

Singelnstein, Tobias, 'Predictive Policing: Algorithmenbasierte Straftatprognosen zur vorausschauenden Kriminalintervention', *NStZ*, (1/2018): 1–9.

Singelnstein, Tobias / Puschke, Jens (ed), D*er Staat in der Sicherheitsgesellschaft*, Wiesbaden: Springer, 2018.

Singelnstein, Tobias / Stolle, Peer, *Die Sicherheitsgesellschaft: Soziale Kontrolle im 21. Jahrhundert*, 3. ed., Wiesbaden: Springer, 2012.

Singer, Natasha / Maheshwari, Sapna, 'European Regulators Ask if Facebook Is Taking Too Much Data', *The New York Times*, 25 April 2017. Available online: https://nyti.ms/2vH7voE [https://perma.cc/9VF8-J7F7], (accessed 1 January 2022).

Sinn, Arndt, 'Vorverlagerung der Strafbarkeit – Begriff, Ursachen und Regelungstechniken', in: Sinn, Arndt / Gropp, Walter / Nagy, Ferenc (eds), *Grenzen der Vorverlagerung in einem Tatstrafrecht – Eine rechtsvergleichende Analyse am Beispiel des deutschen und ungarischen Strafrechts*, Osnabrück: University of Osnabrück, 2011: 13–40.

Sinn, Arndt / Gropp, Walter / Nagy, Ferenc (ed), *Grenzen der Vorverlagerung in einem Tatstrafrecht: Eine rechtsvergleichende Analyse am Beispiel des deutschen und ungarischen Strafrechts*, vol. 1, Osnabrück: University of Osnabrück, 2011.

Skitka, Linda J. / Mosier, Kathleen / Burdick, Mark D. (2000), 'Accountability and Automation Bias', *Int. J. Hum. Comput. Stud.*, 40 (4): 701–717.

Skitka, Linda J. / Mosier, Kathleen L. / Burdick, Mark, 'Does Automation Bias Decision-Making?', *Int. J. Hum. Comput. Stud.*, 51 (5/1999): 991–1006.

Skitka, Linda J. / Mosier, Kathleen L. / Burdick, Mark / Rosenblatt, Bonnie, 'Automation bias and errors: are crews better than individuals?', *Int. J. Aviat. Psychol.*, 10 (1/2000): 85–97.

Skogan, Wesley G., 'Citizen Satisfaction with Police Encounters', *Police Quarterly*, 8 (3/2005): 298–321.

Slobogin, Christopher, 'Why liberals should chuck the exclusionary rule', *U. Ill. L. Rev.*, 1999: 363–446.

Smith, Gavin J. D. / Moses, Lyria Bennett / Chan, Janet, 'The Challenges of Doing Criminology in the Big Data Era: Towards a Digital and Data-driven Approach', *Br. J. Criminol.* 57 (2/2017): 259–274.

Sommerer, Lucia M., 'Geospatial Predictive Policing – Research Outlook & a Call for Legal Debate', *NK*, 29 (2017): 147–164.

Starr, Sonja B., 'Evidence-Based Sentencing and the Scientific Rationalization of Discrimination', *Stan. L. Rev.*, 66 (4/2014): 803–872.

Starr, Sonja B., 'The New Profiling: Why Punishing Based on Poverty and Identity is Unconstitutional and Wrong', *Fed. Sent'g Rep.*, 27 (4/2015): 229–236.

Staubli, Silvia, 'Vertrauen in die Schweizer Polizei', *Soziale Probleme*, 27 (1/2016): 49–74.

Stier, Carolin (2017), *Risikomanagement und wertorientierte Unternehmensführung*, Wiesbaden: Springer, 2017.

Stone, Deborah A., 'Causal Stories and the Formation of Policy Agendas', *Political Science Quarterly*, 104 (1989): 281–300.

Strahilevitz, Lior Jacob, 'Privacy versus Antidiscrimination', *U. Chi. L. Rev.*, 75 (1/2008): 363–381.

Strate, Lance, 'If It's Neutral, It's Not Technology', *Educational Technology*, 52 (1/2012): 6–9.

Stroud, Matt, 'The Minority Report: Chicago's New Police Computer Predicts Crimes, but Is It Racist?', *Verge*, 19 February 2014. Available online: http://www.theverge.com/2014/2/19/5419854/the-minority-report-this-computer-predicts-crime-but-is-it-racist [http://perma.cc/T678-AA68], (accessed 1 January 2022).

Stuckenberg, Carl-Friedrich, 'Die normative Aussage der Unschuldsvermutung', *ZStW*, 111 (1999): 422–460.

Stuckenberg, Carl-Friedrich, *Untersuchungen zur Unschuldsvermutung*, Berlin: de Gruyter, 2012.

Tanneberger, Steffen, *Die Sicherheitsverfassung: Eine systematische Darstellung der Rechtsprechung des Bundesverfassungsgerichts. Zugleich ein Beitrag zu einer induktiven Methodenlehre*, Tübingen: Mohr Siebert, 2014.

Taslitz, Andrew E., 'Police Are People Too: Cognitive Obstacles to, and Opportunities for, Police Getting the Individualized Suspicion Judgment Right', *Ohio St. J. Crim. L.*, 8 (2010): 7–78.

Thomson-DeVeaux, Amelia, 'The Supreme Court Is Stubbornly Analog – By Design', *FiveThirtyEight*, 29 May 2018. Available online: https://fivethirtyeight.com/features/the-supreme-court-is-stubbornly-analog-by-design/ [https://perma.cc/YG65-JAXA], (accessed 1 January 2022).

Tischbirek, Alexander, 'Racial Profiling vor Gericht', *DPolBl* 3 (2019): 17–18.

Tischbirek, Alexander, 'AI and Discrimination: Discriminating against Discriminatory Systems', in: Wischmeyer, Thomas / Rademacher, Timo (ed), *Regulating Artificial Intelligence*, Cham: Springer, 2020: 103.

Tischbirek, Alexander / Wihl, Tim, 'Verfassungswidrigkeit des Racial Profiling', *JZ*, 5 (2013): 219–224.

Tondorf, Günter / Tondorf, Babette, *Psychologische und psychiatrische Sachverständige im Strafverfahren: Verteidigung bei Schuldfähigkeits-und Prognosebegutachtung*, Heidelberg: C.F. Müller, 2011.

Trithemius, Johannes, *De laude scriptorum manualium, 1492 – Zum Lob der Schreiber*, Würzburg, 1973.

Trute, Hans-Heinrich, 'Grenzen des präventionsorientierten Polizeirechts in der Rechtsprechung des Bundesverfassungsgerichts', *Die Verwaltung*, 42 (2009): 85–104.

Tutt, Andrew, 'An FDA for Algorithms', *Admin. L. Rev.*, 69 (2017): 83–123.

Tyler, Tom R., *Why People Obey the Law*, New Haven/London: Princeton University Press, 1990.

Tyler, Tom R., 'Social Justice: Outcome and Procedure', *Int. J. Psychol.*, 35 (2/200): 117–125.

Tyler, Tom R., 'Public Trust and Confidence in Legal Authorities: What do majority and minority group members want from the law and legal institutions?', *Behavioral Sciences & the Law*, 19 (2/2001): 215–235.

Tyler, Tom R., 'Enhancing Police Legitimacy', *The Annals of the American Academy of Political and Social Science*, 22 (2004): 84–99.

Tyler, Tom R. / Huo, Yuen, *Trust in the Law: Encouraging Public Cooperation with the Police and Courts*, New York: Russel Sage Foundation, 2002.

Tyler, Tom R. / Lind, E. Allan, 'A Relational Model of Authority in Groups', *Advances in Experimental Social Psychology*, 25 (1992): 115–191.

Tyler, Tom R. / Rasinski, Kenneth A. / Spodick, Nancy, 'Influence of Voice on Satisfaction with Leaders: Exploring the Meaning of Process Control', *J. Pers. Soc. Psychol.*, 48 (1/1985): 72–81.

Tyler, Tom R. / Sevier, Justin, 'How do the Courts Create Popular Legitimacy – The Role of Establishing the Truth, Punishing Justly, and/or Acting through Just Procedures, *Alb. L. Rev.*, 77 (2013): 1095–1137.

Ulbig, Ellen / Hertel, Rolf F. / Böl, Gaby-Fleur, *Evaluierung der Kommunikation über die Unterschiede zwischen 'risk' und 'hazard'*, Berlin: BfR Wissenschaft, 2009.

Ulbricht, Lena / Haunss, Sebastian / Hofmann, Jeanette / Klinger, Ulrike / Passoth, Jan-Hendrik / Pentzold, Christian / Schneider, Ingrid / Straßheim, Holger / Voß, Jan-Peter, 'Dimensionen von Big Data: Eine politikwissenschaftliche Systematisierung', in: Kolany-Raiser, Barbara / Heil, Reinhard / Orwat, Carsten / Hoeren, Thomas (eds), *Big Data und Gesellschaft*, Wiesbaden: Springer, 2018: 151–231.

University of Cambridge, 'Helping Police Make Custody Decisions Using Artificial Intelligence', 2018. Available online: https://www.cam.ac.uk/research/features/helping-police-make-custody-decisions-using-artificial-intelligence [https://perma.cc/7GCM-E2XA], (accessed 1 January 2022).

Uprichard, Emma, 'Big Data, Little Questions?', *Discover Society*, Focus 1 (2013). Available online: https://discoversociety.org/2013/10/01/focus-big-data-little-questions/ [https://perma.cc/46T8-T34A], (accessed 1 January 2022).

v. Münch, Ingo / Kunig, Philip (ed), *Grundgesetz-Kommentar*, 6. ed., Munich: C.H. Beck, 2012.

Van Wel, Lita / Royakkers, Lambèr, 'Ethical Issues in Web Data Mining', *Ethics and Information Technology*, 6 (2/2004): 129–140.

Verbraucherzentrale Bundesverband, *Verbrauchereinstellungen und Erwartungen zu algorithmenbasierten Entscheidungsprozessen*, Berlin: Verbraucherzentrale Bundesverband, 2017.

Volckart, Bernd, 'Zur Bedeutung der Basisrate in der Kriminalprognose', *Recht und Psychiatrie*, 2 (2002): 105–114.

Vollbach, Alexander, 'Extremismus und kriminelle Gefährdung. Ein Beitrag zur Interventionsplanung und Prävention in der Strafrechtspflege', *NK* 2017, 29 (1(2017): 62–74.

von Liszt, Franz, 'Die deterministischen Gegner der Zweckstrafe', (1893/1905), in: von Liszt, Franz (ed), *Strafrechtliche Aufsätze und Vorträge*, Vol. 2: 1892–1904, Berlin, 2011:25–74.

Wachter, Sandra / Mittelstadt, Brent / Russell, Chris, 'Counterfactual Explanations Without Opening the Black Box: Automated Decisions and the GDPR', *Harv. J.L. & Tech.*, 31(2/2018): 841–887.

Wächtler, Hartmut, 'Strafverteidigung und soziale Bewegungen. Die 1980er Jahre', in: Strafverteidigervereinigungen (ed), ... *kein Grund zu feiern. 30 Jahre Strafverteidigertag*, Berlin, 2007: 129–137.

Waldman, Ari Ezra / Martin, Kirsten, 'Privacy and Algorithmic Decision-Making, (Im-)Perfect Enforcement Conference des Yale Information Society Projects 6 April 2019', (unpublished manuscript).

Wang, A.J., 'Procedural Justice and Risk-Assessment Algorithms, *SSRN*, 2018. Available online: https://ssrn.com/abstract=3170136 [https://perma.cc/KW4M-CVKB], (accessed 1 January 2022).

Wang, Hongjian / Kifer, Daniel / Graif, Corina / Li, Zhenhui, 'Crime Rate Inference with Big Data', *ACM SIGKDD*2016, 635–644.

Weber, Max, *Wirtschaft und Gesellschaft: Grundriss der verstehenden Soziologie*, Tübingen: Mohr, 1972.

Wehrheim, Jan, 'Definitionsmacht und Selektivität in Zeiten neuer Kontrolltechnologien', in: Schmidt-Semisch, Henning / Hess, Henner (eds), *Die Sinnprovinz der Kriminalität. Zur Dynamik eines sozialen Feldes*, Wiesbaden: Springer VS, 2014: 137–153.

Weizenbaum, Joseph, *Computer, Power and Human Reason. From Judgement to Calculation*, New York: W.H. Freeman, 1976.

Wendt, Kai / Rasche, Theresia, 'Fluggastdatenspeicherung im Lichte der EuGH-Rechtsprechung', *ZD-Aktuell*, 05205.

Weßlau, Edda, *Vorfeldermittlungen – Probleme der Legalisierung 'vorbeugender Verbrechens-bekämpfung aus' strafprozessrechtlicher Sicht*, Berlin: Duncker & Humblot, 1989.

Wexler, Rebecca, 'Life, Liberty, and Trade Secrets: Intellectual Property in the Criminal Justice System', *Stan. L. Rev.*, 70 (5/2018): 1343–1429.

Williams, Matthew L. / Burnap, Pete / Sloan, Luke, 'Crime Sensing with Big Data: The Affordance and Limitations of Using Open-Source Communications to Estimate Crime Patterns', *Brit. J. Criminol.*, 57 (2/2017): 320–340.

Wilson, Benjamin / Hoffman, Judy / Morgenstern, Jamie, Predictive Inequity in Object Detection, *arXiv*, 2019. Available online: https://arxiv.org/pdf/1902.11097.pdf [https://perma.cc/ADR5-235J], (accessed 1 January 2022).

Winner, Langdon, *Do artifacts have politics?*, *Daedalus*, 109 (1/1980): 121–136.

Winston, Ali, 'Palantir Has Secretly Been Using New Orleans to Test Its Predictive Policing Technology', *The Verge*, 27 February 2018. Available online: https://www.theverge.com/2018/2/27/17054740/palantir-predictive-policing-tool-new-orleans-nopd [https://perma.cc/84ZW-S7HN], (accessed 1 January 2022).

Wischmeyer, Thomas, 'Formen und Funktionen des exekutiven Geheimnisschutzes', *Die Verwaltung*, 51 (3/2018): 393–426.

Wischmeyer, Thomas, 'Regulierung intelligenter Systeme', *AöR*, 2018: 1–66.

Wischmeyer, Thomas, '§ 21 Regierungs- und Verwaltungshandeln durch KI', in: Ebers, Martin / Heinze, Christian / Krügel, Tina / Steinrötter, Björn (eds), *Rechtshandbuch Künstliche Intelligenz und Robotik*, Munich: C.H. Beck, 2020.

Wischmeyer, Thomas, 'AI and Transparency: Opening the Black Box', in: Wischmeyer, Thomas / Rademacher, Timo (eds), *Regulating Artificial Intelligence*, Cham: Springer, 2020, 75.

Wiseman, Samuel R., 'Fixing Bail', *Geo. Wash. L. Rev.*, 84 (2/2016): 417–479.

Wittgenstein, Ludwig, *Tractatus Logico-Philosophicus – Logisch-Philosophische Abhandlung*, Berlin: Suhrkamp, 1963.

Wolf, Fabiana, *Der Schutz des Betriebs- und Geschäftsgeheimnisses*, Baden-Baden: Nomos, 2015.

Yeung, Karen, "'Hypernudge': Big Data as a mode of regulation by design", *Information, Communication & Society*, 20 (1/2017): 118–136.

Youyou, Wu / Kosinski, Michal / Stillwell, David, 'Computer-based personality judgments are more accurate than those made by humans', *PNAS*, 112 (4/2015): 1036–1040.

Zafar, Muhammad Bilal / Valera, Isabel / Rodriguez, Manuel Gomez / Gummadi, Krishna P., 'Fairness Constraints – Mechanism for Fair Classification', *arXiv*, 2015. Available online: https://arxiv.org/pdf/1507.05259.pdf [https://perma.cc/PQP4-PCE3], (accessed 1 January 2022).

Zafar, Muhammad Bilal / Valera, Isabel / Rogriguez, Manuel Gomez / Gummadi, Krishna P., 'Learning Fair Classifiers', *arXiv*, 2016. Available online: https://arxiv.org/pdf/1507.05259v4.pdf [https://perma.cc/R6M3-5LJZ], (accessed 1 January 2022).

Zalnieriute, Monika / Moses, Lyria Bennett / Williams, George, 'The Rule of Law and Automation of Government Decision-Making', *Mod. L. Rev.*, 82 (3/2019): 425–455.

Zarsky, Tal, 'Transparent Predictions', *U. Ill. L. Rev.*, 4 (2013): 1503–1570.

Zaubermann, Renee (ed), *Self-Reported Crime and Deviance Studies in Europe: Current State of Knowledge and Review of Use*, Brussels: HAL, 2009.

Zedner, Lucia, 'Pre-crime and post-criminology?', *Theoretical Criminology*, 11 (2/2007): 261–281.

Zedner, Lucia (ed), *Security*, London/New York: Routledge, 2009.

Zhao, Jieyu / Wang, Tianlu / Yatskar, Mark / Ordonez, Vicente / Chang, Kai-Wei, 'Men also like shopping: Reducing gender bias amplification using corpus-level constraints', *arXiv*, 2017. Available online: https://arxiv.org/pdf/1707.09457.pdf [https://perma.cc/HV95-G7QN], (accessed 1 January 2022).

Zöller, Mark A., *Informationssysteme und Vorfeldmaßnahmen von Polizei, Staatsanwaltschaft und Nachrichtendiensten: zur Vernetzung von Strafverfolgung und Kriminalitätsverhütung im Zeitalter von multimedialer Kommunikation und Persönlichkeitsschutz*, Heidelberg: Müller, 2002.

Zöller, Mark A., 'Willkommen in Absurdistan: neue Straftatbestände zur Bekämpfung des Terrorismus', *GA 2010*, 607–621.

Zweig, Katharina A., '2. Arbeitspapier: Überprüfbarkeit von Algorithmen', *AlgorithmWatch 2016*. Available online: http://algorithmwatch.org/zweites-arbeitspapier-ueberpruefbarkeit-algorithmen/ [https://perma.cc/98NJ-ZN7M], (accessed 1 January 2022).

Zweig, Katharina A. / Krafft, Tobias D., 'Fairness und Qualität algorithmischer Entscheidungen', in: Mohabbat Kar, Resa / Thapa, Basanta E. P. / Parycek, Peter (ed), *(Un)berechenbar? Algorithmen und Automatisierung in Staat und Gesellschaft*, Berlin: Kompetenzzentrum, Öffentlich IT, 2018: 204–227.